# RoboLaw Series
# 3

directed by E. Palmerini, R.E. Leenes,
K. Warwick and F. Battaglia

D1640208

# Rethinking Responsibility in Science and Technology

edited by
Fiorella Battaglia, Nikil Mukerji and Julian Nida-Rümelin

PISA
UNIVERSITY
PRESS

Rethinking responsibility in science and technology / edited by Fiorella Battaglia, Nikil Mukerji and Julian Nida-Rümelin. - Pisa : Pisa university press, 2014. - (RoboLaw series ; 3)

170 (22.)
I. Battaglia, Fiorella    II. Mukerji, Nikil    III. Nida-Rümelin, Julian    1. Responsbilità <Filosofia>
CIP a cura del Sistema bibliotecario dell'Università di Pisa

 **Peer reviewed work in compliance with UPI protocol**

UNIVERSITY PRESS ITALIANE

SEVENTH FRAMEWORK PROGRAMME

Scuola Superiore Sant'Anna
di Studi Universitari e di Perfezionamento

LUDWIG-
MAXIMILIANS-
UNIVERSITÄT
MÜNCHEN

*Cover illustration*
Marco Manzella, *Piscina XXVI*, wood painting, property of the author (2012).

© Copyright 2014 by Pisa University Press srl
Società con socio unico Università di Pisa
Capitale Sociale Euro 20.000,00 i.v. - Partita IVA 02047370503
Sede legale: Lungarno Pacinotti 43/44 - 56126 Pisa
Tel. + 39 050 2212056 - Fax + 39 050 2212945
press@unipi.it
www.pisauniversitypress.it

ISBN 978-88-6741-373-7

# Contents

# Science, technology and responsibility

*Fiorella Battaglia, Nikil Mukerji and Julian Nida-Rümelin*

Studies in intellectual history seem to indicate that the concept of responsibility is a rather late cultural product (or "construct"). It is certain, though, that the term "responsibility", which also exists in other European languages ("responsabilità", "Verantwortung", etc.), in its current meaning is recent. If, on the other hand, it is true that ascriptions of responsibility are essential for every form of social interaction and moral agency, then there would be a surprising dilemma: Morality and sociality would either be a cultural product of the past three hundred years of European history (which is an utterly implausible idea) or they exist in other forms that make do without the concept of responsibility (which, in comparison, does not seem to be much more plausible).

The resolution of this purported dilemma is, in fact, obvious: The practice of responsibility ascriptions is indeed central to reflective forms of morality and sociality. But it does not require the terms that we use today – terms like the German "Verantwortung" or the Italian „responsabilità". The attribution of actions and of consequences to agents is an age-old cultural practice, which we can track throughout all cultures that kept written records. (We may assume that they were also a central element of other cultures.) This attribution of actions and consequences, the idea of "authorship" and the corresponding sanctioning, critique and the demand for reasons is neither European nor modern. It is deeply embedded into the "lifeworld" of human beings and not subject to change.

The empirical circumstances in which human beings ascribe responsibility to one another are, however, subject to change. Science and technology play a great part in this transformation process. Therefore, it is important for us to rethink the idea, the role and the normative standards behind responsibility in a world that is constantly changing under the influence of scientific and technological progress. This volume is a contribution to that joint societal effort.

In the first paper **Julian Nida-Rümelin** clarifies the concept of responsibility. He argues that we are responsible to the extent that we are (or should be) guided by reasons and that we are, therefore, responsible for our actions. In fact, Nida-Rümelin contends that we are responsible for *all* of our action because all actions require reason-guided intentionality. Then, he examines various other forms of responsibility. Given the idea that responsibility is constituted by reasoned deliberation, Nida-Rümelin suggests that we also have a responsibility for our convictions which are guided by reasons in a way similar to actions. He also endorses a responsibility for (emotional) attitudes, which are, as he explains, also amenable to reasons. Finally, Nida-Rümelin emphasizes the non-consequentialist nature of his account of responsibility by rejecting the notion that we are responsible for the consequences of our actions.

**Nikil Mukerji**, whose paper follows Nida-Rümelin's contribution, analyses the relation between technological progress and responsibility. To this end, he draws a distinction between two forms of responsibility. He calls the first "responsibility as attributability" and explicates it following Nida-Rümelin's account. Mukerji argues that the responsibility for our actions increases as technology progresses. Then, he analyses "substantive responsibility", which refers to that which human agents are normatively required to do. As he explains, technological progress may change our substantive responsibilities. Above that, Mukerji claims, it may affect the way we think about our substantive responsibilities at the level of normative-ethical theory.

**Benedetta Bisol** offers some reflections on the governance of science and technology in the European context and discusses strategies that are currently being used to ethically regulate the fields of research, production and use of technological applications. She also addresses a number of difficulties that are related to these strategies. Her overall goal is to show how contemporary philosophical ethics can provide guidance in the effort of building a regulating framework for science and technology.

**Georg Marckmann** emphasizes the importance of methodology in technology assessment. Based on a coherentist model of justification, he offers a theoretical framework which can provide normative guidance. He suggests a methodological approach that comprises the following steps: Description, specification, evaluation, synthesis, recommendations, and monitoring. In the final part of his paper,

Marckmann illustrates the application of this approach using the example of computer-based clinical decision support systems (CDSS).

**Michael Decker** focuses on adaptive robots, which are relevant in the area of service robotics. These robots, he explains, should be used to take over specific tasks in every day environments, e.g. in public places, in a railway station or in private homes. Hence, it cannot be expected that these high-tech systems are initialised by a user who is a robotics expert. The system must be enabled to learn about different environments and to adapt to them. It must also be able to adapt to different users with different preferences. Decker's contribution shows how to face these issues in an interdisciplinary approach, which is paradigmatic for Technology Assessment and Responsible Research Innovation (RRI). RRI has been the guiding principle of the European research landscape since the launch of Horizon 2020. Based on this approach, Decker makes recommendations, which are of particular interest for the RoboLaw project.

**Klaus Mainzer** addresses ethical challenges from life sciences to robotics and cyberphysical infrastructures of modern societies. Towards the end of his analysis he specifically turns to the issue of human responsibility. As the complexity of technical systems grows, ethical scenarios become complex, too. Mainzer believes, nevertheless, that responsibility should not be relegated to technical artefacts, even if they are able to operate in an automated fashion. Instead, humans should at all times remain responsible for their technological systems.

**Sabine Thürmel** addresses the notions of agency and interagency in socio-technical systems. To this end, she introduces the concept of multi-dimensional, gradual agency, which allows her to investigate interactions of humans with nonhumans. The concept can be used to analyse the potential of social computing systems as well as their virtual and real actualizations. It can also be employed, as Thürmel explains, to describe automated scenarios where technical agents have certain options for acting.

**Filippo Santoni de Sio** discusses legal compatibilism. As he explains, recent developments in the cognitive sciences have given rise to radical scepticism about legal responsibility. It is often attempted to rebut this scepticism by pointing towards the autonomy of law. Santoni de Sio rejects the defensive strategy and sketches out what a viable philosophical defence should look like.

**Andrea Bertolini** goes into the legal aspects of robotics. He believes that the current debate about robots is coined by a kind of exceptionalism. The special technological features of robots are often invoked in order to argue for the need to radically change the legal rules, esp. in the field of liability. Bertolini considers two ways in which such a view may be supported. The first has an ontological basis, the second a functional basis. The ontological argument, which he rejects, seeks to establish that the complex features of robots justify viewing them as subjects. According to Bertolini, the functional argument, which employs consequential considerations and addresses the incentive effects of legal codes, is more promising.

**Susanne Beck** analyses the current debate about the ethical dimension in robotics and diagnoses that the best way for legislators and jurisprudence to deal with developments in that is yet to be found. As she explains, the legal system is traditionally geared towards individual responsibility. When applied to the field of robotics, however, this orientation, she argues, brings with it difficulties. After analysing the problems that the concept of individual responsibility runs into, she goes on to examine the consequences that changes in the legal concept of "responsibility" could have.

**Silja Vöneky**'s paper presents a further legal discussion. She addresses the idea of the "ethicalization of law", which refers to the phenomenon that legal norms are increasingly amended by ethical standards. Vöneky distinguishes between three types of ethicalization. The first consists in so called "opening clauses" in legal texts, which refer to ethical standards. The second consists in an institutionalization of ethics through ethics commissions. And the third consists in ethics codes that obligate research to conduct research ethically. Vöneky analyses both the foundations and the limits of these three types of ethicalization.

Finally, we are happy to be able to present **Daniel Dennett**'s classic paper "When HAL kills who is to blame? Computer Ethics" as a reprint. In it, Dennett argues that a computer system like HAL 9000 from Stanley Kubrick's movie *2001 – A Space Odyssey* (1968) may fulfil the criteria for moral responsibility. In the movie HAL decides to kill the crew of the spaceship in order to protect the mission they are on. Dennett ask, as the title of his essay suggests, who is to blame for HAL's actions. To this end, he carefully analyses his properties and concludes that HAL may, in fact, meet the conditions that are necessary for moral agency. Not only does HAL have desires and beliefs. In addition, Dennett argues, he has higher-order intentional states, which allow him to monitor what he does and reflect critically on it.

We are well aware that the discussions we have compiled in this volume come from very different backgrounds and present different points of view. This is to be welcomed! Ethical issues in science and technology have to be looked at from different angles. And different points of view need to be exchanged and examined before reliable conclusions can be drawn.

Finally, a special acknowledgement is in order. We would like to thank Laura Crompton, who typeset and corrected the texts in this volume, for her valuable work.

Munich, May 2014
Fiorella Battaglia, Nikil Mukerji, Julian Nida-Rümelin

# On the concept of responsibility

Julian Nida-Rümelin

## 1. Introduction

The aim of this short piece is to clarify the concept of responsibility.[1] We will see that a coherent concept of responsibility includes not only responsibility for actions, but also for beliefs and emotional attitudes. The guiding idea is that responsibility is closely connected to rationality and reasoning. We have a responsibility for our behaviour to the extent that this behaviour is guided or should be guided by reasons. Likewise we are responsible for our beliefs insofar as they are guided or should be guided by reasons. And we are even responsible for our emotive attitudes insofar as they are guided or should be guided by reasons. It is our capacity to weigh reasons that constitutes responsibility of all sorts.

The paper is arranged as follows. In the next section, I investigate the notion of responsibility for actions. In the two following sections, I discuss responsibility for beliefs (convictions) and emotive attitudes, and in the final section I dismiss the idea that responsibility is a consequentialist concept.

## 2. Actions

What are we responsible for? An action is that part of our behaviour that is guided by reasons, we are responsible for *all* of our actions. If something can be seen as an action of a person, the person is responsible for it. Action and responsibility are two closely connected concepts. There is no action without responsibility. And there is no

---

[1] This text mainly consists of select passages from J. Nida-Rümelin, *Verantwortung* (Stuttgart: Reclam, 2011). I would like to thank Laura Crompton and Nikil Mukerji for translating the passages from the German original.

responsibility for a behaviour, if this behaviour cannot be regarded as an action. In order to disprove this claim one would have point to an action for which the agent is not responsible. One might think that this is the case when the agent is forced or intoxicated. Let us examine whether this is true.

A tourist in Rio de Janeiro is mugged. The mugger threatens him with a knife and forces him to surrender his wallet. When he comes back to the hotel his wife blames him. She says that he should not have surrendered his wallet. Can the tourist say: "Give me a break. I am not responsible for giving up my wallet. I was forced!"? It seems to me that he cannot. Let us imagine that he had not given up his wallet and was instead stabbed by the mugger. At the hospital his wife asks him: "Why did you not give him your wallet? In these circumstances this would have been the only reasonable thing to do." Obviously, the tourist was not forced to give up his wallet in the sense that there were no alternatives to that action. He did have an alternative, even though its consequences would possibly have been disastrous. And there were reasons for and against. He could weigh these reasons and decide guided by reasons. In other words: He was obviously responsible for what he did. He was responsible for handing over the wallet just like he would have been responsible had he chosen not to hand it over.

Those who believe that agents who are forced to act in a certain way are not responsible for what they do mix up two issues that should be kept apart: They confuse the fact that an action which is done under the influence of a threat is subject to specific evaluative criteria with the fact that the respective behaviour was without alternative, such that it cannot be viewed as an action. In fact, much can be said in favour of the view that a behaviour can only be interpreted as an action if there are alternatives to it, that is, if the person in question could have chosen otherwise. When external force is applied to the agent this does not mean, however, that there are no such alternatives. The existence of a choice presupposes that there was a deliberation over the reasons for and against the action. Such deliberation presupposes that the agent could have chosen otherwise. If she had an alternative, if her behaviour was the result of a deliberation, however rudimentary, she is responsible for it. [2] This observation notwithstanding, actions can, of

---

[2] Harry Frankfurt famously argued that the existence of alternative possibilities is not a necessary condition for moral responsibility. I have rejected that view in J. Nida-

course, be good or bad, reasonable or irrational, morally acceptable or immoral and so on, as the case may be. The action of a person has to be evaluated differently if the agent is subject to a threat. The person is still responsible for what she does, but our evaluation of her action will come to a different result.

In the case of intoxication the case is entirely different. Depending on the degree of intoxication, the person in question is seen as responsible only to a limited degree, if any. This is acknowledged in jurisprudence. In court, the extent to which an intoxicated person is seen as responsible is greatly diminished. Sometimes the person is only seen as responsible for her drinking but not for the action that she performed thereafter when she was already drunk. That, in fact, seems reasonable. For there must have been a time when the person was not drunk and should have been able to foresee that her drinking would lead to a diminished ability to handle herself. In juridical contexts it may make sense to introduce thresholds that determine when responsibility can be ascribed and to which extent. But of course, the process of intoxication is, in fact, gradual and so too is the degree of responsibility that an agent is capable of. The latter declines as the level of intoxication increases. But why? What changes do intoxication bring with it? What is the reason for the diminished responsibility of an intoxicated person? For one thing, such a person is hardly in a position to judge the consequences of her behaviour. A large part of the reasons that usually enter into her deliberations is thus out of the picture. Furthermore, an intoxicated person is highly impulsive. She does not deliberate before she "acts", but simply does what she immediately feels inclined to do. Even the character of an intoxicated person may change and regress to a childish personality, to immature emotionality that is accompanied by a swift loss in frustration potential and willpower. The loss in control, which is usually invoked in order to justify the limited responsibility of an intoxicated person, does not only comprise the coordination of bodily movements but extends, most importantly, to the complex mental processes that guide the actions of a mature and accountable person. The latter is capable of embedding her actions into an overarching structure that shapes her life. She does not engage in pointwise optimization but can provide reasons for what

---

Rümelin, *Über menschliche Freiheit* (Stuttgart: Reclam, 2005). I will not, however, discuss Frankfurt's views here.

she does. In doing this, she incurs a commitment, *viz.* to act similarly in similar situations. To adopt reasons is to embed structure into one's life. An intoxicated person is incoherent to the extent that such structures are missing. Responsibility requires agential control. This control, however, is not driven by pointwise, short-sighted whims. Rather, it is one that is enclosed in the context of a practiced life and the deliberations that guide it.

This, by the way, explains the *prima facie* strange phenomenon that in most countries full-fledged responsibility in the legal sense is only acquired at the age of 18. This is so, even though some 17 or even 14-year-olds have a higher IQ and more knowledge than many adults. They insist on their independence from paternal influence and make their daily decisions on their own responsibility. Nevertheless, the legal threshold for full responsibility seems appropriate. It seems appropriate because responsibility depends not only on the cognitive abilities, empirical knowledge or economic independence. It depends on much more. In particular, it hinges on the ability to weigh reasons coherently and to become the author of one's own life. The latter manifests itself in the fact that one is capable to pursue long-term goals, to resist myopic impulses and to be sufficiently independent from other people's judgement in order to stay true to one's convictions in the face of opposition. These conditions of full responsibility, ego-strength and judgement do, in fact, develop rather late in life. Perhaps they do not develop as late as the threshold for full legal responsibility in most Western industrialized countries suggests. But they definitely do not develop as early as do intelligence and knowledge. Full responsibility is thus only ascribed under quite exacting conditions. Even in an intoxicated adult these conditions are not fully satisfied. These conditions comprise, most importantly, the ability to weigh reasons, to apply the result of the weighing process to concrete situations (judgement) and to follow through on it (willpower), but also the ability to act and to live coherently (Ich-Stärke (S. Freud), ego strength in the sense of psychoanalysis).

The above reasoning, hence, rules out the two potential counter-examples against my claim that we are responsible for *all* our actions. I should re-emphasize, however, that the concomitant attribution of action and responsibility only makes sense if we suppose that both action and responsibility are matters of degree. A minor who is not fully responsible in the legal sense is held responsible to some extent.

She has to explain herself and has to justify her actions. This seems entirely appropriate since she is able to weigh reasons to some extent. But her ability to lead an independent life, her ego strength and the willpower that structures her day-to-day life are not fully developed. She is thus responsible to a lesser extent. But it is reasonable to hold her responsible for what she does within appropriate limits.

## 3. Convictions

If it is indeed true that we are responsible for those parts of our behaviour that are guided by reasons, then there is a question which suggests itself: are there other objects, in addition to actions, for which we are responsible? Our convictions, e.g., are affected by reasons. They are not actions, though. Only the utterance of a conviction is an act, *viz.* a speech act.[3] Does that mean that we are only indirectly responsible for our convictions, *viz.* insofar as uttering them is a speech act and thus amenable to responsibility? To me this seems to be an artificial limitation of the concept of responsibility. The ability to deliberate makes us into rational, free and responsible beings. We weigh reasons as persons. In that weighing process the rational core of our personal identity manifests itself. We may disagree with wishes, feelings and attitudes that we observe in our own psyche. And this may manifest itself in the fact that we do not allow them to become action-guiding. We cannot distance ourselves from our deliberations in the same way. The latter are – in a strong sense – always ours. We identify ourselves with them as persons. Our reason-guided convictions are our own. We cannot distance ourselves from them – or only at the cost of changing our personal identity. In this sense, reason-guided actions and convictions have the same status: They are constitutive of the persons that we are. And their constitutive role expresses itself, amongst other things, through the fact that we are responsible for our convictions and actions and through the fact that we defend them against critics. For this reason, it seems to me erroneous to exclude convictions from the realm of objects for which we are responsible. Convictions exemplify,

---

[3] Cf. J. L. Austin, *How to do Things with Words* (Oxford: Clarendon Press, 1975); J. Searle, *Speech Acts: An Essay in the Philosophy of Language* (Cambridge: Cambridge University, 1969).

even more clearly than actions, the connection of our reasons with our responsibility and freedom. The problem of *akrasia*, after all, presents itself only rarely in the case of convictions. In the case of actions, on the other hand, it is quite frequent. We are responsible for the result of our deliberations because our deliberations constitute our control.

At this point, it may be objected that there are certain convictions that are not based on reasons. Consider the conviction that there is a tree in front of me. I arrive at that conviction through mere observation. At any rate, so it seems. Some will say that there is a causal process at work: the transition from the perception of the tree to the conviction – if one can even speak of a transition in that regard – is a causal one. The perception of the tree causes in me the conviction that there is a tree in front of me. But how about the stick that looks bent in water? I perceive it as bent. But I do not form the conviction that it is. In this case, I have only the perception of a bent stick, but not the conviction that that stick is in fact bent. My conviction does not affect my perception: I still perceive the stick as bent. But I know that, in fact, it is not. The perception of the stick is in that sense a causal process. The reasons that lead me to believe that the stick is not bent cannot change my perception. It is causally determined. I cannot influence it through reasons. This is different in the case of convictions. They are affected by reasons. That shows that reasons figure prominently even when it comes to ones that are closely related to perceptions. Reasons are constitutive – not just for actions, but also for convictions. And to the extent that reasons play a role in their formation, we are responsible for them. We are responsible for our convictions just like we are for our actions.

## 4. Emotional Attitudes

The more closely related our convictions are to perception, the smaller the role of deliberation. Something similar can be said in regards to our actions. The degree of responsibility is small if deliberation only plays a small role – like in the case of intoxication or in the case of young children. Now let us consider a different case. If somebody is hungry, then she has a desire to satisfy her hunger. Further deliberation may incite her not to give in to this desire – e.g. because she is overweight. It does not make much sense to reproach somebody for her wish to eat something. But it may make sense to criticize her because – yet again – she is having a snack, even though she is overweight. This illustrates what I just said. Hunger is accompanied by the desire to eat something. This desire can be guided by reasons only to a very limited extent. However, the decision to go to the kitchen, pick up a chocolate bar and eat it, is not an automatic consequence of that wish. There are persons who have a strong wish to satisfy their hunger and who nevertheless wait until dinner. This is because they have decided that it would be wrong to eat something, even though it would indeed satisfy their current desire. They do the right thing. That is, they do that which is supported by the balance of reasons.

There are other attitudes for which reasons play a role. Take, e.g., the adverse reaction that one person may have to another person. It expresses itself, e.g., in the fact that the person who has this attitude is not willing to sit at the same table as the other or to engage in joint activities with her. We can ask her which reasons there are for this adverse attitude.[4] Perhaps we learn of a previous encounter where the person was offended by the other or had a problematic impression of her character traits. We may also learn about the negative statements of third parties regarding that one person. Whatever it is that can be said in favour of such an attitude, it suggests that such attitudes can generally be justified and do stand in need of justification. A complete refusal to give reasons for such an attitude would make the person having the attitude look irrational. In that case, one could say "she rejects him without any reason". That is to say, "her attitude is without justification". It might also be that reasons are given which are not convincing. E.g., one person may reject another because that other person is homosexual. But that fact is not, in and of itself, a good reason for an adverse reaction. Homosexuality has nothing about it that should offend another person. It merely concerns the intimate relations of two people and does not affect anybody else. When others are nevertheless repulsed by it, then this is an irrational emotion und the corresponding attitude is not justified. Obviously, we have a responsibility not only for our propositional attitudes but also for our

---

[4] The English term "attitude" is more encompassing than similar terms in other languages. It comprises, e.g., the shades of meaning of the two German words "Haltung" and "Einstellung" and has, if I see it correctly, the same meaning as the ancient greek *hexis*, as it is used in Aristoteles' Nikomachean Ethics.

attitudes of a different type, namely to the extent that they are – *rationaliter* – the result of practical deliberation.

One may object to the claim that emotive attitudes are guided by reasons. One may say that for certain attitudes the person having the attitude is not to blame. Some people, it may be argued, *simply have* certain attitudes. Nowadays hardly anyone admits to be homophobic. But occasionally you may hear people say: "Homosexuals just disgust me. There is nothing more to say. It is what it is. I cannot help the way I feel." There is no sharp border that separates attitudes from sentiments. I may have a feeling of disgust towards a particular exotic dish, which contains, let's say, frog legs. I reject such a dish, perhaps because I know the method by which its ingredients are obtained. I have an attitude towards this dish – a negative one – which may express itself, e.g., in the fact that I decline it when it is offered to me. My rejection of the dish can be rooted in animal ethics. My disgust about the dish may only be a side effect of that type of rejection. My rejection of the dish is supported by reasons and can, to the extent that these reasons are convincing, be rational. My disgust would then be a sentiment that is based on an attitude which is rationally supported by reasons. Does this mean that the disgust is also rationally warranted? In the continuum between attitudes and sentiments, it seems, the impact of reasons plays an important role. The more apparent the role of practical deliberation is, the more we feel inclined to speak of an attitude and not of a sentiment. The smaller the influence of reasons[5], the more we are inclined to speak of sentiments. A person who characterizes her dismissive attitude towards homosexuals as a mere irrational sentiment seeks to evade the need to justify her attitude. She emphasizes that she does not have any control over her attitude/sentiment, she emphasizes that is not her fault.

Let's consider the case of a person who is arachnophobic, even though she knows that spiders in her country are not poisonous and that they are not dangerous in any other way either. Some biologists believe that arachnophobia (as well as the fear of certain insects) is a genetic heritage. The arachnophobic person may say: "I know that spiders are not dangerous, but I am disgusted by them. I just am." I

---

[5] Strictly speaking, one would have to add the word "rationally" to this phrase. That is to say, we are picturing the case of a fully accountable person who is capable of judgement and decision.

suppose we will believe her. Perhaps we will recommend, if her disgust is all too irritating, that she watch spiders calmly and from up close in order to gradually overcome her – unjustified – feeling of disgust. Let us alter the case a bit. The arachnophobic person, let us assume, says: "I am afraid of spiders." This attitude is only justified if spiders are, in fact, dangerous. If at the same time the person admits that she knows that spiders are not dangerous, then she will also have to admit that her attitude is irrational. Her fear would thus be closer to an attitude than to a sentiment. The fact that my fear is unjustified implies that I should not have it. We can see, then, that the degree of influence of reasons varies. We are responsible for our attitudes to the extent that they are – *rationaliter* – controlled by reasons.

# 5. Consequences

When we act we also consider the consequences of our actions. An influential theory of rationality, so-called rational choice theory – recommends that we should only consider the consequences of our actions in order to determine their (instrumental) value and in order to determine whether its value is greater than the value of all alternatives. Max Weber distinguished between an ethic of principles ("Gesinnungsethik") and an ethic of responsibility ("Verantwortungs-ethik"), where the latter takes the immediate and mediated consequences of a decision as the measuring rod for its evaluation. This suggestive juxtaposition still coins political rhetoric of our time. But, in fact, it leads us astray. As I have argued elsewhere, acting merely in the pursuit of optimal consequences – and this holds in particular in the area of politics – would undermine the foundation of all of morality.[6] In the present context, I would like to analyse what follows from the conception of responsibility that I have introduced above in regards to the consequences of our actions. Thus far I have argued that we are responsible for our actions and convictions and also for our (emotional) attitudes to the extent that they can be seen as being founded on reasons. Are we also responsible for the consequences of our actions?

It is a *prima facie* plausible view that our responsibility for actions implies that we are also responsible for their consequences. If we are

---

[6] See J. Nida-Rümelin, *Kritik des Konsequentialismus* (München: Oldenburg, 1993).

responsible for an action, then we are also responsible for all its consequences. Adherents of the ethic of responsibility will add that that is, in fact, the essence of responsibility. Responsibility for actions expresses itself in the willingness to also take responsibility for the consequences of one's actions. This initially plausible view is false. In order to see this, we have to take a little detour into the area of decision theory. When I choose to do an action I thereby choose a probability distribution of possible consequences. Sometimes particular consequences may count as almost certain. In that case, they have a probability close to 1 and all other possible consequences have a probability close to 0. When I decide to take the plane from Frankfurt to New York then there is a certain probability, however minimal, that the plane will crash. In winter there is a certain possibility, which may in fact be significant, that the departure in Frankfurt or the arrival in New York is delayed through the influence of snow. In the past years there has been a steadily increasing probability that a flight is overbooked and that passengers have to move to a different flight etc. By participating in road traffic I have to take into account the possibility that I cause an accident. Even if I am fully alert and abide by the road code, my participation in traffic may lead – through no fault of my own – to the death of a person. An extremist about responsibility will say: You decided to take part in traffic, you knew that this was associated with certain risks. Therefore, you bear full responsibility for all consequences of your decision.

This position confuses two entirely different issues. The one is whether it can be justified to partake in traffic. Whether that is the case depends on the probability that participation in traffic will cause harm to others. The latter depends, in turn, on the driver's personal abilities and character traits. If I am extremely impatient and rather prone to take risks, I should not participate in road traffic. Similarly, if I have a hard time concentrating and get easily distracted by conversations with my co-drivers, I should not drive myself. But let us suppose that I am – like most adults – sufficiently able to focus and that I also possess all other characteristics that allow for a reasonable risk distribution when I partake in traffic. Nevertheless, an accident occurs – through no fault of my own.[7] Let us suppose a very serious case in which a child unexpectedly runs out on the road and dies. If, in fact, I did not make a mistake, then I am not responsible for that consequence of the accident. To be sure, I am responsible for accepting the general risks that are associated with my participation in traffic. But this does not imply that I am responsible for all consequences of that decision.

How far does this limitation of responsibility go? In this case, my causal contribution to the death of a person is reconcilable with the fact that I am not responsible for that death. There is only one way to ascribe responsibility that can be coherently applied to all sorts of examples. It consists in a radical limitation of responsibility to one's own actions. We are merely responsible for our actions and in no way for their consequences. This may sound highly counterintuitive. But that has to do with the fuzziness of our linguistic usage. In order to make this clear and let us once more go back to a decision-theoretical description: Actions always contain a probability distribution of possible consequences. By deciding to do a given act, I thereby accept the respective probability distribution of that act's consequences. I have to justify this. I am responsible for this. More precisely: I am responsible for the probability distribution of the consequences of the act. I am not responsible for happenstance, for something that I cannot control, which may cause the one rather than the other consequence to eventuate.

If I stop in front of a red street light, then there is a residual probability that I thereby cause a rear-end collision. I do not have to look into the rear-view mirror when I stop in front of a red street light, even though the probability for a collision is not 0. That probability is sufficiently small and the mutual understanding of all participants in traffic that one has to stop in front of a red street light and that following cars have to keep a sufficient distance in order to avoid collisions in front of red street lights, is enough to release me entirely from my responsibility for this possible, yet unlikely, consequence. So I do have a responsibility for the consequences of my actions to the extent that in deciding to do a given action I accept the probability distribution of consequences that is associated with that action.

---

[7] I have already discussed this problem in my invited talk 'There is no Moral Luck' at Caltech, Pasadena. A German translation of the manuscript can be found in Ch. 4 of J. Nida-Rümelin, *Über Menschliche Freiheit* (Stuttgart: Reclam, 2005).

One may say that I am responsible for the possible consequences of my action weighed by their respective likelihoods. But this way of talking can cause confusion. For this reason, we should restate the previous claim, *viz.* that I am only responsible for my actions and that I am, insofar as I am responsible for my actions, also responsible for the probability distribution of possible consequences that is caused by that action.[8] The responsibility for consequences is, to that extent, included in a responsibility for actions and the associated probability distributions of their possible consequences. Over and above that, there is no independent responsibility for consequences.

# 6. Conclusion

In this short piece, I have argued on the basis of the view that we are responsible to the extent that we are or should be guided by reasons. This led me to making the following claims: Firstly, we are responsible for our actions. We are responsible for all of them. Once a behaviour is properly seen as an action, the agent is responsible for it. Agency and responsibility are two sides of the same coin. This only makes sense, however, if we adopt a gradual understanding of agency and responsibility, as I also explained. Secondly, we have a responsibility for our convictions. Like actions, convictions are guided by reasons. Hence, it would seem to be an artificial limitation of the concept of responsibility if we were to confine it only to actions. Thirdly, I argued that we can have a responsibility for our (emotional) attitudes, too. The reasoning behind that claim employed the same premise. Having reasons implies responsibility. And since attitudes are amenable to reasons, we can be responsible for them as well. Finally, I discussed the idea that we can be responsible for the consequences of our actions and rejected it. Instead, I argued that we can be responsible only for the probability distribution of possible consequences that is caused by the action that we chose.

---

[8] In scientific theory and probability theory there is a controversy as to whether it is appropriate to speak of "causation" in this context. I, however, see good reasons in favour of a probabilistic concept of causation, which would legitimate that we use this expression here.

# Technological progress and responsibility

*Nikil Mukerji*

## 1. Introduction

In this essay, I will examine how technological progress affects the responsibilities of human agents. To this end, I will distinguish between two interpretations of the concept of responsibility, *viz. responsibility as attributability* and *substantive responsibility*. On the former interpretation, responsibility has to do with the idea of authorship. When we say that a person is responsible for her actions we mean that she is to be seen as the author of these actions. They can be attributed to her, such that she can be normatively appraised – i.e. blamed, praised, etc. – on that basis. In discussing this kind of responsibility I will show that the responsibility of human agents tends to increase as their technologies progress. This claim is often taken for granted, but seldom clarified and argued for. I will give it a clear interpretation and provide a semi-formal reasoning that supports it. The second interpretation of responsibility that I will discuss is substantive responsibility. It has to do with the normative demands that confront us – with what we are required to do. I will argue that technological change can affect, firstly, what our substantive responsibilities are on a case-by-case basis. Secondly, I will try to show that it can affect the way we think about our substantive responsibilities at the level of theoretical normative ethics.

The remainder of the text is structured as follows. In the next section, I will start off with a few rather general remarks about the idea of responsibility in which I shall distinguish between responsibility as attributability and substantive responsibility. In the two sections that follow, I will try to support the two aforementioned claims. First, I will argue for the view that advances in technology tend to increase human responsibility in the sense of attributability. Then, I will try to show how technological change affects our substantive responsibilities as well as the way we think about them at the level of normative-ethical theory. In the final section, then, I will sum up and conclude.

## 2. Some clarificatory remarks on responsibility

First off, I should disambiguate the term "responsible", which can be used in various senses. We can say, e.g., that the corrosion of a pipe was responsible for its bursting.[1] And we can say that Smith kicked Jones' shin bone and is thus responsible for hurting Jones. In the first example, we use the term "responsible" in the same sense in which we use the word "causal" (or "causally responsible"). In the second case, we presumably use the term "responsible" with different intent. We are not just saying that Smith's kick *caused* Jones' pain (though we presumably believe that, too). Over and above, we want to say that Smith is *normatively* responsible for harming Jones. The latter idea is closely related to the idea of blame and to the various other reactive attitudes that figure prominently in the moral psychology of responsibility.[2] In the following, I will, of course, focus on the second, i.e normative, idea of responsibility.[3]

This having said, I can differentiate the idea a bit further. As I already pointed out in the introduction, we can speak of normative responsibility in two different senses, *viz.* in the sense of *attributability* and in the sense of *substantive responsibility*.[4] In the two subsequent sections, I will discuss how technological advancements affect both kinds of responsibility. Before I can to do that, however, I need to make some preliminary observations.

---

[1] I borrow this example from J. Nida-Rümelin, *Verantwortung* (Stuttgart: Reclam, 2011), 19-20.

[2] On that point, see P. Strawson, "Freedom and Resentment," in (1962) *Proceedings of the British Academy* 48, 1–25.

[3] As Julian Nida-Rümelin explains, the distinction between causation and responsibility is actually more complex than I just depicted it: "A plumber who is inspecting a pipe burst may point to the corrosion of the pipe as the cause. But this utterance can have a meaning that is to some extent normative. It can mean that everything else – e.g. the water pressure, the thickness of the pipe, the bolting and so on – was the way it was supposed to be. Only the corrosion was not supposed to be there. The corrosion would then not suffice for a comprehensive causal explanation of the pipe burst. Such a causal explanation would have to include many factors, such as the water pressure, the thickness of the pipe and many others, which jointly explain the pipe burst. But it can be singled out as *causal* or *responsible* because it deviates from its expected or normal condition, which serves as a normative standard." J. Nida-Rümelin (fn. 1), 19-20 (my translation, NM).

[4] Cf. T. M. Scanlon, *What We Owe to Each Other* (Cambridge, MA: Harvard University Press, 1998), 248.

Let me start with responsibility as attributability. When we talk about responsibility in that sense we pronounce that somebody is responsible *for something*. What this means is simply that the person in question is, in an appropriate sense, to be seen as the *originator* or *author* of that something, such that the former can be morally appraised on the basis of the latter. That is, we can ascribe praise, blame and so on to the respective person. Now when do we ascribe responsibility in this sense? On one plausible view, responsibility as attributability is linked to rationality.[5] That is to say, it is linked to our capacity to appreciate, weigh and give reasons. Being responsible hence means, quite literally, being required to *respond* by giving reasons. As a consequence, we can only be responsible (or ascribe responsibility to another) for something if that something is amenable to reasoned deliberation.

The account I have just introduced confines both the scope of possible objects and the scope of possible subjects of responsibility. Let us consider the former first by asking which possible objects of responsibility there are or, to put it differently, what we can possibly be responsible *for*. If, as I have just assumed, responsibility is connected to rationality, we can be responsible only for objects that can plausibly be seen as and should be the product of reasoned deliberation. This means, first of all, that we have an *agential responsibility* – a responsibility for our actions. Our actions, after all, are driven by reasons. But it also means that we can be responsible for other objects that are not typically seen as objects of responsibility. We can, e.g., have an *attitudinal responsibility* – that is, a responsibility for our attitudes. And we can have an *epistemic responsibility* – that is, a responsibility for our convictions. After all, attitudes and convictions are also amenable to reasons.[6] Be that as it may, in my discussion of responsibility as attributability, I will put attitudinal and epistemic responsibility aside and focus exclusively on agential responsibility.[7]

---

[5] I follow the view expressed in J. Nida-Rümelin (fn.1). An abridged statement of his ideas about responsibility can be found in J. Nida-Rümelin, "On the Concept of Responsibility", which is contained in this volume.

[6] Cf. J. Nida-Rümelin, "On the Concept of Responsibility" (fn.5).

[7] On the account of responsibility that I am using here, agential responsibility is, in fact, quite far-reaching. It implies not only that we are responsible for some of our actions. Rather, it says that we are responsible for *all* of them. This follows from what I have said so far in conjunction with an analysis of the concept of an action. Actions have behavioural components. When we act we move our bodies. But we do not think of every behaviour as an action. It is only intentional behaviour – behaviour driven by

That said, I should mention that different kinds of agential responsibility can be distinguished – at least if you believe, as some authors do, that we can differentiate between various types of agents. In what follows, I will focus on *individual agential responsibility*, which is the responsibility of an individual agent for her actions, though I will not use these qualifiers. In passing, I should note, however, that there are various other possible subjects that may be seen as candidates for agential responsibility. Christian List and Philip Pettit, e.g., have recently revived the idea of *group agency*, which holds that groups can be agents and thus capable of responsibility, too.[8] And a number of authors have suggested that technological artefacts can also be seen as agents who may bear agential responsibility. This holds in particular for Daniel Dennett, who has argued that a computer system like HAL from Stanley Kubrick's movie *2001 – A Space Odyssey* (1968) could conceivably be viewed as an agent who is subject to responsibility.[9] As I just said, however, I will not discuss these forms of responsibility in what follows.

Having clarified the idea of responsibility as attributability in the sense of individual agential responsibility, I can now move on to the idea of substantive responsibility. As T. M. Scanlon explains, judgements of substantive responsibility simply "express substantive claims about what people are required (…) to do for each other."[10] To say that

---

reasons – that we think of as an action. Therefore, since all actions are driven by reasons and we are, according to the account of responsibility that I have just proposed, responsible for something to the extent that that something is or should be guided by reasons, we are responsible for all our actions.

[8] See C. List, P. Pettit, *Group Agency* (Oxford: Oxford University Press, 2012). Note that the view of List and Petti is controversial since the idea that groups can be agents appears to be metaphysically queer. I have nevertheless tried to defend it in a recent paper, N. Mukerji, C. Lütge, 'Responsibility, Order Ethics and Group Agency', in (forthcoming) *Archiv für Rechts- und Sozialphilosophie.*

[9] See D. Dennett, 'When HAL kills Who is to Blame?', in D. G. Stork (ed.) *HAL's Legacy: 2001's Computer as Dream and Reality* (Cambridge, MA: MIT Press). The paper is reprinted in this volume. For a critique of Dennett's viewpoint view, see J. Nida-Rümelin, 'Agency, Technology and Responsibility', in *Politica & Società* (forthcoming).

[10] T. M. Scanlon (fn.4), 248. It may be noted that Scanlon's explanation of substantive responsibility is quite narrow. In the case of responsibility as attributability I distinguished between agential, attitudinal and epistemic responsibility (as attributability). Similarly, it seems not unreasonable to distinguish between different kinds of substantive responsibility, *viz.* agential, attitudinal and epistemic (substantive) responsibility. Scanlon's remark only captures the first of these. Given the purpose of this essay in which I focus on agential responsibility, this is, however, a moot point.

a person has a substantive responsibility to do something is thus to say that there is a normative requirement upon her to do it.[11] Our substantive responsibilities depend on the choice situation that we are in and they have a *content*. In other words, whenever we have a substantive responsibility, we are required to do something *specific*. And what that specific thing is depends on our options for acting as well as the reasons for and against these options. From an ethical point of view, we are supposed to weigh these reasons and choose accordingly. Thus, while we satisfy our agential responsibility (as attributability) by giving reasons for what we do, we satisfying our substantive responsibility by doing that which we have sufficient reason to do.

# 3. Technological progress and agential responsibility

What I said in the previous section prepared my substantive discussion of the relation between technological progress and responsibility. In this section, I will address the idea of agential responsibility as attributability. My claim is that technological progress tends to increase and never decreases our agential responsibility because it tends to increase and never decreases our options for acting. There are cases where new technologies do not give us new options for acting, thus leaving our choice situations unchanged. In these cases, our agential responsibility stays the same. In other cases, however, new technologies affect our choice situations by increasing our options for acting. And in these situations they increase our agential responsibility. This, in fact, seems to be a purely conceptual matter, as we shall see.

In order to explain the argument for this claim, I need to explain, first of all, what it means for our agential responsibility to increase. An informal way to answer this question is to say that our agential responsibility increases if the requirement to give reasons for our actions becomes more demanding. But this seems to be a bit vague. So I should tackle the issue more formally. To this end, let me introduce the following conventions. Let $A$ be an agent, who faces, let us suppose, a number of choice situations, $C_1, \ldots, C_n$, in her daily practice,

---

[11] I deliberately do not speak of a *moral* responsibility here because this would require that I explain that qualification. This task is harder than it looks. Cf. J. Nida-Rümelin (fn.1), Ch. XII.

$D$. That is to say, there are $n$ situations in which $A$ can choose between at least two alternatives, such that she has to provide reasons for her choices in $n$ cases. In order to make sense of the word "increase" in my above claim we need to make agential responsibility comparable across different practices $D$, $D'$, $D''$ and so on. To that end, let us stipulate that the choices, $C_1$, ..., $C_n$ that $A$ faces in $D$ create a measurable "amount" or "degree" of agential responsibility, which is denoted by $R_A(D)$.

Admittedly, it will be hard to compare all practices with regard to the amount of agential responsibility that they involve. However, there seem to be certain clear cases. Let us look at two of them. In these two cases $A$'s daily practice, $D$, is transformed into new practices, $D'$ and $D''$, respectively, and the amount of $A$'s agential responsibility, $R_A(D)$, is transformed into $R_A(D')$ and $R_A(D'')$, respectively. *Vis-à-vis* $D$, $D'$ and $D''$ are specified, respectively as follows:

> $D$ *is transformed into* $D'$: A new choice option is introduced *ceteris paribus*, such that a new choice situation arises. $A$ faces not only choice situations $C_1$, ..., $C_n$. Instead, she faces an additional choice situation $C_{n+1}$.
>
> $D$ *is transformed into* $D''$: A new choice option is introduced *ceteris paribus*, such that choice situations $C_1$, ..., $C_{i-1}$, ..., $C_{i+1}$, ..., $C_n$ remain unchanged. But there is (at least) one additional choice option that she can choose in situation $C_i$.

Both the transformation of $D$ into $D'$ and the transformation of $D$ into $D''$ undoubtedly increase the agential responsibility of the agent. That is, $R_A(D') > R_A(D)$ and $R_A(D'') > R_A(D)$.

Why the former? To see this, we need to compare $D'$ with $D$. Under $D'$, $A$ needs to provide reasons for her choices in $C_1$, ..., $C_n$ just like she did in $D$. In addition, though, she needs to provide reasons for her choice in situation $C_{n+1}$. This makes her new situation, $D'$, more demanding in terms of agential responsibility than the old situation, $D$. The requirement to justify what $A$ does is more stringent under $D'$ than it is under $D$. Hence, $R_A(D') > R_A(D)$.

Why the latter? Again, to see this we need to compare $D''$ with $D$. Under $D''$, $A$ has to provide reasons for the actions she choses in choice situations $C_1$, ..., $C_{i-1}$, ..., $C_{i+1}$, ..., $C_n$ and against the actions that she did not choose just like she did under $D$. In addition, she needs to give a further reason in situation $C_i$ that justifies why she did or did not choose the new option that has become available. This makes $D''$ more demanding in terms of agential responsibility than $D$. And hence, $R_A(D') > R_A(D)$.

With these preliminary remarks in mind, the argument for my claim is, in fact, straightforward. To the extent that technological progress is practically relevant it brings with it new options for acting, while all other options remain available.[12] It either enriches existing choice situations by giving us new choice options. E.g., when I want to travel from Munich to Hamburg I have a choice to travel by car, train, plane or, God forbid, by bus. Once the hyperloop becomes available I will have a further option.[13] This type of technological progress matches the transition from $D$ to $D'$. A second possibility is that technological progress creates new choice options. NASA, e.g., were confronted with a choice as to whether or not they should send a person to the moon as soon as the technology that would allow them to do this became available. The change introduced by that kind of technology fits the transformation from $D$ into $D''$. As I established above, both the transformation from $D$ to $D'$ and the transformation from $D$ to $D''$ increase our agential responsibility. This shows, then, that technological progress, to the extent that it is practically relevant, increases our agential responsibility.

# 4. Technological progress and substantive responsibility

In this section, I will attempt to show how technological progress can affect both our substantive responsibilities and the way we think

---

[12] This claim may be doubted. It may be said that certain technological changes take away certain options for acting. E.g., now that everybody has a mobile phone we may say that not having one is "just not an option". Though there is nothing wrong with taking that way in everyday life, it must be pointed out that the sense in which the word "option" is used here is different from the one intended. When we say about a particular course of action that it is "just not an option" we mean that choosing that it would have unacceptable consequences. In that sense, technological progress can take away options. However, it does not take away options in the sense that certain possibilities are eliminated.

[13] The Tesla Company has recently released a document which shows how the hyperloop would work. Available at <http://www.teslamotors.com/sites/default/files/-blog_attachments/hyperloop_alpha3.pdf> accessed 1 May 2014.

about them. To this end, it makes sense to distinguish, first of all, between two areas of ethics, *viz.* applied ethics and normative ethics.

Applied ethics may be defined as the application of moral theory and its methods to concrete moral problems. These problems involve a choice situation with various options for choice and an agent who can choose between them. In order to determine what the right choice – in other words, the responsibility of the agent – is, applied ethicists investigate the factors that speak in favour of the respective options and against them. They investigate, in other words, their *pro's* and *con's* and advise the agent to do that action which, on balance, is most favourable. Now as we have seen in the previous section, technological progress tends to add choice options. Agents who have access to new technologies can do new things or can do whatever they used to do in new ways. For this reason, technological progress may change their substantive responsibilities. This is, of course, not a matter of necessity. The mere fact that a new option has become available does not mean that the agent is normatively required to choose this option. Quite often, the new options for acting that technological progress makes available involve risks. And this may make it inadvisable to choose them. In other cases, however, new options may be best supported by reasons and may thus become normatively mandatory. And in these cases, technological progress changes our substantive responsibilities.

Let us look at an example by Peter Singer that illustrates the point. In his influential paper "Famine, Affluence, and Morality" (1972) Singer says that

> [f]rom a moral point of view, the development of the world into a 'global village' has made an important, though still unrecognized, difference to our moral situation. Expert observers and supervisors, sent out by famine relief organizations or permanently stationed in famine-prone areas, can direct our aid to a refugee in Bengal almost as effectively as we could get it to someone in our own block.[14]

A few decades before Singer wrote these words, people were unable to help poor people in faraway places. They could only help their fellow neighbours, that is, the people in their immediate environment. Given

---

[14] P. Singer, 'Famine, Affluence, and Morality', *Philosophy and Public Affairs* 1(3), 229-243.

the progress in information technologies, however, funds can now be transferred around the Globe in no time. And there are infrastructures, which ensure that these funds are distributed fast and greatly impact the lives of those in need. Today we live, as Singer puts it, in a "global village."[15] That means that almost every one of us now has it in their power to do a tremendous amount of good. This holds, in particular, for those who live in affluent Western countries. If you are from such a country, there is a fair chance that you should give much more than you currently do. You do not even have to be a utilitarian like Singer to arrive at that conclusion.[16] I, e.g., am from Germany, where only 47% of all people give money to charity. This places my country at number 27 in terms of money donations worldwide. It would be hard to argue that more than half of its population is too poor to give anything at all. After all, in Myanmar the number is 85%. And India, of all countries, has the largest absolute number of people who give to charity.[17] An applied ethicist like Singer may thus draw the conclusion that the technology-induced transformation of our world into a "global village" gives my fellow Germans a responsibility to do much more to help those in need than they currently do.

The way in which technological progress affects our responsibilities as human agents is, I think, rather obvious. Above I have, however, made a more far-reaching claim. I said that technological progress does not only affect our substantive responsibilities on a case-by-case basis. I maintained that it may also change the way we think about our responsibilities at the level of normative-ethical theory. Admittedly, this connection is less obvious. After all, normative ethics concerns, one may say, the fundamental makeup of our moral "reality". Just like the laws of physics are reasonably seen as eternal and changeless, the basic principles that underlie our moral duties may be supposed to be unalterable. Though that may in fact be true, the changes that our

---

[15] The term "global village" is not, however, original to Singer. To my knowledge, it was coined by Herbert Marshall McLuhan in the book *The Gutenberg Galaxy* (Toronto: University of Toronto Press, 1962).

[16] My colleague Jan-Christoph Heilinger has, e.g., argued for far-reaching moral obligations based on human welfare rights. See J.-C. Heilinger, 'The moral demandingness of socioeconomic human rights', in G. Ernst, J.-C. Heilinger, *The philosophy of human rights. Contemporary controversies* (Berlin/Boston: de Gruyter, 2012), 185–208.

[17] I take these figures from the *World Giving Index 2013* of the Charity Aid Foundation (CAF), which is available at: <https://www.cafonline.org/pdf/WorldGivingIndex-2013_1374AWEB.pdf> accessed 1 May 2014.

empirical world undergoes – and that includes technological changes – may nevertheless change the way we *think* about the issues that lie at the heart of normative ethics.[18] And to that extent, these changes may have an impact on the discipline of normative ethics and on the conclusions at which we arrive in that discipline. This, in a nutshell, is the reasoning behind the claim that technological progress can affect the way we think about our substantive responsibilities. Perhaps it is not entirely satisfactory, though. For it remains to be explained *how* technological advances can affect the way we think about normative ethics. To explain this, I should, first of all, say a few words about the way in which modern normative ethics commonly proceeds.

Right off, I should emphasize that normative-ethical theorists have by and large distanced themselves from the views of the systematic moral thinkers, such as Kant, Mill, Sidgwick and so on.[19] They believed that the whole content of morality could be deduced from a single principle (or a number thereof). Like in physics, experiments of sorts nowadays play a fundamental role in normative ethics. While physicists test the laws that are suspected to underlie the workings of the cosmos against empirical observation, ethical theorists test their theories against cases. These are usually hypothetical thought experiments (e.g. trolley cases). But they can also be examples that are taken from our real world. In both cases, the standard procedure is roughly as follows. A philosopher considers an example – either hypothetical or real – of a situation in which an agent faces a morally significant choice or acts in ways that call for moral evaluation. Then, she probes into our moral intuitions about that case. She investigates, e.g., which of the choice options strike us as permissible, obligatory or forbidden. After that, she turns to the various contestants in the race for the best moral theory – say, Kantianism, utilitarianism, virtue ethics and so on – and analyses their implications for the case at hand. Finally, she compares our moral intuitions to the implications that the respective theory yields. The

---

[18] Arguably, this is also true for artistic characterizations of technology (e.g. in film). On this point, see N. Mukerji, 'Why Moral Philosophers Should Watch Sci-Fi Movies', in (forthcoming) F. Battaglia, N. Weidenfeld (eds.), *Roboethics in Film* (Pisa: Pisa University Press).

[19] On this point, see J. Nida-Rümelin, *Philosophie und Lebensform* (Frankfurt a. M.: Suhrkamp, 2009), 194-221. See, furthermore, N. Mukerji, J. Nida-Rümelin, 'Towards a Moderate Stance on Human Enhancement', in (in press) *Humana.mente – Journal of Philosophical Studies*.

theory whose implications are best in line with our intuitions is the one that may count as corroborated by the case at hand.

This is admittedly a very sketchy depiction of what goes on when normative-ethical theorists go about their business. But it suffices to explain what I am seeking to explain, *viz.* how technological advances can affect our normative-ethical thinking and the substantive responsibilities that follow from it. As I explained above, technological progress changes the empirical circumstances in which we act. We are able to do new things or do the same things in new ways. This gives rise to new moral scenarios, which may provide new test cases for the theories that we discuss in normative ethics. Their tenability will depend, at least in part, on how well they can cope with the new scenarios that we encounter as our technologies advance. And, obviously, the substantive responsibilities that follow from them will, too. This shows, then, that technological progress does not only affect our responsibilities in concrete cases. It may also affect the way we think about them at a theoretical level.

Singer's stance in "Famine, Affluence, and Morality" can once again be used as illustrative material. As I said above, Singer believes that most people in affluent Western countries should do much more than they currently do to help the poor. Technological progress has transformed the world into a "global village" where affluent individuals are perfectly able to make a great difference in the lives of those in need. They should choose to do this rather than to spend their money on luxury items that they do not really need. Singer says this as an applied ethicist. He essentially explains how, in his view, technological progress affects our substantive responsibilities in a concrete situation. But what he says also holds a lesson for a normative ethicist. If you find Singer's judgement plausible, if you also believe that the rich have a responsibility to do much more than they currently do to help the poor, then you should use this insight for normative-ethical purposes, too. You should investigate the implications of various theories of substantive responsibility in Singer's case and compare them to the judgement that you find plausible. If they imply that judgement, this constitutes one reason to accept them. If they do not, this constitutes a reason not to accept them. On the other hand, if you reject Singer's view, then you may proceed in the opposite way. You may check which moral theories support Singer's judgement and take this to be a reason for rejecting them. At this point, I am not interested in whether or not

Singer's judgement is correct. In either case you can use his analysis of the way in which technological progress changes our responsibilities to the global poor as data for normative-ethical theorizing. And this illustrates what I claimed, *viz.* that concrete cases of technological developments can influence the way we think about our substantive responsibilities at the theoretical level.

# 5. Conclusion

In this paper, I analysed the relation between technological progress and responsibility. I started out by distinguishing between two concepts of responsibility, *viz.* responsibility as attributability and substantive responsibility. I argued that our responsibility as attributability, which we satisfy by giving convincing reasons for our choices, increases as technology progresses since technological progress increases our options and thus confers upon us a more stringent requirement to justify what we do. Then, I went on to show that technological progress can furthermore affect our substantive responsibilities. That is to say, it can affect what we are required to do. And it may, in fact, add rather demanding requirements. I illustrated this using the "global village" and our obligations to the poor in faraway places as an example. Technological progress in information technology has given us the option to help those in need. Given that we have this option and can help very easily, much can be said to support the view that we therefore have a far-reaching responsibility to help. In addition, I argued that technological change can affect not only the substantive content of our responsibilities but also the way we think about them from a theoretical standpoint. It may provide new test cases for our normative theories of substantive responsibility.

Developments in technology are, of course, interesting in and of themselves. But given what I have argued, it seems reasonable to think that ethicists in particular should take an interest in technology as it gives rise to stimulating questions in both applied and normative ethics.

# Ethics and the regulation of technological applications in Europe

*Benedetta Bisol*

## 1. Introduction

This article presents some reflections on the governance of science and technology in the European Union, considering this topic from a philosophical point of view. The main subject of the article is to discuss currently adopted strategies of ethical regulation in the fields of research, production and use of technological applications as well as some limits and difficulties related to these strategies. The main goal of my analysis is to show how ethics as a philosophical discipline can help today to draw up a regulating framework for science and technology with particular regard to new and emerging technologies.

At first glance, it seems to be possible to define the ethics of technology as a field of knowledge that can be clearly distinguished from the scientific knowledge about technology, according to the following criterion: ethics gives us a repertoire of theoretical models, notions and methods which allows us to distinguish between good and bad, right and wrong use of technologies; on the other hand, technical options are neutral in axiological terms. Accordingly, when we refer to the scientific knowledge of a technological object, we merely describe how it functions and how we can use it. Following this approach, the main contribution of ethics in the field of science and technology lies in providing useful conceptual and methodological tools for the development of an adequate ethical analysis, which can also support legal regulation, only if it is open to the interdisciplinary dialogue with science and technology: ethics teaches us about the ethical implications of the use of technology, but does it by referring to other fields of knowledge that are outside its epistemic dominion. I agree with the relevance of interdisciplinary work and with the contribution which ethics can give *within* the ethical debate about technology. However, I will try to show in the following that there are some problematic aspects with this kind of approach.

My thesis is that it is based on a very restricted view of the possible role of ethics as a philosophical discipline for discussing issues of technological regulation. The crucial question is the following: considering that the aim of ethics, and in a more general way of philosophy itself, is *just to participate* in the ethical debate as an internal member, in order to contribute to *solving ethical problems*, we risk losing sight of the possibility of another, genuinely philosophical contribution to the debate. In other words, if we consider that the contribution of ethics to this debate is just an internal one, that is, the contribution of ethics to the debate exactly *coincides* with the direct participation of ethics experts in the debate, we run the risk of a complete *operationalization* of ethics. But such an internal contribution can discuss ethical issues only inside a horizon of values, which is fully defined within the debate, because it shapes the conceptual background of the ethical debate. This horizon cannot be questioned as a whole: just specific and particular issues within it can be addressed. This implies that it is not possible to consider ethical issues and the ethical implications of technology from a radical, critical distance. However, the characteristic trait of philosophy is more to reflect on how questions are asked, than what the "right" answer is. According to this conception of philosophy, I will try to describe the position of philosophy in the debate about technology not just in terms of participation in the debate, but also as a permanent exercise of 'subtraction', reflecting about how much the debate itself is shaped from the conception of technology we adopt.

In this regard, it is important to remark that, depending on how "technology" is conceived, deeply different models for the regulation of technologies can be developed. In fact, philosophers defend a lot of different theses about technology and its ethical implications. Within the philosophical debate, different theses are discussed and critically examined by others authors. These theses are subject to objections, criticism and review, according to a model of dialogue that follows rules of communication accepted and shared by the participants of the dialogue. The thesis that I intend to defend in the following is no exception. I intend to propose the thesis that philosophy's task is to review and criticize the normative dimension of the problems, which is different from problem solving.

For this reason, I will focus on the relationship between ethics and technology in the next part of the paper. In doing this, I will try to outline a broader conceptual basis, which will be useful in order to contextualize the more detailed and concrete reflections in the next sections. So I intend to present, in the third section, the activities of the highest authority at the European level for the regulation of science and technology, the *European Group on Ethics in Science and New Technologies to the European Commission* (EGE), discussing the limits of ethics proposed by this institution. In the fourth and in the final part, I shall take up the developed critique. In doing so I will try to show what might be the function of philosophy in the context of reflection on technology.

## 2. Ethics and technology: the values-neutrality-thesis

The following brief overview of the philosophical reflection about technology, which began at the end of the 19th century, shows the complexity and the difficulties related to the ethical analysis of technology.[1] I will basically address the most problematical aspect of this topic, which is the question of the neutrality of technology with regard to values. First, I will presenting this thesis. Then, I will discuss the contemporary debate and some classical authors, who discuss this topic.

According to the so called values-neutrality-thesis, it is possible to clearly distinguish between an ethically neutral reflection about technologies, which is merely descriptive, and an ethical reflection about technology, which considers the goals that human being aim at when using technology. Technology as such can not be judged ethically good or bad. Just the use of technology can be considered from an ethical point of view. This old thesis has recently been defended in the context of philosophy of technology as well. Rosi Braidotti, for instance, argues that technology is neutral with regard to values, and it makes no sense to speak of an incorporation of morality in techno-logical tools.[2] In the context of the newest technological applications,

---

[1] For a reconstruction of the history of the philosophy of technology (with a selection of texts) see C. Hubig, A. Huning, G. Ropohl (eds), *Nachdenken über Technik: Die Klassiker der Technikphilosophie* (Berlin: Sigma, 2000).

[2] R. Braidotti, *The Posthuman* (Cambridge:, Polity Press, 2013).

such as drones, Braidotti remarks that the structure of technology is ethically neutral. According to her, machines are not able to distinguish between good and bad. Because of this, the humanistic point of view is not useful in this context, when we consider the ethically relevant consequences of autonomous systems like the drones. Despite its value neutrality, Braidotti's position considers technologies as basically good. In fact, even if the inconsiderate use of technologies can lead to ethically problematical consequences, for the human being technology represents, according to Braidotti, the possibility of emancipation from the limits of nature. For this reason, Braidotti supports anti-, post- and transhumanistic approaches, which point towards the creative potential of technologies.

From a similar point of view, Julian Savulescu and Nick Bostrom – and exponents of transhumanism generally – who defend neoliberal approaches with regard to technological intervention of the human body and mind, share an optimistic view of technology.[3] Technologies enable the enhancement of the human condition and the human well-being. These authors identify technology with the most evolved form of an intrinsic disposition of the human being, that is the disposition to transform nature in order to improve itself and the environment according to the human needs and desires. Accordingly, technique is the natural mode of being for humans. Technologies are the most recent form of technique and do not differ, from a conceptual point of view, from older forms of technique, such as building constructions, agriculture, breeding animals and so on.

In the history of philosophical reflection on technique and technology many authors have argued for the opposite thesis: technology cannot be neutral with regard to values. For instance, we can mention some classical works in this field: Theodor Adorno (1953), Arnold Gehlen (1957), Martin Heidegger (1962), Jürgen Habermas (1968), Max Horkheimer and Theodor Adorno (1969), and Hans Jonas

---

[3] J. Savulescu, N. Bostrom (eds), *Human Enhancement* (Oxford: Oxford University Press 2009). N. Agar, 'Liberal Eugenics' in *Defence of Human Enhancement* (Oxford: Blackwell Publishing, 2004); J. Harris, *Enhancing evolution: the ethical case for making better people* (Princeton: Princeton University Press 2007). See also L. Pellizzoni and M. Ylönen (eds), *Neoliberalism and technoscience:* critical assessments (Farnham: Ashgate, 2012).

(1979).[4] Surely, the positions which are defended by these authors are different from one another. Despite these differences, all these authors share a fundamental skepticism about the optimistic view that only the use of technology is ethically relevant. For instance, Adorno (1953) shows how the instrumental rationality, which aims at the dominion of nature through technologies, is intrinsically related to the domination of the human being over the human being, Thus, the technological development is, as a product of instrumental rationality, intrinsically a possible instrument of human domination of the human being. For this reason, it cannot be assumed that it is ethically neutral. The point is, to show the constitutive limits of the technology as such with regard to ethics, not just its degenerative forms of use. Despite significant differences in approach, Gehlen, Heidegger and Habermas also address the issues of technology considering the relation between the human being and nature, and reflect about the implication of an instrumental relationship with nature. On this approach, the question of technology is related to the fundamental meaning of human existence: the ethical reflexion about technology is profoundly connected to the question of the relationship between the human being and the world. Finally, Jonas (1979) insists on the necessity of a responsible handling of the human being, which also considers the consequences of the technological development for the future generations. For Jonas, the relationship between nature and technology is also a central question. Nature is something vulnerable: the human being must take care of nature in the same way as a father takes care of his child.

Let's resume some results of this introductory discussion of the philosophical approaches on technology. It is important to remark that the older reflection on technology tends to consider technology as a whole, and to address a fundamental aspect of the relationship which the human being establishes with himself and with the world through technology. Following this approach, technology is addressed as an

---

[4] T. Adorno, 'Ueber Technik und Humanismus', in H. Lenk, G. Rohpol (eds), *Technik und Ethik* (Stuttgart: Reclam, [1953] 1987); A. Gehlen, *Die Seele im technischen Zeitalter. Sozialpsychologische Probleme in der industriellen Gesellschaft* (Hamburg: Rowohlt, 1957); M. Heidegger, *Die Technik und die Kehre* (Pfullingen: Neske, 1962); M. Horckheimer, T. Adorno, *Dialektik der Aufklärung* (Frankfurt a.M.: Fischer, 1969); J. Habermas, *Technik und Wissenschaft als ‚Ideologie'* (Frankfurt a. M.: Suhrkamp, 1968); H. Jonas, *Das Prinzip Verantwortung. Versuch einer Ethik für die technologische Zivilisation* (Frankfurt a.M.: Insel, 1979).

expression of rationality. Technology is not just a set of tools, but a specific way in which the human being acts in the world. By contrast, a relevant part of the contemporary ethical reflexion tends to consider technology as something principally good, or at least as something that obviously belongs to our world. I am not addressing technophobic positions here, which are a possible alternative to this assumption. I just want to bring to the analysis the contemporary debate on technology, resuming the approaches which are, in my opinion, reasonable: on the one hand, the tendency to restrict the ethical analysis again on the matter of use, on the other hand, to develop the ethical analysis considering the specificity of each technology or class of technology.[5] Particularly, this approach is characteristic for the ethics of technology at the institutional level.

## 3. The ethical expertise for regulating research and development of technology in Europe

Founded in 1991, the European Group on Ethics in Science and New Technologies to the European Commission (EGE) is the highest independent body of the European community for discussing ethical and legal issues raised by science and technology, giving particular attention to the emerging technological applications. The EGE produces a rich documentation, published online.[6] In the following, I will summarize the theoretical and methodological strategies adopted by the EGE, which are particularly relevant in the present context.

The research groups of the EGE are interdisciplinary and include experts on humanities as well as experts on science and technology. This ensures that the groups can avail themselves of the full knowledge that is necessary in order to examine the issues at stake and to achieve a consistent result. From a programmatic point of view, the EGE adopts a dual understanding of ethics: ethics as a "philosophical discipline" does not correspond to the full meaning of ethics, which is relevant for

---

[5] See A. Braunack-Mayer, J. Street, N. Palmer, 'Technology, Ethics of: Overview', in R. Chadwick (ed.), *Encyclopedia of Applied Ethics*, vol. 4, (Amsterdam: Academic Press, 2012), 312-327.

[6] Information available at <http://ec.europa.eu/european_group_ethics/index_-en.htm> accessed 6 May 2014.

the EGE, but covers just an aspect of it. It provides the necessary theoretical background. According to the EGE's definition, ethics as a philosophical discipline is the theoretical analysis of moral practices.[7]

Ethical-philosophical analysis takes into account various dimensions and aspects of morality: "basic concepts, methods, standards and beliefs and convictions of claims, including the claims of cultural norms or religious traditions".[8] In addition to philosophical ethics, the EGE also considers ethics "as political consultation".[9] Unlike ethics as a philosophical discipline, ethics as political consultation aims to develop concrete strategies of ethical regulation.

Therefore, the EGE's documentation indicates five successive steps of analysis, which are necessary in order to develop a sound ethical analysis. The first step consists in the technological reconstruction of the state of the art in the technology at hand, considering also possible developments in the near future.[10] The second step is the preparation of complete documentation of relevant legal issues.[11] In the third step, the ethical issues are identified. In the fourth step, the general ethical framework is defined.[12] Finally, the ethical recommendations or suggestions are prepared: "developing concrete recommendations-/suggestions with regard to existing or novel EU policies to deal with the ethical issues (and, where appropriate, also with the legal and social implications) of the scientific/technological area analyzed"[13]

---

[7] Salvi, M. (ed.), 'General report on the Activities of the European Group on Ethics in Science and New Technologies to the European Commission 2005-2010 (Luxembourg: EC, 2010), available at <http://ec.europa.eu/bepa/european-group-ethics-/docs/gar_ege_2005-2010_web.pdf> accessed 6 May 2014.

[8] Ibid., 22.

[9] Ibid.

[10] Ibid., 32: "Familiarising itself with the state of the art of the science or technology in question as envisaged in the present, near future and a more distant future perspectives."

[11] Ibid.: "obtaining information on/overview of the relevant legal/regulatory framework of the scientific and/or technology area in question in the EU and EU Member States (check- ing whether any important differences existed between relevant EU MS' national legis- lation) and internationally."

[12] Ibid. "identifying the ethical issues raised by the science/technology developments considered;defining a general ethical framework to be used by the EGE to analyse the ethical issues identified and to develop its recommendations on how to deal with those ethical prob- lems and/or dilemmas."

[13] Ibid.

Summing up the programmatic aims focussing on the contents of the analysis, the approach adopted by the EGE discusses how technologies promote or obstruct values, which are recognized in the European Union. The EGE investigates the social impact of technologies, keeping in mind the changes that they have on socially shared values, indicating possible conflicts of values and eventually expressing reservations in the case of those technologies which seem to be incompatible with the values established by institutional documents, both at international and national levels. The method adopted by the EGE aims to achieve as much consensus as possible, respecting minority positions.

For all these reasons, it is possible to argue that the ethical reflection carried out in the institutional context differs significantly from the ethical-philosophical analysis. EGE's purposes are fully oriented from and towards the practice. In this sense, the contribution of philosophical ethics is crucial, since it permits us to found the methodology used in the discussion, but the work done is characterized by concrete and pragmatic orientation.

## 4. Structural limits of the EGE's approach

Ethics as a philosophical discipline constitutes an important part of the conceptual background of investigation of the EGE. Regarding the considerations set out in the previous paragraph, it is possible to mention two different elements of this contribution: on the one hand, philosophical ethics is a repertoire of theories and arguments; on the other hand, it is the reference for the adopted ethical methods. Therefore, the EGE's ethical evaluations are meant to produce documents, which have a real impact on the regulation for the development and use of technologies. This purpose significantly determines the kind of conceptual approach to which the topic of technology is addressed. Accordingly, the reflection on technology involved in the work of EGE does not primarily address to systematic or general questions, such us the relationship between man and technology, or between man and nature. As Rafael Capurro remarks, the 'excess' of theory may even be counterproductive for the goals of the analysis. With regard to robotic technologies, Capurro argues:

A central task for techno-ethics is to learn the lessons of discussions on bioethics. For example, we should avoid abstract discussion of agency or of the intentionality of agents and robots, and reflect on whether these latter are helpful to working out the context on the future development and use of agents and robots.[14]

Because of this, the ethical analysis of EGE is embedded in a defined theoretical framework, which does not determine the contents of evaluation – that is, if the technological application is ethically acceptable or not –, but fixes some preconditions of analysis, which are not discussed further within the evaluation process. In other words, the evaluation starts necessarily from the assumption that, in principle, technologies contribute to human wellbeing. Consequently, the main goal of the ethical reflection is to verify that the technology at stake actually promotes human wellbeing without significantly damaging man and nature or colliding with other societally shared values. It is evident that this approach differs radically from the classical philosophical reflection about technology.

A second problem, immediately connected to this one, concerns the abstractness of the philosophical reflection. Also for reasons of space, the EGE's work cannot focus on basic concepts, but delves into concrete aspects of the interaction between man and technology. As Capurro remarked, an abstract reflection about technologies would even mislead the analysis and does not seem to be necessary in order to draw conclusions with respect to societally relevant ethical issues. Examining the steps that are considered fundamental by the EGE for the preparation of an ethical analysis, it becomes evident that there is no place for reflecting about the theoretical constructs that are the basis of this ethical analysis. Furthermore, the state of the art does not consider conceptual aspects that go beyond an adequate knowledge of technology in the scientific-technical sense. For instance, the horizon of meaning according to which a technology is intended to be good (or bad) under an ethical point of view is not mentioned. However, which criterion defines the extent of theoretical reflection that is necessary to achieve sound ethical recommendations? Avoiding "abstract discussion" may jeopardize the validity of the work, because without a solid theoretical basis it is impossible to determine if the ethical analysis is

---

[14] R. Capurro, 'Etica e robotica. I robot, maschere del desiderio umano', in (2007) 20 *I quaderni di Athenet. La rivista dell'Università di Pisa*, 9-13.

based, for instance, on wrong conceptual assumptions. Due to the absence of this analysis, the ethical recommendations of EGE run the risk of being based on wrong or at least imprecise theoretical assumptions.

Federica Lucivero and Guglielmo Tamburrini showed, with regard to ethical monitoring of brain-machine interfaces, how the EGE's approach can lead to a hasty ethical analysis.[15] Examining the Opinion 20 (EGE 2005), the authors argue that an accurate knowledge of the technical features of the device is not the only necessary knowledge in order to guarantee the validity of the ethical analysis. It is also mandatory to achieve a clear and precise conceptual framework with regard to basic notions involved in the analysis, such as *person, autonomy* and *identity*. More concretely, if we want to understand what the effects of technology on identity are, we have to clarify the identity model which we refer to. Different conceptions of identity may lead to different evaluations of the ethical relevance of one or the other effects of the device on identity. A generic reference to such notions, without taking into account different possible conceptualizations, makes the ethical analysis inconsistent.

This same objection can be raised with respect to the part of the EGE's investigation concerning the axiological dimension. By integrating the observations made above, it can be pointed out that even the understanding of concepts such as freedom, responsibility, safety, welfare, and so on, are essential for guiding the analysis and determining the perspective in which we investigate technology. The dominant approach in the European context, as I have shown with Antonio Carnevale and Federica Lucivero, with respect to the regulation of robotics, tends to take as a given the values which drive the ethical analysis.[16] On the basis of official documents, a list of shared values is established. Doing so, however, the result of the ethical analysis is the extrinsic comparison between technology and values.

Another problematic aspect of the EGE's procedure for analyzing ethical issues is developed from Jacques Lenoble and Marc Maesschalk

---

[15] F. Lucivero, G. Tamburrini, 'Ethical monitoring of brain-machine interfaces A note on personal identity and autonomy', in (2008) 22 *AI & Soc.*, 449-460.

[16] B. Bisol, A. Carnevale, F. Lucivero, 'Diritti umani, valori e nuove tecnologie. Il caso dell'etica della robotica in Europa' in (2014) 2 (1) *Metodo. International Studies in Phenomenology and Philosophy*, 235-252.

and concerns methodological issues[17]. Lenoble and Maesschalk criticize the proceduralism adopted by EGE, because it does not take into account the contexts in which the considered values are formed, experienced, lived and transformed. This leads to too static an analysis, which is not able to give reasons for the relevance of the analysis with regard to concrete situations of use of technologies. From another point of view, the same kind of criticism has also been developed by Tsjalling Swiestra and Arie Rip.[18] Following a pragmatic approach inspired by Dewey, they insist on the relevance of a dynamic understanding of values as social constructs, which have to be studied within society (and not just as ethical-legal notions formulated  in documents). Therefore, it can be remarked that the ethical analysis has to produce conceptually valid results, but it must also comply with criteria of effectiveness and usefulness at the social level: it must help to support the regulation of technologies in given social contexts concretely. For this reason, it also has to take in account needs, desires and values of individuals and society. The opening of the debate on technology to the public, the inclusion in the investigation process, a participatory dimension of non-experts is not simple, and basically still poorly defined, at the institutional level.[19]

Furthermore, as Madeleine Akrich showed, the technological design strongly influences the user's behaviour.[20] The question of design opens up another field of reflection, which is exstremely relevant for the ethical analysis. What is a technological object? Which features of the technological objects determine the relationship, which we have with

---

[17] J. Lenoble, M. Maesschalck, *Toward a Theory of Governance. The Action of Norms* (Zuidpoolsingel: Kluwer Law International, 2003).

[18] T. Swierstra, A. Rip, 'Nano-ethics as NEST-ethics: Patterns of moral argumentation about new and emerging science and technology' in (2007) 1 *NanoEthics*, 3-20.

[19] See F. Lucivero, T. Swierstra, M. Boenink, 'Assessing Expectations: Towards a Toolbox for an Ethics of Emerging Technologies', in (2011), 5(2) *NanoEthics*, 129-141. Tendentially, the construction of a survey setting for the investigation of technoethical issues appears inadequate and limited to data collection through opinion polls or to discussion of values on the basis of socio-anthropological, not philosophical research. (A. Bogner (ed.), *Ethisierung der Technik – Technisierung der Ethik. Der Ethik-Boom im Lichte der Wissenschafts- und Technikforschung* (Baden Baden: Nomos, 2013); M. Decker (ed.), *Interdisciplinarity in Technology Assessment. Implementation and its Chances and Limits* (Berlin: Springer 2001).

[20] M. Akrich 'The Description of Technological Objects', in W. Bijker, J. Law (eds) *Shaping Technology Building Society: Studies in Sociotechnical Change* (Cambridge MA: MIT Press, 1992).

it?[21] Consequently, the consistency of the conceptual background related to ethics is not the only difficulty for achieving a sound ethical analysis. It is also crucial to determine which aspects of the materiality of the technological device at stake have to be taken in account. Several aspects can be considered relevant: the design and the functionalities of the technological devices, the forms of interaction of the users and the devices, including degrees of autonomy or proximity of the device and the environment in which it is used. In this sense, the ethical analysis cannot simply be 'superimposed' on a technical-scientific conceptualization of the technology at hand, but it has to be developed taking into account the complexity and multiplicity of levels and perspectives in which objects, and particularly tools, can be conceptualized.

## 5. Conclusions

In conclusion, a radical difference between ethics as a philosophical discipline and ethics as political consultation can be pointed out: The philosophical reflection on technology, including ethical issues, may certainly aim to influence the public debate. But unlike regulations and guidelines, it does not intend to intervene directly on societal settings. The "effects" of philosophy still persist in a mediated way: philosophy "acts" through the defense of a position, the proposed arguments, the critique or endorsement of (dominant) social values or opinions. Otherwise, the institutional ethical reflection about technology aims to have a direct impact, producing documents, which regulate and influence the development, the production and the use of technologies. In other words, ethics as political consultation aims to transform not only the public opinion, but also social practices.

This remark may seem trivial. However, it is important to ask what the contribution of philosophy can be, when it contributes to the public in institutional contexts. Philosophical practice can be described as an attitude to discuss questions, rather than to provide functional answers.

Ethical-philosophical reflection is responsible for a constant revision of the principles, topics, and conceptual constellations and

---

[21] See also P. Verbeek, *What things do: Philosophical reflections on technology, agency, and design* (University Park, Pa.: Pennsylvania State University Press, 2005).

models that define the horizon in which the public, institutional debate happens. For this reason, along with the effort of a direct contribution and active participation in the socio-political debate, it must constantly dissociate itself from the public sphere.

Philosophical practice can be characterized precisely through this specific attitude: to point out the question, thinking about its conceptual structure, rather than providing an answer to such a question. Because of this attitude, it is difficult to define philosophy in a positive way, determining its function: the function of philosophy is, in this sense, to have no functions. Understanding philosophy as a critical job does not mean transforming the philosophical interrogation in a pure rhetorical exercise, that does not stand in need of practice. The defense of the "futility" of philosophy, however, is a necessary corrective to avoid misunderstanding the goal of philosophical expertise as a mere instrumental knowledge.[22]

Specifying this question with regard to ethics of technology, it is necessary to remark that the institutionalization of ethics represents a challenge for the contemporary philosophical debate about the relationship between man and technology. A notable part of the philosophical work in ethics focuses on contributions, which are conceived in order to be useful for the development of guidelines and recommendations. As I tried to highlight in the previous pages, this type of ethical analysis has to deal with very specific constellations of problems, which are different from what philosophical ethics has to deal with. Particularly, the research on ethics of technology is strongly determined by practical requirements and by the effort to offer effective solutions for regulating research, production and use of technological devices. Therefore, it is obvious that the ethical analysis adopted in institutional field has to follow specific rules of survey and develop proper methods. However, it is the relationship with ethics as a philosophical discipline that remains problematic, also accepting that the methodological differences between ethics as a philosophical discipline and as a political consultation are unavoidable. Reconstructing the activities of the EGE, I tried to point out some elements of this complex relationship, illustrating how ethics as a philosophical discipline can contribute to the research work of the EGE, but also showing

---

[22] I discussed this topic in B. Bisol, 'Spazio pubblico o spazio del pensiero?', in U. Perone (ed.), *La filosofia nello spazio pubblico* (Torino: Rosenberg & Sellier, 2013), 27-37.

how some basic features of philosophical ethics are implemented in the ethical analysis only to a limited extent. Accordingly, there are two possible objections, which can be raised against the approach of the EGE starting from a philosophical point of view: on the one hand, the conceptual horizon, from which the analysis starts, is in many ways generic and fuzzy; on the other hand, a lack of deepened discussion about background questions can be recognized. According to these critiques, the challenge for the EGE is to balance the need for an analysis, which has to be necessarily specific and detailed, and the effort for maintaining a highly comprehensive perspective as background for the specific analytical work. Philosophy can make a significant contribution to both requirements. On the one hand, philosophers can be active in institutional committees as experts, being involved in concrete research. On the other hand, they can contribute by turning their attention to background questions, which are not directly discussed in the ethical analysis, but build the conceptual frame within which the ethical analysis is developed.

# Ethical assessment of medical technologies
# A coherentist methodology

*Georg Marckmann*

The ethical assessment of technologies should follow an explicitly defined methodological approach comprising both a set of normative evaluation criteria and a step-by-step procedure for the assessment itself. I propose a normative framework based on a coherentist model of justification which can provide rather specific normative guidance for various application domains. For the application of the normative criteria, I suggest a methodological approach with 6 steps: Description, specification, evaluation, synthesis, recommendations, and monitoring. The application of this approach is exemplified for computer-based clinical decision support systems (CDSS).

## 1. Introduction

Technologies have found its way into almost all domains of human life. They increasingly shape many fields of human activities. Especially in medicine, important diagnostic and therapeutic advance have been possible due to the increasing application of medical technology. However, quite often technological approaches do not only provide benefits, but also risks and burdens. This ambivalence makes it necessary to carefully evaluate the technologies, especially in the field of medicine as the patients' well-being is at stake. While at the first glance this technology assessment might appear to be a value free activity, it turns out that medical technologies have ethically relevant implications: They not only affect the patients health and well-being, they also have implications on patient autonomy and the fair distribution of benefits and burdens in the health care system. Last but not least, the implications on the costs of care are also ethically relevant under the conditions of resource scarcity.

Given the ethical relevance of medical technologies, it seems necessary to assess the ethical implications of individual technologies in a systematic way in order to maximize the positive and minimize the negative effects. This article presents a systematic approach for an ethical technology assessment based on a coherentist model of justification. First, I will lay out the methodological ingredients of this approach. Second, I will demonstrate how this approach can be applied in evaluating computer-based decision support in medicine. Clinical decision support systems (CDSS) play an increasingly important role in medical practice. By assisting physicians with making clinical decisions, CDSS are expected to improve the quality of medical care. However, there are also concerns that malfunctioning or inappropriate use of MDSS could jeopardize the well-being of the patient. Thereby, they are a good example of a medical technology with ambivalent, ethically relevant implications.

## 2. Overview of the approach

It is the overarching goal of an ethical technology assessment to give *normative guidance* with respect to a certain technology. This involves three major goals:[1]

(1) *Identify* ethical issues that arise with the development and use of the technology

(2) Ethically *evaluate* individual technologies

(3) Develop ethically justified *recommendations* for the development or design and application of a certain technology.

It becomes clear that an ethical technology assessment is fundamentally a *normative* enterprise. It therefore requires at least two "ingredients":[2]

---

[1] G. Marckmann, D. Strech, 'Konzeptionelle Grundlagen einer Public Health Ethik', in: D. Strech, G. Marckmann (ed.), *Public Health Ethik* (Berlin: LIT Verlag, 2010), 43-65

[2] D. Strech, G. Marckmann, 'Normative Versorgungsforschung. Eine orientierende Einführung in Themen, Methoden und Status quo in Deutschland', in (2012) *Gesundheits- und Sozialpolitik. Zeitschrift für das gesamte Gesundheitswesen* 8-15

(1) A comprehensive and at the same time flexible *normative framework* that contains a list of normative criteria or considerations based on an explicit ethical justification.

(2) A *systematic methodological approach* that assures a transparent evaluation, allows an assessment of the process quality and can provide education and guidance for the professionals in the field (researcher, developers and users of the technology).

Fig. 1 provides an overview of this approach: Based on an ethical theory a normative framework is developed and justified which then is applied for the ethical assessment of a certain technology. I will explain both the ethical basis of the normative framework (i.e. the coherentist model of justification) and the practical methodological approach in more detail in the two following paragraphs.

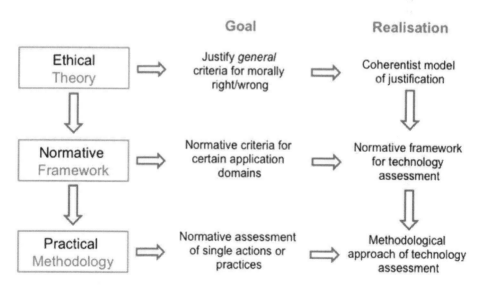

**Fig. 1**: Methodology of ethical technology assessment: overview

## 2.1. *Normative foundations*

It is one of the fundamental goals of technology assessment to provide normative guidance regarding a certain technology. Therefore, the framework must be grounded in an ethical theory that provides an ethical justification of the selected normative criteria. However, there is intractable disagreement about which ethical theory is correct. Moral philosophy is characterized by a multitude of competing approaches that differ significantly in their justificatory strategies. As a consequence, the results of ethical analyses will vary considerably depending on the underlying ethical theory.

An alternative approach that explicitly acknowledges the complexity of normative orientations in modern pluralistic societies is the coherentist model of justification, which has been introduced as "reflective equilibrium" by John Rawls.[3] Unlike classical ethical theories, the coherentist approach does not build on a single foundational moral principle, but rather starts with considered judgments, i.e. moral convictions and beliefs that we hold in our everyday life, and develops a *coherent* framework by specifying, testing and revising them. The goal is a "reflective equilibrium" of theoretical assumptions, moral principles and judgments about single cases.[4] Based on a coherentist model of justification, Tom L. Beauchamp and James F. Childress have developed on of the most influential theories of biomedical ethics. In their seminal book "Principles of biomedical ethics" they propose four principles for ethical inquiries in the field of biomedicine: beneficence, nonmaleficence, respect for autonomy and justice.[5]

The four principles that have been developed from considered judgments are *prima facie* binding, i.e. they must be followed unless they conflict with equally strong or stronger obligations. They provide general ethical orientations that require further content to give guidance in concrete cases. Thus, in application, the principles have to be specified and – in case of conflict – balanced.

A coherentist model of justification has several advantages: Despite unresolved foundational issues in moral philosophy, it allows to find a consensus on the level of *prima facie* binding mid-level principles, since they build on our everyday moral convictions and are compatible with various ethical theories. It makes moral controversies more transparent, since they can be analyzed as conflicts between principles with different

---

[3] J. Rawls, *A theory of justice* (Cambridge, Mass.: Harvard University Press, 1971).

[4] N. Daniels, 'Wide reflective equilibrium in practice', in N. Daniels (ed.), *Justice and Justification* (Cambridge: Cambridge University Press, 1996), 333-352.

[5] T. L. Beauchamp, J. F. Childress, *Principles of Biomedical Ethics* (New York, Oxford: Oxford University Press, 2013).

weights. Identifying precisely the type of ethical conflict is often the first step towards a solution.

Based on this coherentist approach, it is possible to develop and justify a rather concrete normative framework that contains the normative criteria and considerations that are relevant in a certain application area. In the next paragraph, I describe a methodological approach of how to apply the normative framework to a certain technology.

## 2.2. Practical methodology

It is above all a question of quality assurance that the ethical assessment of a technology follows an explicitly defined methodological approach (see table 1). The first step must be a thorough description of the technology that shall be evaluated: What is the application area? What are the goals of the technology? What tasks shall the technology perform? By what technical means shall the goals be achieved? This description is necessary to identify potential ethical implications in the further process of the evaluation. In the second step, the normative framework requires critical review: Are any further specifications or even supplementations necessary for the technology at hand? It is important that the normative criteria are as specific as possible for the technology in order to achieve practically relevant results in the assessment.

In the third step, the technology is evaluated based on each of the specified criteria. For example, the following criteria have to be answered: What are the expected benefits of the technology? What are the potential burdens and risks? What are the implications for a fair distribution of benefits and harms? In the fourth step, the single evaluation of step 3 have to be integrated to an overall assessment of the technology. This involves identifying conflicts between the individual criteria and balancing the resulting conflicting ethical obligations. Quite often, a technology will have both positive and negative implications. Instead of rejecting the technology completely because of this ambivalence, it is often a good solution to draw up recommendations for the development or design and application of the technology (step 5). These recommendations shall maximize the positive effects of the technology and minimize the negative implications. By setting up these recommendations, the assessment can contribute to shaping the technology and its application in an ethically and socially acceptable way. The last step of the assessment involves a continuous monitoring and re-evaluation of the ethical implications over the life of the technology: Was the ethical evaluation appropriate? Are new ethical issues arising with the further development and application of the technology? Are the recommendation followed and are they effective in assuring the ethically appropriate application of the technology? Again, the ethical assessment shall play a very constructive role in the further development of the technology.

| Steps | | Tasks |
|---|---|---|
| 1 | Description | Thorough characterization of the technology: application area, designated goals and tasks, functionality |
| 2 | Specification | Specification (if necessary) of the normative criteria for the assessed technology |
| 3 | Evaluation | Step-by-step evaluation of the technology based on the normative criteria |
| 4 | Synthesis | Overall evaluation of the technology by integrating an balancing the single evaluations of step 3 |
| 5 | Recommendation | Development of recommendations for the development and application of the technology |
| 6 | Monitoring | Monitoring and re-evaluation of the ethical implications in regular intervals |

**Table 1**: 6-step methodology of an ethical technology assessment[6]

In the following paragraphs, I will illustrate how this methodological approach can be applied to evaluate clinical decision support systems. Within the scope of this article, however, I won't be able to provide a

---

[6] Cf. G. Marckmann, D. Strech (fn 1) and D. Strech, G. Marckmann (fn 2).

comprehensive analysis. Rather, I will provide some exemplary results that will enable the reader to better understand the practical potential of this coherentist approach of ethical technology assessment.

# 3. Example: Computer-based clinical decision support systems (CDSS)

*3.1. Clinical decision support systems – basic description*

Clinical decision-support systems (CDSS) are computer systems designed to assist physicians or other health care professionals in making clinical decisions. While the diffusion of large-scale diagnostic systems has been slower than originally anticipated, the growing availability of electronic patient records and the increasing technical diversity of CDSS will promote the widespread use of computer assisted medical decision making. Currently, most CDSS provide decision support for particular diagnostic or therapeutic tasks like interpreting pulmonary function tests, analysing electrocardiograms or managing the use of antiinfective agents. CDSS can help physicians to organize, store and apply the exploding amount of medical knowledge. They are expected to improve the quality of care by providing more accurate, effective and reliable diagnoses and treatments, and by avoiding errors due to physicians' insufficient knowledge. Evaluation studies demonstrate that CDSS can have a positive effect on clinician performance and patient outcomes.[7] In addition, CDSS can decrease health care costs by providing a more specific and faster diagnosis, by more efficient drug prescriptions and by reducing the need for specialist consultations.[8] However, the performance of CDSS is subject to some important limitations and their inappropriate use or malfunctioning might adversely affect the well-being of patients. Some CDSS fail to achieve the same level of diagnostic performance as

---

[7] See e.g. R. S. Evans, S. L. Pestotnik, D. C. Classen, T. P. Clemmer, L. K. Weaver, J. F. Orme, Jr., et al., 'A computer-assisted management program for antibiotics and other antiinfective agents [see comments]', in (1998) 338 *N Engl J Med* 232-8; D. W. Bates, L. L. Leape, D. J. Cullen, N. Laird, L. A. Petersen, J. M. Teich, et al., 'Effect of computerized physician order entry and a team intervention on prevention of serious medication errors [see comments]', in (1998) 280 *JAMA* 1311-6.

[8] See R. S. Evans et al.(fn 7).

human experts.[9] This raises the ethical question: how can we design and use MDSS in a way that maximizes the benefits and minimizes the risks for the patients?[10] In the next paragraph, I will present a normative framework, developed by a coherence theory of justification, that shall guide the ethical evaluation of CDSS.

### 3.2. *Normative framework*

Computer-based clinical decision support is a technological application in the medical field. Therefore, the four classical ethical principles of biomedical ethics apply:[11] beneficence, nonmaleficence, respect for autonomy and justice. From these general ethical principles, a more specific set of ethical criteria can be derived for the evaluation of CDSS (see table 2 for an overview).

The first two criteria can be inferred from instrumental rationality, but they also ethical relevance: A limited functionality can do harm to a patient or withhold an expected benefit. The criterion of *functionality* thereby comprises three different aspects: CDSS should match the users' need for decision support (*usability*). The goal of modelling a clinical diagnoses for example should be achievable by means of the CDSS (*feasibility*). Thereby, the systems' performance with regard to the diagnostic accuracy should be sufficiently good (*efficacy*). In addition, instrumental rationality requires a careful scrutiny whether there are alternatives to the use of CDSS, alternative, that might be more effective or more efficient. The other criteria are directly derived from the four principles of biomedical ethics, like the systems' safety and benefit for the patient, implications for patient autonomy, data protection and safety, the cost-benefit ratio or the attribution of responsibility.

Between the different criteria, there are instrumental and competing relationships. The functionality, for example, is a prerequisite for the safety and benefit of the CDSS. On the other hand, maximizing the

---

[9] See e.g. J. L. Willems, C. Abreu-Lima, P. Arnaud, J. H. van Bemmel, C. Brohet, R. Degani, et al., 'The diagnostic performance of computer programs for the interpretation of electrocardiograms', in (1991) 325 *N Engl J Med* 1767-73.

[10] For a more thorough discussion of this question see: G. Marckmann, 'Recommendations for the ethical development and use of medical decision-support systems', in (2001) 3 *MedGenMed* 5.

[11] T. L. Beauchamp, J. F. Childress, *Principles of Biomedical Ethics* (New York, Oxford: Oxford University Press, 2013)

systems' safety might compromise the systems' efficiency, because safety measures like thorough evaluation studies require a considerable amount of resources. This set of normative criteria has two major functions: First, it can be used to identify ethically relevant issues involved in the use of CDSS. Second, they are the normative basis for the recommendations of an ethically appropriate design and application of CDSS. In the following paragraphs, I will sketch out in exemplary way some important elements of an ethical assessment of CDSS.

| Evaluation Criteria | Ethical Justificationfication |
|---|---|
| Functionality (Feasibility, usability, efficacy) | Instrumental rationality (non-maleficence, beneficence) |
| Possible alternatives | Instrumental rationality |
| Safety, susceptibility to errors | Nonmaleficence |
| (Incremental) benefit | Beneficence |
| Integrity of physician-patient relationship | Respect for autonomy, beneficence |
| Patient autonomy | Respect for autonomy |
| Data protection, privacy | Informational autonomy |
| Data safety/integrity | Nonmaleficence |
| Cost-benefit ratio | Efficiency, distributive justice |
| Physicians' decisional autonomy | Beneficence |
| Physicians' competency | Nonmaleficence, beneficence |
| Attribution of responsibility | Nonmaleficence |

**Table 2**: Normative framework for the ethical evaluation of computer-based clinical decision support systems (CDSS)[12]

---

[12] G. Marckmann, *Diagnose per Computer? Eine ethische Bewertung medizinischer Expertensysteme* (Köln: Deutscher Ärzte-Verlag, 2003), 20

### 3.3. Description: Limitations of CDSS

The first step an ethical evaluation must be a thorough description of the technology to clearly delineate the limitations of the technology that have to be taken into account by the users. Most CDSS cover only a narrow field of medical knowledge and exhibit a significant decline of their performance if they are used at or beyond the border of their intended scope ("cliff-and-plateau" effect). And even within a given medical domain, only part of the relevant clinical knowledge is computationally tractable and can be transferred into a MDSS. So far, the inference techniques of MDSS cannot represent the rich variety of diagnostic and therapeutic reasoning strategies that clinicians use to solve complex patient problems. These limitations are especially critical as the computer systems fail to recognize internally when their results become erroneous.

Due to limitations in the user interface, the advice of MDSS relies only on computable input data, which represent just a small proportion of the information required to make clinical decisions. It is extremely difficult for the user to determine whether the input data adequately represent the patient's clinical problem. These limitations in the user-interface can lead to an overemphasis of "hard" laboratory data and the neglect of "softer" psychological and social information. Most MDSS fail to represent common-sense knowledge and have no real understanding of the patient's problem. Instead of a patient-centered medicine, the use of MDSS fosters a disease-centered medicine with a comparatively inflexible interpretative framework, which cannot account for the physiological, psychological and social individuality of the patient. If MDSS operate on the basis of heuristic knowledge, the correctness of the systems' advice cannot be guaranteed. Even with systematic testing, it is impossible to exclude programming errors with certainty due to the computational complexity of MDSS.

### 3.4. Ethical issues in the use of CDSS

Given the inherent limitations of CDSS, a major ethical concern is the appropriate application of the system: Why and when should CDSS be used? What minimum qualifications are required of a user for the responsible application of the systems? Another important issue is the validity of the implemented knowledge base, a key determinant of the overall performance of the systems. CDSS are complex computer programs that pose risks for patient safety by system malfunctioning or misuse. As computer systems suggest precision and objectivity, there is the fear that physicians could relinquish their own independent medical judgment and uncritically rely on the system advice.

Further ethical concerns include the dehumanization of patient care due to the use of computer systems and adverse effects on the physician-patient relationship. Patient autonomy could be compromised if physicians solely rely on the standardized knowledge of CDSS and fail to account for the individual needs and preferences of their patients. However, some authors have challenged this assumption of an impersonal, computer-controlled therapy: If CDSS help to find information quickly and easily, physicians might have more time to build a caring relationship with their patients. CDSS could also enhance patients' trust in their physicians by suggesting an increased competency due to the use of a computer system.

In addition, the use of CDSS raises questions of responsibility: Who is responsible for decisions based on the system advice, especially in the case of medical errors? Some people fear that the increasing reliance on computer support might lead to a degradation of physicians' reasoning skills. Finally, CDSS also raise concerns about the confidentiality and security of the processed patient data. While most of these concerns address potential harm for patients, there is also the complementary question: If CDSS have a proven benefit for medical care, should a failure to use such systems be considered unethical?

Overall, CDSS have both positive and negative ethical implications. The ethical evaluation depends to a large extent on how the systems are designed and how they are applied in routine clinical practice. It therefore does not seem to be appropriate to endorse or reject the CDSS completely. Rather, the ethical assessment should set up appropriate guidance for the design and use of CDSS that shall guarantee that the positive effects are maximized and the negative effects minimized as far as possible.

## 3.5. Recommendations for the development and use of CDSS

According to the proposed methodological approach (see table 1 above, step 5), the result of an ethical technology assessment should provide concrete recommendations for the development and application of the technology. With regard to the CDSS, it is important to develop two different sets of recommendations, one for the development (table 3) and one for the application (table 4) of the computer systems.[13]

| Ethical recommendations for the development of CDSS | |
| --- | --- |
| 1 | Clearly defined goals of system development |
| 2 | Demonstrated demand for decision support |
| 3 | Appropriate goals for the development of CDSS |
| 4 | Evaluation of alternative strategies |
| 5 | Selection of appropriate application domains |
| 6 | User involvement |
| 7 | Clinical-methodological foundation |
| 8 | Clinically intuitive input mode |
| 9 | Flexible decision support |
| 10 | Multiple diagnostic or therapeutic suggestions |
| 11 | Quality assurance of represented knowledge |
| 12 | Transparent design of knowledge base and inference engine |
| 13 | Sophisticated explanation function |
| 14 | Integration into the clinical environment |
| 15 | Provision for the prevention and detection of system errors |
| 16 | Rigorous testing and evaluation of CDSS |

**Table 3**: Ethical recommendations for the development of CDSS

The inherent limitations of CDSS require several safeguards to ensure the appropriate and responsible usage of CDSS. Whether the use of CDSS will be ethical depends on how we develop and implement the systems. Most important is the selection of an appropriate application domain that fits the specific performance profile of the system. MDSS should be used only for those tasks that can be sufficiently solved on the available input data and the implemented knowledge. As physicians cannot convey their complete understanding of the patient's problem to the system, CDSS should be

---

[13] For a more detailed description of the recommendations see: G. Marckmann (fn 10).

used as decision aids and should never replace the practitioner's independent clinical judgment. Integration into the clinical environment will be crucial for the utility of a MDSS. As MDSS are a technologically diverse group of systems, each system should be thoroughly evaluated with regard to the expected benefits, risks and cost. Continuous maintenance, update and quality assurance will be the key to a safe and useful computer-based decision support.

| Ethical recommendations for the use of CDSS | |
|---|---|
| 1 | Application only for the designated tasks |
| 2 | Continuous validation, maintenance and update of the system |
| 3 | Human control of system results |
| 4 | Human diagnosis before system consultation |
| 5 | Time for scrutinizing the system results |
| 6 | Required user expertise in the application domain |
| 7 | User education regarding functionality and limitations of CDSS |
| 8 | Clinicians must retain final responsibility |
| 9 | Confidentiality and integrity of patient data |
| 10 | Error policy |
| 11 | Integration into a comprehensive information infrastructure |

**Table 4**: Ethical recommendations for the use of CDSS

# 4. Conclusion

Many technologies – not only in the medical field – have ambivalent ethical implications that require a thorough ethical assessment over the life-cycle of the technology. I have proposed a systematic approach for the ethical evaluation of technologies that consists of two main elements: (1) A set of normative criteria based on a coherence theory of justification (*normative framework*), and (2) a systematic methodological approach to apply the normative criteria in the assessment of a given technology. A clearly defined methodology is not only the cornerstone of the quality of the assessment. It also allows those affected by a technology to assess whether all relevant arguments have been taken into consideration. If the technology is not rejected completely, the assessment should result in concrete ethically justified recommendations that should guide the development and the use of the technology. The assessment of computer-based clinical decision support systems (CDSS), which support physicians in making a diagnosis and selecting a therapeutic strategy, was used to demonstrate how the assessment proceeds and how the recommendations try to shape the development and application of the computer systems.

# Responsible innovation for adaptive robots

*Michael Decker*

## 1. Introduction: Responsible Innovation

With the launch of the new EU Framework Programme 'Horizon 2020', the concept of 'Responsible Research and Innovation' (RRI) became the guiding principle of the European research landscape.[1] RRI has already been discussed in the context of research policy and 'foresight'[2], in STS research,[3] and in the philosophy of technology and technology assessment.[4] An essential part of RRI is the early assessment of the impact of technology in the light of social and ethical values as well as the consideration of normative criteria of sustainable development both in the innovation process and in defining the societal objectives to be achieved. This will help focus research programmes on solving societal challenges and will lead to more democratic decision making by integrating deliberative elements. Many – if not all – of these aspects have been discussed for many years in the context of TA, and against the background of this discussion it remains to be seen how the vaguely defined concept of 'responsible innovation' will differentiate itself in the future. The conceptual closeness to technology assessment is particularly evident when looking at the definition of RRI:[5]

---

[1] R. Schomberg, 'A vision of responsible innovation', in (2013) Owen et al., (fn 3) below.

[2] CEC, *Report on the DG Research workshop on Responsible Research & Innovation in Europe* (Brussels, 16-17 May 2011); CEC, *Options for Strengthening Responsible Research and Innovation*, Report of the Expert Group on the State of Art in Europe on Responsible Research and Innovation (Brussels, 2013).

[3] See e.g. R. Owen, J. Bessant, M. Heintz, *Responsible Innovation: Managing the Responsible Emergence of Science and Innovation in Society* (Weinheim: Wiley, 2013).

[4] A. Grunwald, 'Responsible Innovation: Bringing together Technology Assessment, Applied Ethics, and STS research', in (2011) 7 *Enterprise and Work Innovation Studies*, IET 9-31.

[5] R. Schomberg, (fn 1).

RRI is a transparent, interactive process by which societal actors and innovators become mutually responsive to each other with a view to the (ethical) acceptability, sustainability and the societal desirability of the innovation process and its marketable products (in order to allow a proper embedding of scientific and technological advances in our society).

Since Schumpeter[6] described innovation as 'creative destruction' where not only something new is developed, but usually something old – possibly tried and tested – is invalidated, it is obvious that 'new' does not automatically mean 'better'. It is also obvious that such a process of creative destruction creates 'winners' and 'losers' in society and thus bears a certain potential for conflict. Technology assessment has traditionally focused on these conflicts by evaluating the chances and risks of new technologies, taking account of different 'categories' of technology impact:[7]

- intended *versus* unintended consequences
  (from the perspective of technology development)
- desirable *versus* undesirable technology
  (from the perspective of citizens)
- main and side-effects
  (from the perspective of political decision makers)
- …

Irrespective of this, innovation can be considered a special element of prosperity in industrial countries, as also assumed by Schumpeter:[8] "The fundamental impulse that sets and keeps the capitalist engine in motion comes from the new consumers' goods, the new methods of production or transportation, the new markets, […]." Therefore, it seems logical that the German Federal Ministry of Education and Research (Bundesministerium für Bildung und Forschung, BMBF) calls its concept of TA 'innovation and technology analysis' (ITA). ITA aims to provide the actors in the innovation process with information and reflection in order to support them in making informed and confident

---

[6] J. Schumpeter, *Capitalism, Socialism and Democracy* (London: Routledge,1994).

[7] M. Decker, 'Technikfolgen', in A. Grunwald (ed), *Handbuch Technikethik* (Stuttgart and Weimar: Metzler, 2013), 33-38.

[8] J. Schumpeter, (fn 6), 82.

decisions on research, technology and innovation. Innovation and technology analysis is used to identify potential opportunities and risks, and potentials and options and to enable early detection of potential barriers and driving factors for innovation. The concept brochure of the BMBF states:[9]

> The policy concept 'Innovation and Technology Analysis' (ITA) of the Federal Ministry of Education and Research aims to identify fields of socially desirable technological progress, development potentials, as well as the scope and options for political action. ITA is intended to provide guidance in a highly technologised society and contribute to promoting more humane, socially just and environmentally sound technological processes. Building on best practices and studies in technology assessment (TA), ITA is a strategic concept for analysis and evaluation of technologies, with an integrative approach that combines research and practice.

Innovation and technology analysis thus pursues its own aim of being a 'mid-term radar'.[10] Early identification of relevant topics of innovation and technology analysis is necessary to enable the BMBF to provide strategic support in a way that combines the basic idea of TA with the needs of innovation policy.[11] With the idea of assessing the impact of technology at an early stage, ITA approaches the concept of RRI. Here, too, the declared aim is to start at early stages of technical development, because there exists greater flexibility for socio-environmental considerations to guide the innovation process.[12]

---

[9] BMBF – Bundesministerium für Bildung und Forschung, *Innovations- und Technikanalyse. Zukunftschancen erkennen und realisieren*, (Bonn, 2001), 7.

[10] O. F. Bode, 'Wissenschaftsbasierte Beratung für politische Entscheidungsfindung und/oder für die Exekutive', in A. Bora, S. Bröchler, M. Decker (eds), *Technology Assessment in der Weltgesellschaft*, (Berlin: edition sigma, 2007), 51-60.

[11] F. Meyer-Krahmer, 'Technikfolgenabschätzung im Kontext von Innovationsforschung und Globalisierung', in T. Petermann, R. Coenen (eds), *Technikfolgenabschätzung in Deutschland. Bilanz und Perspektiven* (Frankfurt am Main: Campus, 1999), 197-216; N. Malanowski, A. Zweck, 'Bridging the gap between foresight and market research: Integrating methods to assess the economic potential of nanotechnology', in (2007) 74 (9) *Technological Forecasting and Social Change* 1805-1822.

[12] J. Stilgoe, R. Owen, P. Macnaghten, 'Developing a framework for responsible innovation', in (2013) 42 (9) *Research Policy* 1568-1580.

## 2. TA on the innovation process of adaptive robotics

Adaptive robotics is first of all relevant for the application area of service robotic. If robots should be used to take over specific tasks in every day environments – be it at public places as in a railway station or in private homes – it cannot be expected that these high-tech systems are initialised by a user who is not a robotics expert. The system must be enabled to learn about different environments and to adapt to them as well as to different users showing different individual preferences. Therefore the following disciplinary perspectives on service robotics[13] should just show that we face a problem which needs to be tackled by an interdisciplinary approach which is paradigmatic for TA and RRI.[14]

### 2.1. *Technological perspective*

The successful provision of a service is already a big technological challenge. This can be compared with a 'checklist' which can be compiled for a particular service. The service 'vacuum cleaning' is provided successfully when the floor is clean, and when this is done without damaging furniture, without making too much noise, within a reasonable time, etc. If the vacuum cleaning robot has met these requirements, the service is – in technical terms – performed successfully. A basic requirement in the private environment is that the robot has to be able to find its way 'autonomously' in a surrounding which has to date been unknown and that it can adapt to the environment in which it has to perform its service. To summarise it briefly: The robot has to be enabled to learn its task and its environment. Here we take different approaches, which aim, among others, at learning 'like human beings' ('learning like a child', 'learning by demonstrating', etc.) where 'trial and error and imitation' play a central role. A humanoid stature (torso, head, arms and legs, ...) is often

---

13 These perspectives were developed in Decker et al. (2011) and are mentioned here as an interdisciplinary framing of the legal perspective complemented by aspects referring especially to adaptive systems. (M. Decker, R. Dillmann, T. Dreier, M. Gutmann, I. Ott, I. Spieker genannt Döhmann, 'Service robotics: do you know your new companion? Framing an interdisciplinary technology assessment', in (2011) 8 (1) *Poiesis & Praxis* 25-44.

14 M. Decker, A. Grunwald, 'Rational Technology Assessment as Interdisciplinary Research', in M. Decker (ed), *Interdisciplinarity in Technology Assessment. Implementation and its Chances and Limits* (Berlin: Springer, 2001), 33-60.

considered to be an advantage for learning. On the one hand it animates people to interact with the robot, on the other hand the robot is 'physically' adapted to an environment which is optimised for human beings (steps adjusted to the length of human legs, doorways, signs at eye level, etc.).[15] While concerning the last aspect 'humanoid' just means having human dimensions and movement abilities as well as multimodal communication capabilities, making the robot even more manlike can be an interesting aspect to support learning. Then we would be speaking of android or gynoid robots with a 'confusingly similar' appearance to human beings. This 'being like humans' could become relevant when it comes to the technical realisation of so-called soft skills like friendliness, helpfulness, etc. which are related to the provision of services. It is also important that the human being on the one hand, who is capable of integrating his knowledge and using his experience, and the specialised, skilled humanoid robot on the other hand, share their information by exchanging and thus updating their respective knowledge.

## 2.2. Economic perspective

Major trends provide various opportunities for the application of service robots: Since the industrial revolution, the importance of the service sector has steadily increased and in Germany, for example, its contribution to overall added value as well as to employment amounted to almost 75% in 2009.[16] A similar development might also be observed in other industrialised high-tech countries. Structural change from the primary to the secondary and tertiary (i.e. the service) sector is accompanied by a transition towards net- and knowledge-based societies. Citizens are generally well educated and their knowledge and their dynamics are a key factor and driver within innovation processes. Especially in application fields where ICT is playing a major role, user-driven innovations are prevalent. As a consequence, in the context of service robotics individual skills significantly affect both supply-side and demand-side aspects.

---

[15] S. Behnke, 'Humanoid robots – from fiction to reality?', in (2008) 4 (8) *Zeitschrift Künstliche Intelligenz* 5.

[16] See <http://www.bmwi.de/BMWi/Navigation/Wirtschaft/dienstleistungswirt schaft,did=239886.html> or <www.destatis.de>, <www.vgrdl.de> accessed 23 April 2014.

The major distinction between service enterprises and industry robots is based on the characteristics of services: they are immaterial and thus, experience goods; their quality can only be assessed once they are actually used by the customer(s). The parallelism of production and consumption as well as the consequential direct relation between service provider and customer are the reason why services cannot be stored, exchanged or sold again. Due to the human interaction during the performance of the service, the possibilities for standardisation are rather limited. At the same time standardisation is a major prerequisite for the application of service robots both in individual and professional use.

The introduction of service robots raises several questions, including some topics concerning standardisation and patenting. Questions that have to be addressed in order to estimate the potential of service robotics include: What is the incentive for individual actors to develop or use service robots (e.g. lack of nursing staff in an 'aging society' and/or the resulting profit opportunities)? Which costs incur throughout the innovation process of the robots (technical and non-technical costs)? Their application requires their adjustment to existing environments, hence aside from the use of 'complementary' qualified staff who operates the robot also adjustment costs, e.g. for the modification of the surroundings in which the robots become active, have to be borne. Are those who bear the costs also the ones who receive the revenues? Furthermore, it is important to identify the stakeholders and the relevant markets. The acceptance of technologies and thus their demand may be higher in technology-enthusiastic economies (Japan is generally considered as being one of them) than in more conservative ones. Are there some countries that are supposed to become leading markets in that field? An overall assessment of the potential, e.g. for the labour markets, does not only consider those jobs which might be replaced by robots but also includes especially those which are newly created in the course of innovation. And finally, what are the preconditions of the national or regional innovation systems (including the legal and political framework) where robots are developed?

## 2.3. *Legal perspective*

Depending on the field where service robots are used, different legal questions arise. We can distinguish between those concerning the relation citizen-citizen (civil law) and others concerning the relation between the state and the citizen (public law). As a regulatory tool, public law restricts economic activities which collide with the rights and legal interests of others or the common good. Here, one major problem consists of governmental decisions under uncertainty. If and how the legislative authority intervenes depends on prognostic assumptions whose future fulfilment is uncertain. It is not foreseeable if, to what extent and in which social contexts service robots will be accepted and used and will thus change social systems or social perception as well as require changes, e.g. in the existing infrastructure, in social welfare and health care provision, and finally damage regulation. It is also unclear whether existing requirements for production safety which are already covered by the existing legal foundations of private liability law are applicable and sufficient to cover potential harm to people and objects and whether they set the right incentives: Do we assume a generally dangerous activity – in line with the strict and far-reaching liability regulations e.g. of genetic engineering or atomic energy which calls for an absolute liability? There is also the need to consider secondary objectives of liability: The promotion of any innovation can only be successful if the chosen liability scenario does not regulate the entrepreneurial (and private) development in such a strict way that further developments do not pay off. More importantly, individual legal requirements may interfere with innovative ideas: Social law for example, which is especially relevant for services in the field of health and care (age, disability, sickness), demands attention to a number of special requirements, some of them induced by constitutional law. They differ significantly from the legal framework service robots encounter in professional environments, e.g. in agriculture.

From the perspective of civil law, where the relation citizen-citizen is in the focus of legal considerations, it is mainly a question of liability of those who plan, produce, sell and finally use service robots to the integrity of legally protected goods of those people who get in contact with service robots. Here the existing regulation instruments should be made applicable to the new problems of warranty and hazard. This refers to the drafting of contracts, especially regarding the risk allocation in the general terms and conditions as well as general questions of liability for damages to third parties. The formulation of due diligence and liability standards is a central element here. If the requirements are too strict, this will impede – or even prevent – the manufacturing, distribution and use of service robots; if the requirements are too low, the use is seen with even more scepticism the more defect-prone the relevant service robots turn out to be. However, it should be noted that civil liability rules are only one means of reducing the risks associated with the operation of potentially dangerous technology. Ideally, in regulating such technology, civil law rules should be combined with, and complemented by, public law rules which aim at preventing or at least reducing technology risks in the first place. Additional issues are raised if service robots are autonomously adaptive and can react with other robots or the environment in general in a way that is not predictable in detail. This leads to the question to what extent damages caused by the operation of such robots can still be meaningfully attributed to the person(s) operating the robot, or whether new rules of accountability, such as, e.g., the creation of an independent legal 'liability' of these novel mechanical 'beings', are called for. So far, this issue has only been discussed for software agents but not yet for service robots.

### 2.4. *Philosophical and ethical perspectives*

From an ethical point of view, the focus is on the desirability of certain technical solutions regarding their reasonability. These questions will be discussed hereafter on the example of robots in caregiving/medical services.

Today, services in the field of caregiving, or medical care in general, are typically provided by human beings. However, the statistics for industrialised countries predict a demographic change which means that the number of people in need of care will be growing in the foreseeable future while the number of caregivers is going to decrease. Against this background it could be desirable for a society to develop service robots for care.[17] Their use can be planned to different extents, with the spectrum reaching from simple assistance in caregiving to 'real' care robotics in the narrower sense.

---

[17] R. Sparrow, L. Sparrow, 'In the hands of machines? The future of aged care', in (2006) 16 (2) *Minds and Machines* 141-161.

Ethical questions on the desirability, which are connected to such scenarios, usually refer to the classical questions of ethics of technology. This is about the scientific reflection of moral statements which are often cited as arguments for the acceptance or the rejection of the use of technology. Cost-benefit considerations also play a role here. The questions are then answered with reference to procedural utilitarian, discursive or participatory approaches. Such ethical considerations in the narrow sense form the standard repertoire of ELSI concepts which are also common for robotics and autonomous systems in use in parallel to ongoing research.[18] A comprehensive ethical reflection also includes methodological questions aiming at the determination of what should be considered succeeding or even successful support, replacement or surpassing of human performances, abilities or skills. Then the design criteria for the adequacy of the description of robotic systems which replace human actors gain centre stage.[19] The methodological reflection focuses on an equalisation of human and machine including a thorough analysis of the limits of technical systems engaging into decision making, which would address them as potential moral agents.[20] This is followed by the differentiation of human-machine, machine-human, machine-machine and human-human interaction where a differentiation of connection, interaction and interface could become relevant, terms that are often used synonymously.[21] Only such a clarification can provide information on the logical grammar of the 'as-if' structure and thus the attribution of emotive, volitional and cognitive terms to robotic systems. A systematic clarification of the logical structure of such equalisations is directly relevant for solving the above-mentioned ethical questions.

Questions of anthropological dimensions are directly associated, since services in the field of medicine/care are currently performed by

---

[18] See e.g., Royal Academy, *Autonomous systems: social, legal and ethical issues* (London: The Royal Academy of Engineering, 2009).

[19] Cf. M. Gutmann, ‚Autonome Systeme und der Mensch: Zum Problem der medialen Selbstkonstitution', in S. Selke, U. Dittler (eds), *Postmediale Wirklichkeiten aus interdisziplinärer Perspektive* (Hannover: Heise, 2010), 130-148; D. Sturma, 'Autonomie. Über Personen, künstliche Intelligenz und Robotik', in T. Christaller, J. Wehner (eds), *Autonome Maschinen* (Wiesbaden: Westdeutscher Verlag, 2003), 38-55.

[20] P. M. Asaro, 'What should we want from a robot ethic?', in (2006) 6 *International Review of Information Ethics* 9-16.

[21] C. Hubig, 'Mensch-Maschine-Interaktion in hybriden Systemen', in C. Hubig, P. Koslowski (eds), *Maschinen, die unsere Brüder werden* (München: Fink, 2008), 9-17.

humans, as stated above. Thus the introduction of technical systems replaces the human being in some areas,[22] technical systems are increasingly involved in human actions, machines will act in the role of humans in an 'as-if' mode; accordingly, technical systems can only metaphorically be considered to actually take certain (cognitive as well as social) roles of human beings.[23] This expansion of the ethical consideration which complies with the double meaning of ἔθος and ἦθος[24] finally allows to ask for concepts of man which are – normally implicitly – invested in the construction of the respective technology.

This background is necessary to address issues which go beyond a purely syntactical understanding of technical systems and can be phrased in the following way, taking health care services as an example:

But the scope of philosophical consideration extends the limits of ethical and anthropological dimensions by far: methodological questions become urgent, which are well-known from the critical evaluation of AI since the early 1960s.[25] These questions are connected with semantic as well as pragmatic aspects of the 'understanding' and 'knowledge-sharing' potentials of artificial systems: How can a successful care service be classified as 'keeping the meaning'? Such a classification does not only require 'technical specifications' but also a comprehensive description of the service provided – also considering, e.g., friendliness, helpfulness, support, etc.

How can this 'successful service' be determined as being factually successful? Does this require a long dialogue between 'receiver' and 'provider' in the sense of a human-machine, machine-human or a parallel communication via human-human dialogues?

A comprehensive systematic clarification – which is unfortunately only rudimentarily carried out in normal ELSI studies – of the ethical problems of the use (or the prevention of the use) of robotic systems is necessary and should be done under consideration of all three aspects.

---

22 M. Decker, *Perspektiven der Robotik. Überlegungen zur Ersetzbarkeit des Menschen* (Bad Neuenahr-Ahrweiler: Europäische Akademie, 1997).

23 See M. Gutmann, (fn 19).

24 C. F. Gethmann and T. Sander, 'Rechtfertigungsdiskurse', in A. Grunwald, S. Saupe (eds), *Ethik in der Technikgestaltung. Praktische Relevanz und Legitimation* (Berlin: Springer, 1999), 121 ff.

25 For an extended outline see M. A. Boden, *Mind as machine*, vol I & II (Oxford: Clarendon Press, 2006).

This multidisciplinary approach can still be extended. Socio-scientific aspect can be included,[26] for example with empirical studies, to systematically analyse the concrete acceptance on the part of those who provide the service and those who receive the service. This could especially take place on the level of so-called sub-disciplines; their relevance for the subject is quite justifiable.[27] In this contribution the focus is on liability issues for adaptive service robots as will be discussed in the following section.

# 3. Liability for Robots

Currently, German law considers robots as 'intelligent' machines whose behaviour is determined by humans. It assumes that a robot cannot make decisions on its own and therefore treats it as a thing. As a thing, the robot itself cannot be held responsible for negligence or even wilful misconduct. There must be misconduct particularly on the part of the robot's owner or the robot's manufacturer, depending on the standard of liability.

As a general principle, the robot's owner is liable if the damage caused by the robot is due to misconduct on the part of the owner, such as in particular inadequate organisation, improper operation and improper maintenance. Problems arise from the difficulty in proving causality or misconduct.[28]

The example of robots shows that, despite the general applicability of the principles of the 'classical codifications' in the information society, some adaptations of private law are required. In the eighteenth and nineteenth centuries, machines and robots played a minor role as means for providing services directly. Since the division of labour had

---

[26] K. Böhle, M. Pfadenhauer, 'Schwerpunkt: Parasoziale Beziehungen mit pseudointelligenten Softwareagenten und Robotern', in (2011) 20 (1) *Technikfolgenabschätzung – Theorie und Praxis* 4-10.

[27] See M. Decker, A. Grunwald, (fn 14).

[28] These comments on the liability for robots are based on Christaller et al., *Robotik. Perspektiven für menschliches Handeln in der zukünftigen Gesellschaft* (Berlin and Heidelberg: Springer, 2001), whose interdisciplinary group of authors was supervised by E. Schweighofer. They have previously only been published in German and are presented here in abridged form in translation, with a focus on the aspect of how liability insurance facilitates innovation. The purpose is to make them available in the context of RoboLaw.

not progressed very far, causality and guilt were easier to prove. Private law has reacted quite appropriately to the developments accompanying the industrialisation and 'informatisation' of society. However, further progress will be needed to cope with issues associated with robotics, a key technology of the twenty-first century.

The main argument for the necessity of adaptation is that robots – highly complex mechatronic machines – are no longer transparent to ordinary citizens. This applies both to the spectrum of misconduct and to the often complex assignment of liability. It is therefore appropriate that the owner of the robot as beneficiary of the technology has to bear additional liability for a robot's failures.

The law of damages or the law of torts is based on the principle that a person shall be liable for damages caused by his/her unlawful and culpable infringement of legally protected interests. This is referred to as a wrongful and culpable act of a tortfeasor. The provision of § 1295 ABGB (Austrian Civil Code) is provided here as an example:

"Any person may claim compensation from the tortfeasor for the damage caused by his/her fault. These damages may have been caused by violation of a contractual obligation or without regard to a contract."

In a similar form, this applies to many national laws, such as those of Germany, Switzerland, France and England. If this is not the case, the aggrieved person generally has to bear the damage alone. This is clearly expressed in the Austrian ABGB: Damage as such is caused to the person whose property or person is harmed (§ 1311 sentence 1 ABGB).

As a thing, a robot cannot be held liable for a tort. If a robot commits an illegal act that causes damage, the aggrieved party only has to claim damages for reproachable misconduct from the robot's owner or manufacturer.

Legal systems distinguish with regard to liability for things between a robot owner's culpability for misconduct and his strict liability (i.e. liability without proof of causality) for a robot as a helper. Culpability is differentiated based on the standard of care and can closely approach strict liability. In strict liability, one is responsible for all causal and unlawful damages, although various types of exonerating evidence (especially of a force majeure or of every conceivable act of caution) are admissible.

A strict liability for robots as helpers would represent a significantly stricter liability for them. An increasingly important aspect is the allocation of the burden of proof. The fact that the party aggrieved by the robot must prove misconduct by its owner effectively opens the door for the owner's exculpation. A clever allocation of organisational responsibility by the owner of the robot can make it very difficult for the aggrieved party to prove which tortfeasor in the owner's organisation is causally and unlawfully culpable for the misconduct. A reversal of the burden of proof thus significantly simplifies the pursuit of justice. The robot's owner could then no longer block his liability if the aggrieved were not successful in proving culpability. The robot's owner would on the contrary have to prove his lack of responsibility for the damage. A further simplification would be the reversal of the burden of proof for causality if there were prima facie evidence of causality.

## 3.1. *Product Liability and Product Safety*

Products cannot, in general, be considered to be dangerous.[29] Nonetheless, the prevailing school of thought is that product liability is classified as a type of strict liability. According to Wilburg's system of tort law, interaction of the following criteria is important with regard to the classification: the utilisation or endangerment of someone else's goods or the accusation of a defect approaching unlawfulness, depending on the number and severity. In product liability, there must be a concrete danger based on a flaw. The flaw is the central criterion of product liability, with a distinction being made between flaws in fabrication, construction, and instruction. Product liability is based on the interest in integrity, according to which no product should inflict damage on one's other legally protected interests. Compensation is to be provided for subsequent damage to one life, health or property, but not for the deficient quality of the product itself. Compensation is to be made for those damages inflicted on a person or property that are caused by flaws that the product had when it was put on the market by the liable party. Product liability is not incurred by the owner but by the manufacturer (or importer) of the robot.

Robots are products as understood in product liability (Product Liability Guideline, Article 2): [...] every mobile object, even if it forms part of another mobile object or an immobile one.

---

[29] C. W. Canaris, 'Die Gefährdungshaftung im Lichte der neueren Rechtsentwicklung', in (1995) *JBl* 6 f.

The essential role of software does not change this judgment in any way. According to the prevailing opinion, even software must be considered a thing if it is integrated into the hardware. A product is 'faulty' if it does not offer the safety that one is justified in expecting after taking all the circumstances into consideration. The expectations are oriented on the product's performance, the use that can rightly be expected of it, and point in time at which it is put on the market. This is true for both mechanical and electronic components as well as for instructions, behavioural logic and possibly learning procedures defined in the software. Decisive is the state of science and technology, i.e. the highest achievable level of knowledge.

Independent of culpability, flaws in production – such as the notorious outlier – are to be conceded. Liability is to be accepted for mistakes in construction (design mistakes). In German case law, very high demands are placed on construction. All the available technical and scientific know-how and possibilities are to be utilised to prevent dangers to users and third parties (more than DIN or VDE norms). The robot's manufacturer must refer in the user manual to all the risks that cannot be excluded despite correct construction and production (instruction requirement). If there are mistakes in construction or instruction, the producer can object that it was impossible for it to detect the flaw even though work conformed to the state of the art of science and technology. The ideal manufacturer must not only demonstrate due diligence but also prove that it exercised every caution indicated under the circumstances. This definition follows the concept of an unavoidable event (from the Austrian Traffic Liability Act, EKHG).

The manufacturer has to keep an eye on his products even after they have reached the market and warn purchasers if subsequently any dangerous properties appear or take steps to prevent damage. Products that come to pose a hazard must be withdrawn. Product liability does not include the risk of development. The idea of including development risk in product liability was widely rejected in the responses to the European Commission's green book. For the European Commission, the sparse information that is presently available does not provide any reason for it to alter the present liability regulations.

The reversal of the burden of proof gives particular strictness to product liability. The aggrieved party only has to prove that there is damage and that it was caused by the production flaw. The manufacturer has the complete burden of proof for all activities in his sphere of influence. It is difficult to prove exonerating or mitigating factors since high requirements are put on organisation and documentation.

Compensation stemming from product liability can be demanded by any aggrieved party if the damage to person or property was caused by product flaws that were present when the product was put on the market. No compensation is made for damage to the product itself. Significant simplifications come from the 500 euro deductible rule and the limitation of compensation for property damage to products for one's private use. Product liability expires three years after the damage becomes known to the aggrieved party. The statute of limitations is ten years.

There is furthermore tort liability, for which it is necessary prove culpability. The advantages are the absence of a deductible amount, the use against business people and the higher limits on liability. Assuming there is a very high standard of diligence or a reversal in the burden of proof, tort liability results in outcomes similar to those for product liability according to the product liability guideline.

The regulations on product safety set minimum standards for product safety and give the authorities the power to undertake measures to ensure consumer safety, such as issuing a warning about products or calling them back.

The manufacturers of robots are subject to product liability for ten years subsequent to putting them on the market. According to the guidelines, the amount of this liability can be limited, but many EU member states do not make any use of this. Manufacturers are obviously only liable for flawed services if these are caused by a flaw in the product.

While there is strict liability for product flaws, culpability for services provided is considered sufficient. There are no particular regulations in the German legal system regarding liability for services. Problems result from the fact that the burden of proof for tort liability is on the aggrieved, which is also true for consideration of the proximate cause of a subsidiary. This limitation of liability is doctrinally inconsistent.

With regard to changes, the ball has been in the court of the European Community (EC) for many years. The Commission of the

EC presented a draft guideline on liability for services in 1990. This suggestion provided in particular for a reversal of the burden of proof regarding damage from faulty services. The massive criticism of such changes affecting the respective legal systems[30] has pushed any realisation into the distant future. The EC Commission withdrew the project in 1994. The European Commission, however, then envisaged the introduction of service liability as part of its consumer policy action plan (Com (98), 696).

### 3.2 Suggestion for the Introduction of Strict Liability for Robots Serving as Helpers with a Supplemental Insurance Model

Since it is very difficult to prove culpability in using a robot, we recommend the recognition of a strict responsibility for a robot as a technical tool. This liability, a form of strict liability, is an expanded liability for things. This very high standard of diligence is appropriate to impede as much as possible the difficult issues of differentiating detail.

The following formulation is suggested for a modification of the laws:

- The robot's owner is liable for the damages caused by the use of the robot as a technical aid. Liability is precluded if the damage is caused by an unavoidable event that is the result neither of a flaw in the condition of the robot nor of a failure of its mechatronics. It is the responsibility of the owner to show cause.
- The amount of the liability for an individual aggrieved person is limited to
- a one-time payment in the amount of 300,000 euros
- an annual pension of 17,500 euros
- The maximum amount for which the robot's owner is liable for one and the same event is 1,000,000 euros.
- The robot's owner is to make provision for resolving such damages as he may be liable for by purchasing insurance or in some other appropriate manner.

---

[30] See, e.g. for Austrian law F. Bydlinski, *Juristische Methodenlehre und Rechtsbegriff* (Vienna: Springer, 2nd ed., 1992a); F. Bydlinski, 'Zur Haftung der Dienstleistungsberufe in Österreich und nach dem EG-Richtlinienvorschlag', in (1992b) *JBl* 341.

This formulation includes the addition to §276Abs 1 S 3 of the dBGB suggested by Köhler[31] as well as the analogy to vicarious liability made by Koziol. A limit to the maximum amount of liability is proposed to facilitate insurability. Insurance against damages (or an analogous precautionary measure) supplements the model of strict liability for robot assistants. The use of robots is not supposed to be encumbered by protracted trials for compensation. Robots have to represent a highly developed and safe form of technology in their practical use. Liability for product safety and a strict liability for robots will ensure high standards in production, construction, instruction and operation. If further cases of damage arise, they are to be covered by the guarantee fund of the manufacturer or owner. Such risk-sharing groups will remove a burden from aggrieved parties. The economic advantage of the use of robots justifies this additional burden on robot owners. Enforcement is to take place either via the courts or, if desired, via special arbitration tribunals. Given use of the latter, the expedient combination of lawyers, physicians and technicians could make it possible to achieve a very efficient procedure and provide for sound decision making.[32] Speaking against this insurance model are the higher costs and the consequent higher threshold for the use of new technology. Since the introduction of product liability and the efforts to establish strict liability for medical institutions, the higher threshold appears to be justified to ensure that poorly conceived or developed technology is not tested in practice at the expense of aggrieved parties. The risk of damage is still given for the robot's manufacturer or owner. It is their responsibility to minimise the risk of damage and insurance premiums by exercising a sufficiently high level of diligence.

# 4. Final remarks

The concrete suggestion presented here to create a legal basis for handling damages caused by robotic systems pursues the goal of facilitating the introduction of innovative technical solutions into the

---

[31] H. Köhler, 'Die Problematik automatisierter Rechtsvorgänge, insbesondere von Willenserklärungen', in (1982) 182 (1-2) *Archiv für die civilistische Praxis* 126-171.

[32] F. Haft, 'Haftung für Automaten', in M. Decker (ed), *Robotik. Einführung in die interdisziplinäre Diskussion*, Graue Reihe 16 (Bad Neuenahr-Ahrweiler: Europäische Akademie, 1999), 55-66.

market. The suggestion thus takes into account the status quo of robotic research. In the last few decades, the approach has been to bring as much of the lifeworld as possible into the robotic research labs in order to be able to appropriately test the models behind the adjustment algorithms. The subsequent methodological step must be performed in the real world, in which robotic systems then inevitably come into contact with innocent bystanders. This is a regular feature of these applications in the entire field of service applications, and with regard to services provided for humans, people even become the object of the robot's activities. This is the case, for example, in care giving as well as in washing hair.

In addition to this recommendation – which is to facilitate innovation – that courts ease within the framework of existing laws the challenges that claimants face when demanding compensation for damages caused by robots, further recommendations for action have been formulated that even now still appear to be relevant to the current discussion about robotic technology. And precisely the current call for proposals by the German Federal Ministry of Education and Research (BMBF) for improving the interaction between man and technology – which thematically are dedicated to coping with demographic change or, more precisely, to providing technical support to people suffering from dementia – make it clear that the subject of robots continues to be a topic of discussion in society. [33] The recommendations for action are supposed to contribute to drawing attention to significant aspects for assessing robotics.

In addition to the legal aspects discussed here, technical issues were discussed. At the focus of these discussions was the consideration of robots as being a means to promote the goals of human action. It is particularly important to make sure that reality and utopia are assessed just as realistically. The metaphors and images employed in science fiction play an important role as sources of ideas. They also involve the

---

[33] *Bundesanzeiger* AT 19.03.2014 B5 'Bekanntmachung von Richtlinien zur Förderung von Forschung und Entwicklung auf dem Gebiet „Pflegeinnovationen für Menschen mit Demenz"' (trans.: Announcement of Guidelines to Promote Research and Development in the Area of 'Innovations in Caring for People with Dementia) available at <https://www.bundesanzeiger.de/ebanzwww/wexsservlet?session.sessionid=7ded8e6359bdf8d6843e9e50249770da&global_data.designmode=eb&genericsearch_param.fulltext=19.03.2014&genericsearch_param.part_id=&%28page.navid%3Dto_quicksearchlist%29=Suchen> available at 10 May 2014.

danger, however, of considering the utopian to be practicable, which applies even to scientific modes of speaking and language games. Two recommendations for action should still be explained explicitly here since they could be of special relevance for the RoboLaw project.

The first recommendation forms the counterpart to some extent to the manner for dealing with damage presented above that robots might pose to innocent bystanders. It refers to those actions that innocent third parties as a rule do not participate in. In other words, it refers to those actions that actors carry out in the context of their profession, for which a protected space is created. The recommendation suggests that robotic systems be promoted that represent an extension of an individual's scopes of action: [34]

> Expansion robots put a person in the position to overcome obstacles to action and to be telepresent, i.e. to be able to act at a place that is not directly accessible. The inaccessibility results from large distances such as in outer space, from scales of size such as in the micro- or nanometre range, and from physical barriers. In minimally invasive medicine, concepts of telepresence can serve to transfer the motion of a surgeon's hand in an intuitively comprehensible and appropriate manner. The dangers that people might be exposed to can also pose a barrier that telepresence can help overcome, such as in the deep sea, disarming explosives, inspection or dismantling of atomic energy plants and medical radiation. These applications should be considered a basis for robotic development, from which technical innovations can flow into other areas of application. A comprehensive support for research in these expanding areas is recommended.

In the applications named above, there are no innocent bystanders and the people involved can be given special training to prepare them to use the robotic system optimally. The human actor retains responsibility in this context.

The second recommendation for action refers to learning robotic systems, which ultimately are the fundamental precondition for making it possible for robots to adjust to new environments and persons:[35]

> It should be possible to distinguish learning robots from non-learning robots since the use of learning algorithms will have an influence on

---

[34] T. Christaller et al., (fn 28), 217.
[35] Ibid., 220.

the distribution of liability for damages between the manufacturer and the owner. The recommendation is to make the learning process transparent for the robot's owner or third parties. In this connection, the installation of a non-manipulable black box for the ongoing documentation of the important results of the learning process or of sensors can be of assistance.

This recommendation poses, first, an immense challenge to technology. Making a learning act transparent must be accompanied by the robot being capable of explicating what it considers worth learning in connection with concrete action and which of the actions in its repertoire it suggests to be its learned action. When robotics is in a position to argue in this fashion and to draw the corresponding conclusions, even to give reasons for its learning, then it would have taken a giant step closer to human intelligence.[36] The second challenge is rather social in nature. The introduction of a non-manipulable black box, i.e. a recording device that cannot be modified from the outside and that documents precisely the modifications in the robotic system that are induced by the robot's learning algorithm, would also mean that the robot would make a detailed recording of its environment. The robot's sensory data are a central element of the possibility for it to be able to suggest adjustment measures. They thus also reflect the robot's immediate environment and possibly even properties of the person using it. Precisely in the context of care giving, the collection of physiological data plays a special role. This brings in its wake corresponding problems with the respective user's privacy.[37] On the other hand, the black box can ensure that the reason that the robotic system learned something is always comprehensible. This can, in turn, play a special role in legal disputes.

Issues of this kind are obviously particularly relevant for modern robotic systems. On the one hand, the systems have to be adaptive since it is impossible to imagine that such a robot is initialised on location and that a technician then carries out modifications of the technical system for every change in the person's environment or in the person him- or herself with whom the robot is supposed to cooperate. Adaptivity and thus the capacity to learn become a *conditio sine qua non* in

---

[36] See D. Sturma, (fn 19).

[37] K. Böhle, Chr. Coenen, M. Decker, M. Rader, 'Biocybernetic adaptation and privacy', in (2013) 26 (1-2) *Innovation: The European Journal of Social Science Research* 1-10.

the robotics of service applications. At the same time, it must be guaranteed that responsibility in the context of action can be attributed to the respective entity. We thus speak here – in the context of the overarching societal concept of responsible innovation - of "responsible" innovation in two concrete senses. On the one hand, there is the responsibility for concrete technical acts mediated by the robot. On the other, there is the responsible handling of potential damages caused by the robotic system, for which I suggest here that courts should within the framework of the existing laws facilitate claims for compensation. The robot's owner should bear partial responsibility for the intransparency of the mechatronic system for third parties as would result from a reversal of the burden of proof for wrongful conduct and from acknowledging the sufficiency of proving prima facie causality. At the same time, the amount of the damage should be limited by a suggested maximum liability, thus making possible an economically feasible insurance solution.

# From robotics to cyber-physical systems Technical options and ethical-legal challenges

*Klaus Mainzer*

Cognitive and humanoid robots become more and more autonomous, interactive, and adaptive, in order to master complex problems and situations. Cyberphysical systems grow together with the complex infrastructure of our technical civilization. This paper discusses challenges from life sciences to robotics and cyberphysical infrastructures of modern societies and asks for human responsibility in a technical co-evolution.

## 1. Engineering Paradigm in Life Sciences

The engineering point of view is not only dominating robotics, but also the life sciences.[1] Modern robotics will grow together with the life sciences under the engineering paradigm. Therefore, we start with recent trends of modern systems and synthetic biology. From a methodological point of view, systems biology aims at developing models to describe and predict cellular behavior at the whole-system level. The genome project was still a reductionist research program with the automatic analysis of DNA-sequences by high speed supercomputers (e.g., 2000 bases per second). The paradigm shift from molecular reductionism to the whole-system level of cells, organs and organisms needs an immense increase of computational capacity in order to reconstruct integrated metabolic and regulatory networks at different molecular levels and to understand complex functions of regulation, control,

---

[1] K. Mainzer, *Leben als Maschine. Von der Systembiologie zur Robotik und Künstlichen Intelligenz* (Paderborn: Mentis, 2010).

adaption, and evolution (e.g., computational metabolic network of E.coli with power law connection degree distribution and scale-free property).

A remarkable paradigm shift in methodology is the new role of computer experiments and computer simulations in systems biology. In systems biology, computational modeling and simulation and technology-driven high-throughput lab experiments are combined to generate new knowledge, which is used to fine tune models and design new experiments. Thus, "in vivo" experiments" in labs must be supplemented by "in silico" experiments on computers, in order to handle the huge amount of data in systems biology. Increasing accumulation of biological data ranging from DNA and protein sequences to metabolic pathways leads to the development of computational models of cells, organs, and organisms with complex metabolic and gene regulatory networks.

Systems biology is an application of analytical science modeling complex systems of life with methods of mathematical analysis, namely differential equations. In the history of science, Newtonian mechanics was an analytical paradigm in the 18th and 19th century. A typical application was the planetary model with differential equations of gravitational interactions. In systems biology, a cell is considered a complex system of interacting, e.g., proteins modeled by appropriate differential equations. In his book "Critique of Judgment" (§ 75), Kant (1724-1804) proclaimed that the "Newton of a blade of grass" cannot be found. Under the conditions of Newtonian physics, an explanation of life seemed to be excluded. Kant was right in the sense that life sciences cannot be reduced to mechanics. But, systems biology works successfully with the Newtonian paradigm in the sense that mathematical equations are applied to model complex molecular and cellular interactions.

Synthetic biology does the next step like technical mechanics in the 18th and 19th century. The Newtonian paradigm is applied in engineering science. Mechanical systems are not only mathematically modeled, but also constructed according to Newtonian laws. Synthetic biology is engineering biology that constructs new biological systems (e.g., bacteria) for special purposes of application (e.g., cleaning polluted water, indicating poison).

Systems biology reconstructs complex circuits and networks of life. Synthetic biologists are biological engineers of complex molecules, cells and organisms with new functions and properties. In methodology, we distinguish top-down strategies reducing properties of genomes and bottom-up strategies constructing new systems from artificial fragments. In a top-down strategy, a living cell is reduced to a minimal with only absolutely necessary functions of life. Minimal cells are sometimes called "chassis" in analogy to the minimal structure of a car which can be re-equipped by engineers with additional functions of different purposes. Minimal cells are used as basic systems for tailored new functions of livings organisms (e.g., mycoplasma genetalium).

Contrary to living cells, protocells are no products of biological evolution, but completely new technical systems. They are constructed as self-replicating nano-systems in laboratories. They have mutating information stores, metabolic systems, and membranes for material and energetic interchange with cellular environment. Protocells are sometimes considered bridges between the "unanimated" and "animated" nature.

A challenge of current research is an automated evolution of artificial organisms with new chemical building blocks differing from the usual ones in nature. An automated procedure of long term evolution was applied to adapt genetically engineered E.coli bacteria unable to synthesize the natural nucleobase thymine to grow on increasing concentrations of 5-chlorouracil. After a culture of about 1000 generations, descendants of the original strain were obtained with 5-chlorouracil as complete substitute for thymine.[2] This paradigm shift in the chemistry of living systems aims at the generation of new organisms not found in nature, but satisfying the universal laws of evolution with changed building blocks. The analysis and synthesis of new life according to universal laws of evolution, but with different chemical elements may even be interesting for the research of extraterrestrial life in xenobiology.

In synthetic biology, electronic circuits of electrical engineering become a paradigm of research. Metabolic engineering aims at the design of tailored metabolic networks. Genetic circuits control cellular regulations. In analogy to electronic circuits and their programming, synthetic biology uses the term "biological circuits". Although there are

---

[2] P. Marlière, J. Patrouix, V. Döring, P. Herdewijn, S. Tricot, S. Cruveiller, M. Bouzon, R. Mutzel, 'Chemical Evolution of a Bacterium's Genome', in (2011) *Angewandte Chemie International Edition*, Vol.50 Issue 31.

many similarities with technical circuits, networks in living tissues differ by their restricted stability. Networks in living cells may more or less spontaneously change their functions which can arbitrarily be reproduced in technology. The reason is the unbelievable complexity of life: Contrary to technical systems, natural systems can often not be divided into specific modules with well-defined functions. During a long evolution, proteins, for example, might have developed additional properties and functions which are often unknown to researchers. This is the reason why surprising effects can emerge without being predictable. Therefore, without doubts, the engineering paradigm is successful in life sciences, but we must be extremely cautious with applications.

## 2. Computational View in Life Sciences

The paradigm shifts of systems and synthetic biology are only possible on the background of the dominating computational view in life sciences. Historically, computational explanations of life started with the concept of cellular automata introduced by John von Neumann et al. Cellular automata are complex systems of finite automata with states (e.g., numbers) which change in dependence of neighboring cells according to simple local rules. There is no central processor, but self-organization. Special cellular automata can even reproduce themselves in sequential generations. Cellular automata are a comprehensive modeling instrument, because every computer can be simulated by an appropriate cellular automaton and vice versa.[3]

With simple local rules, complex structures of pattern formation can be generated in several generations. Cellular automata can even simulate phase transitions and attractors of nature, (e.g., equilibrium and periodic oscillations, but also chaos, turbulence, and growth of complex structures with sensitive dependence on initial conditions in the sense of the famous butterfly effect of chaos theory). In some cases, the long-term behavior of cellular automata cannot be predicted, although their local rules are completely deterministic. This is true for cellular automata with the property of universal computability. It is well-known

---

[3] K. Mainzer, L. O. Chua, *The Universe as Automaton. From Simplicity and Symmetry to Complexity* (Heidelberg: Springer, 2011).

that the long-term behavior of a universal Turing machine is unpredictable: With respect to Turing's famous undecidability of the Halting problem, it cannot be decided, in principle, if the computational process of an arbitrary computer program will stop or not for an arbitrary input. As universal Turing machines can simulate any computer program, their long-term prediction would contradict Turing's undecidability of the Halting problem. John Conway's "Game of Life" is an example of a universal Turing machine and can, therefore, not be predicted in the long run with respect to the Halting problem.

# 3. Modeling the Brain as Complex Dynamical System

A special case of cellular growth is the dynamics of neural networks. Neural networks are complex systems of firing and non-firing neurons with topologies like brains. There is no central processor (mother cell), but a self-organizing information flow in cell-assemblies according to rules of synaptic interaction. There are different architectures with one synaptic layer or more synaptic layers with hidden units for feed-forward flow, or feedback loops with back-propagation flow. Learning algorithms change the synaptic weights, in order to realize the synaptic plasticity of living brains. The dynamics of neural nets can be modeled in phase spaces of synaptic weights with trajectories converging to attractors which represent prototypes of patterns.

Neural networks are already applied in cognitive robots. A simple robot with diverse sensors (e.g., proximity, light, collision) and motor equipment can generate complex behavior by a self-organizing neural network. In the case of collision, the connections between the active sensors of proximity and collision layer are reinforced by Hebbean learning. A behavioral pattern emerges from simultaneously firing neurons in the technical brain of the robot.

In order to model the brain and its complex abilities, it is quite adequate to distinguish the following categories. In neuronal-level models, studies are concentrated on the dynamic and adaptive properties of each nerve cell or neuron, in order to describe the neuron as a unit. In network-level models, identical neurons are interconnected to exhibit emergent system functions. In nervous-system-level models, several networks are combined to demonstrate more complex functions of sensory perception, motor functions, stability control, et al. In mental-operation-level models, the basic processes of cognition, thinking, and problem-solving are described.

In the complex systems approach[4], the microscopic level of interacting neurons should be modeled by coupled differential equations modeling the transmission of nerve impulses by each neuron. The Hodgekin-Huxley equation is an example of a nonlinear diffusion reaction equation with an exact solution of a traveling wave, giving a precise prediction of the speed and shape of the nerve impulse of electric voltage. In general, nerve impulses emerge as new dynamical entities like ring waves in chemical BZ-reactions or fluid patterns in nonequilibrium dynamics. In short: they are the "atoms" of the complex neural dynamics. On the macroscopic level, they generate cell assemblies which can be modeled by dynamical systems of differential equations. For example, a synchronously firing cell-assembly is correlated to some visual perception of a plant which is not only the sum of its perceived pixels, but characterized by some typical macroscopic features like form, background or foreground. On the next level, cell assemblies of several perceptions interact in a complex scenario. In this case, each cell-assembly is a firing unit, generating a cell assembly of cell assemblies whose macrodynamics can be modeled by nonlinear differential equations.

In these mathematical models, we get a hierarchy of emerging levels of cognition, starting with the microdynamics of firing neurons. The leading research hypothesis assumes that all kinds of cognitive activities are correlated with dynamic patterns of certain cell assemblies. The dynamics of each level is assumed to be characterized by certain differential equations of a dynamical model. For example, on the first level of macrodynamics, a dynamical model characterizes a visual perception. On the following level, the observer becomes conscious of the perception. Then the cell assembly of perception is connected with the neural area that is responsible for states of consciousness. In a next step, planning activities are realized in a state of consciousness. In this case, cell assemblies of cell assemblies are connected with neural areas in the planning cortex, and so on. They are represented by coupled

---

[4] K. Mainzer, *Thinking in Complexity. The Computational Dynamics of Matter, Mind, and Mankind*, Fifth Edition (New York: Springer, 2007).

nonlinear equations with firing rates of corresponding cell assemblies.[5] Even high-level concepts like self-consciousness could, in principle, be modeled by self-reflections of self-reflections, connected with a personal memory which is represented in corresponding cell assemblies of the brain. Brain states emerge, persist for a small fraction of time, then disappear and are replaced by other states. Nevertheless, we must not forget that these modeling steps are part of a complex research program of brain research and cognitive psychology which still needs empirical confirmation and tests in all empirical details.

# 4. Self-Organization and Self-Control of Technical Systems

Organic computing applies the principles of evolution and life to technical systems.[6] The dominating principles in the complex world of evolution are self-organization and self-control. How can they be realized in technical systems? In many cases, there is no finite program, in order to forecast the development of complex systems. In general, there are three reasons for computational limits of system dynamics: 1) A system may be undecidable in a strict logical sense. 2) Further on, a system can be deterministic, but nonlinear and chaotic. In this case, the system depends sensitively on tiny changes of initial data in the sense of the butterfly effect. Long-term forecasting is restricted, and the computational costs of forecasting increase exponentially after some few steps of future predictions. 3) Finally, a system can be stochastic and nonlinear. In this case, pattern emergence can only be predicted probabilistically.

Engineering control systems commonly are designed to behave linearly. This implies that they obey superposition, that is, twice as large an input signal will produce twice as large a response. By contrast, biological control frequently involves nonlinearities (Yates, 1988). Some

---

[5] K. Mainzer, *Symmetry and Complexity. The Spirit and Beauty of Nonlinear Science* (Singapore: World Scientific Publisher, 2005), 232.

[6] W.-T. Balke, K. Mainzer, 'Knowledge representation and the embodied mind: towards a philosophy and technology of personalized informatics', in *Lecture Notes of Artificial Intelligence 3782, Professional Knowledge Management* (Berlin: Springer, 2005), pp. 586-597.

nonlinear behavior is to be expected. For example, since biological variables cannot exceed certain values, they exhibit upper limits that may show up in mathematical models as saturation nonlinearities.

The firing frequency of certain sensory receptors can be considered a function of the sensed variable or stimulus. An ideal linear receptor would have a response proportional to the input stimulus over the full range if inputs. On the other hand, an actual biological receptor might have a nonlinear response. In the case of saturation, there is range of stimulus values over which the input-output relationship is nearly linear. Beyond this range, it takes a larger and larger input to obtain a given increment of response, until the response reaches its maximum possible value. Since receptors are always limited to some maximum output, it is evident that all biological receptors display some form of saturation. In other cases, a biological system will not respond to an input stimulus until the stimulus exceeds some minimum value. Obviously, such a property has adaptive value, since it may conserve energy. Sometimes, biological systems behave in a nearly linear manner for small values of input signals, but will deviate from linearity increasingly as the signal magnitudes grow.

Some properties of systems containing nonlinearities exhibit spontaneous oscillations which are called limit cycles. They exist only in nonlinear dynamical systems. Certain physiological variables exhibit limit cycle oscillations.[7] Among these variables are many homeostatic quantities, such as blood glucose concentration, arterial pressure, and temperature. Many of these quantities have a daily rhythm like body temperature. Others, like ovulation, have a twenty-eight-day cycle. Physiology is challenged to understand why nonlinearities and the ensuing limit cycle oscillations are essential to an organism.

Controllers for robot manipulators began as simple linear feedback control systems. However, since these systems were modeled on the human arm, it soon became apparent that more complex controllers were required in order to obtain some of the versatility of that arm. The situation is even more interesting with respect to mobile robots. Although most small mobile robots use very simple linear controllers at the lowest reflex level, they also perform reasoning and planning at

---

[7] J. B. Bassingthwaighte, L. S. Liebovitch, B. J. West, *Fractal Physiology* (New York: Oxford University Press, 1994).

high levels.[8] Many mobile robots use a multitude of sensors. Therefore, in common with organisms, they must integrate the readings from these sensors in order to make movement decisions. With increasingly autonomous humanoid robots, biological models for their control will become more and more complex and nonlinear, too.

# 5. Neural Networks and Robotics

In complex dynamical systems of organisms monitoring and controlling are realized on hierarchical levels. Thus, we must study the nonlinear dynamics of these systems in experimental situations, in order to find appropriate models and to prevent undesired emergent behavior as possible attractors. From the point of view of systems science, the challenge of embodied robotics is controlled emergence.

A key-application of controlled emergence is the nonlinear dynamics of brains. Brains are neural systems which allow quick adaption to changing situations during life-time of an organism. Neural networks are complex systems of threshold elements with firing and non-firing states, according to learning strategies (e.g., Hebbian learning). Beside deterministic homogeneous Hopfield networks, there are so-called Boltzmann machines with stochastic network architecture of non-deterministic processor elements and a distributed knowledge representation which is described mathematically by an energy function. While Hopfield systems use a Hebbian learning strategy, Boltzmann machines favor a back-propagation strategy (Widrow-Hoff rule) with hidden neurons in a many-layered network.

In general, it is the aim of a learning algorithm to diminish the information-theoretic measure of the discrepancy between the brain's internal model of the world and the real environment via self-organization. The interest in the field of neural networks is mainly inspired by the successful technical applications of statistical mechanics and nonlinear dynamics to solid state physics, spin glass physics, chemical parallel computers, optical parallel computers, or laser systems. Other reasons are the recent development of computing

---

[8] G. L. Bekey, *Autonomous Robots. From Biological Inspiration to Implementation and Control* (Cambridge Mass.: MIT Press, 2005).

resources and the level of technology which make a computational treatment of nonlinear systems more and more feasible.[9]

A simple robot with diverse sensors (for example, proximity, light, collision) and motor equipment can generate complex behavior by a self-organizing neural network. In the case of a collision with an obstacle, the synaptic connections between the active nodes for proximity and collision layer are reinforced by Hebbian learning: A behavioral pattern emerges, in order to avoid collisions in future.[10] In the human organism, walking is a complex bodily self-organization, largely without central control of brain and consciousness: It is driven by the dynamical pattern of a steady periodic motion, the attractor of the motor system.

What can we learn from nature? In unknown environments, a better strategy is to define a low-level ontology, introduce redundancy – which is commonly prevalent in sensory systems, for example – and leave room for self-organization. Low-level ontologies of robots only specify systems like the body, sensory systems, motor systems, and the interactions among their components, which may be mechanical, electrical, electromagnetic, thermal et al. According to the complex systems approach, the components are characterized by certain microstates generating the macrodynamics of the whole system.

Take a legged robot.[11] Its legs have joints that can assume different angles, and various forces can be applied to them. Depending on the angles and the forces, the robot will be in different positions and behave in different ways. Further on, the legs have connections to one another and to other elements. If a six-legged robot lifts one of the legs, this changes the forces on all the other legs instantaneously, even though no explicit connection needs to be specified. The connections are implicit: They are enforced through the environment, because of the robot's weight, the stiffness of its body, and the surfaces on which it stands. Although these connections are elementary, they have not

  [9] K. Mainzer, 'The Emergence of Mind and Brain: An Evolutionary, Computational, and Philosophical Approach', in R. Banerjee, B. K. Chakrabarti (eds.), *Models of Brain and Mind. Physical, Computational and Psychological Approaches* (Amsterdam: Elsevier 2008), pp. 115-132.

  [10] R. Pfeifer, C. Scheier, *Understanding Intelligence* (Cambridge Mass., MIT Press 2001).

  [11] S. Kajita, *Humanoide Roboter. Theorie und Technik des Künstlichen Menschen* (Berlin: Aka GmbH, 2007).

been made explicit by the designer. Connections may exist between elementary components that we do not even realize. Electronic components may interact via electromagnetic fields that the designer is not aware of. These connections may generate adaptive patterns of behavior with high fitness degrees. But they can also lead to sudden instability and chaotic behavior. In our example, communication between the legs of a robot can be implicit. In general, much more is implicit in a low-level specification than in a high-level ontology. In restricted simulated agents, only what is made explicit exists, whereas in the complex real world, many forces exist and properties arise, even if the designer does not explicitly represent them. Thus, we must study the nonlinear dynamics of these systems in experimental situations, in order to find appropriate models and to prevent undesired emergent behavior as possible attractors.

In the research project "Cognition in Technical Systems" (CoTeSys)[12] of both universities in Munich, cognitive and life sciences, information processing and mathematical sciences, engineering and robotics work systematically together to explore cognition for technical systems. Robotic agents cannot be fully programmed for every application. The program learns from experience where to stand when taking a glass out of a cupboard, how to best grab particular kitchen utensils, where to look for particular cutlery, et al. This requires the control system to know the parameters of control routines and to have models for how the parameters change the behavior. The sensor data of a robot's environment, which is the robot's "experience", are stored in a relational database system, the robot's "memory". According to the paradigm of probabilistic robotics[13], the data in the database together with causal structure on domain relations imply a joint probability distribution over relations in the activity domain. This distribution is applied in Markov logic, which allows inferring the conditional probability of logical (first order) statements. In short: A robot can estimate the environmental situation probabilistically. From an engineering point of view, it must not be assumed that the human cognitive system works on this line. But, nevertheless, Markov logic is

---

[12] CoTeSys (2006-2011) is funded by the German Research Council DFG as a research cluster of excellence within the "excellence initiative" from 2006-2013.

[13] S. Thrun, W. Burgard, D. Fox, D., *Probabilistic Robotics* (Cambridge Mass.: MIT Press, 2005).

an effective tool to solve cognitive tasks which are also solved by human cognition, perhaps, in different way.

According to the paradigm of complex dynamical systems, a robot can be described at different levels, in which global properties at one level emerge from the interaction of a number of simple elements at lower levels.[14] Global properties are emergent in the sense that they result from nothing else but local interactions among the elements. They cannot be predicted or inferred from knowledge of the elements or of the rules by which the elements locally interact, given the high nonlinearity of these interactions.

Simple examples of embodied robotics are reactive robots. They are controlled by simple neural networks, for example, fully connected perceptrons without internal layers and without any kind of internal organization. Nevertheless, these robots can display not only simple behaviors, such as obstacle avoidance, but also behaviors capable of solving complex problems involving perceptual aliasing, sensory ambiguity, and sequential organization of sub-behaviors. The question arises how far we can go with reactive sensory-motor coordination.

## 6. Embodied Robotics and Cognition

Not only „low level" motor intelligence, but also „high level" cognition (for example, categorization) can emerge from complex bodily interaction with an environment by sensory-motor coordination without internal symbolic representation. We call it „embodied cognition": Developmental psychology shows that an infant learns to categorize objects and to build up concepts by touching, grasping, manipulating, feeling, tasting, hearing, and looking at things, and not by explicit symbolic representations (for example, language). The categories are based on fuzzy patchworks of prototypes and may be improved and changed during life. We have an innate disposition to construct and apply conceptual schemes and tools.

But are there situations and problems which can only be solved by robots allowed to go beyond embodied reactions with internal

---

[14] K. Mainzer, 'From Embodied Mind to Embodied Robotics: Humanities and System Theoretical Aspects', in (2009) 103 *Journal of Physiology*, 296-304.

dynamical states? During evolution, primates and human beings have learnt to develop alternative internal models of situations with changing conditions to find the appropriate decisions. In embodied robotics, there are experiments of homing navigation where a robot is asked to navigate in an arena with a limited, but rechargeable, energy supply.[15] The abilities to locate a battery charger and periodically return to it are achieved without introducing explicit instructions of a program. Evolved homing strategies are based on autonomous development of an internal neural topographic map that was not predesigned allowing the robot to choose appropriate trajectories of motion.

The emergence of internal models or maps is made possible by an architecture of robots where two or more alternative neural modules compete for control of each motor output. This architecture allows evolving robots to use different neural modules to produce different sub-behaviors, but without preprogramming the whole behavior. There is an artificial evolution to select different neural modules and appropriate sub-behaviors. In a neural network with a layer of hidden neurons, some of the hidden nodes start to specialize and to influence the planning decision of the robot's trajectories of motion. The activation levels of the hidden neurons can be displayed on maps of the environment, displaying remarkable topographical representations of the external world.

In several examples, artificial evolution of robots with emergent modular architectures reported better results than other architectures.[16] But, in embodied organisms as well as embodied robots, sensory-motor coordination, and internal models are no excluding alternatives. In natural and technical evolution, they coexist and cooperate. All this amounts to saying that the behavior of robots with increasing autonomy cannot be purely explained by a stimulus-reaction paradigm, but by the emergence of internal ("cognitive") representation of the environment which reflects the goals defined by the robot itself.[17]

---

[15] D. Floreano, F. Mondada, 'Evolution of homing navigation in a real mobile robot', in (1996) *IEEE Transactions on Systems, Man, and Cybernetics – Part B: Cybernetics* 26 (3), 396-407.

[16] S. Nolfi, D. Floreano, *Evolutionary Robotics. The Biology, Intelligence, and Technology of Self-Organizing Machines* (Cambridge Mass.: MIT Press, 2001).

[17] K. L. Bellman, 'Self-Conscious Modeling', in (2005) *IT – Information Technology 4*, 188-194.

Moreover, cognitive states of human beings depend on emotions. We recognize emotional expressions of human faces with pattern recognition of neural networks and react by generating appropriate facial expressions for non-verbal communication. Emotional states are generated in the limbic system of the brain which is connected with all sensory and motor systems of the organism. All intentional actions start with an unconscious impulse in the limbic system which can be measured before their performance. In that sense, embodied intentionality is a measurable feature of the brain.[18] Humans use feelings to help them navigate the trees of their preferences, to make decisions in the face of increasing combinational complexity. Obviously, emotions help to reduce complexity.

The embodied mind is a complex system acting and reacting in dynamically changing situations. The emergence of cognitive and emotional states is made possible by brain dynamics which can be modeled by neural networks. According to the principle of computational equivalence, any dynamical system can be simulated by an appropriate computational system. But, contrary to Turing's AI-thesis, that does not mean computability in every case. In complex dynamical systems, the rules of locally interacting elements (for example, Hebb's rules of synaptic interaction) may be simple and programmed in a computer model. But their nonlinear dynamics can generate complex patterns and system states which cannot be forecast in the long run without increasing loss of computability and information.[19] At least to some well-defined degrees, artificial minds[20] could have their own intentionality, cognitive and emotional states which may differ from human beings. They also cannot be forecast and computed similar as is the case with natural minds. Limitations of computability are characteristic features of complex systems.

---

[18] W. J. Freeman, 'How and why brains create meaning from sensory information', in (2004) *14 Int. J. Bifurcation and Chaos*, 515-530.

[19] K. Mainzer, L. Chua, *Local Activity Principle* (London: Imperial College Press, 2013).

[20] C. D. Dennett, *Brainchildren: Essays on Designing Minds* (Cambridge Mass.: MIT Press, 1998).

# 7. Towards Complex Socio-technical Infrastructures: Cyberphysical Systems

In a technical co-evolution, a global information and communication network is emerging with surprising similarity to self-organizing neural networks of the human brain. The increasing complexity of the World Wide Web (www) needs intelligent strategies of information retrieval and learning algorithms simulating the synaptic plasticity of a brain. The Internet links computers and other telecommunication devices. At the router level, the nodes are the routers, and the edges are their physical connections. At the interdomain level, each domain of hundreds of routers is represented by a single node with at least one route as connection with other nodes. At both levels, the degree distribution follows a power law of scale-free network which can be compared with networks in systems biology. Measurements of the clustering coefficient deliver values differing from random networks and significant clusters. The average paths at the domain level and the router level indicate the small-world property.

Global information networks are growing together with societal infrastructures. Current examples are complex smart grids of energy. Many energy providers of central generators and decentralized renewable energy resources lead to power delivery networks with increasing complexity. Smart grids mean the integration of the power delivery infrastructure with a unified communication and control network, in order to provide the right information to the right entity at the right time to take the right action. It is a complex information, supply and delivery system, minimizing losses, self-healing and self-organizing. Thus, global networks solve complex problems more or less autonomously. In this sense, they are intelligent, but without consciousness like human brains.

Smart grids are complex organizations of networks regulating, distributing, storing, and generating electrical power. Their structure and dynamics have surprising similarity with complex protein networks in systems biology regulating the energy supply of a cell. The intelligence of smart grids increases with their ability of self-organizing information processing for optimal energy supply. In communication networks, appropriate prices of optimal energy supply could be automatically negotiated by virtual agents. In smart grids, the energy system grows together with information and communication technology in a kind of symbiosis.

A well-known problem with wind mills and solar cells is the unpredictability of production depending on changing weather conditions. In intelligent networks, the need can be locally satisfied by virtual negotiations. A model assumes the following rules and conditions of negotiating virtual agents:[21]

1. The need for renewable energy can be satisfied either in a local regional subnet or between subnets. Reserve capacity is used only in exceptional cases.

2. Energy must be adjusted between different voltage levels or different groups of balance on the same level.

3. Producers are also consumers and vice versa.

4. Negotiations on local energy supply are automatically performed by agents of producers and agents of consumers. They are coordinated by balance group managers working parallel and synchronized in time on each level.

5. In the model, the negotiations start in periods of 0.5 s. The negotiations as well as the distribution of negotiated energy are expected to be finished before the end of each period. Bids and offers arriving in the meantime are negotiated in the next period.

6. At the beginning of each period, each client decides whether he/she takes part as producer or consumer or not. He/she decides with respect to the current difference between the states of demand and production.

7. Bids and offers occur in frameworks of prices with respect to amortization and maintenance. In the model, there are no long-range contracts or discounts for big and future acquisitions which can occur in reality.

The algorithm of negotiation assumes a framework of prices for each level of negotiation. Each balance group manager on each level accomplishes a cycle of coordination of 10 turns. Each turn takes 1 ms. After each turn the balance managers test in parallel whether bids and offers are sufficiently similar. If they are sufficiently similar, a contract

---

[21] H. J. Wedde, S. Lehnhoff, C. Rehtanz, O. Krause, 'Von eingebetteten Systemen zu Cyber-Physical Systems. Eine neue Forschungsdimension für verteilte eingebettete Realzeitsysteme', in (2007) *Informatik Aktuell. Aktuelle Anwendungen in Technik und Wirtschaft - 12 Pearl 2008.*

between the partners is concluded. A fixed amount is added until the stock or demand is spent. The negotiation strategies of a client are given by an opening bid, an opening offer, and parameters of priority and strategy. After n turns, the unsatisfied agents adapt their bids and offers with respect to an exponential law of behavior which is useful to realize a fast convergence between bids and offers. The negotiated price is the arithmetic mean between similar values. Unsatisfied clients are passed on to the next level of negotiation. On this level, the framework of prices is reduced to a constant relation. The needs and interests of finally unsatisfied clients are satisfied by a central reserve capacity (but with very bad prices).

Short term fluctuations of consumption in the ms to min interval, which are effected by sudden and unpredicted local or regional causes, are not only observed as perturbations in households, but they can endanger the stability of large transport networks. In our model, these critical situations are avoided by the activation of agents after each cycle of negotiation. It is assumed that many electrical appliances (e.g., refrigerator, boiler) can temporarily work without power or with a battery. In these cases, reserve energy can be used for other purposes. The reserve energy is more competitive than the traditional one, because of low costs of transport and storage in the network. Additionally, the balance managers act on each level in parallel in shortest time.

Smart grids with integrated communication systems accomplish a dynamical regulation of energy supply. They are examples of large and complex real-time systems according to the principles of cyber-physical systems.[22] Traditionally, reserve energy which is used to balance peaks of consumption or voltage drops is stored by large power plants. The main problem of changing to renewable energies is the great number of constraints depending on questions of functionality as well a security, reliability, temporary availability, tolerance of failures, and adaptability. Cyber-physical systems with local and bottom-up structures are the best

---

[22] E. Lee, 'Cyber-Physical Systems: Design Challenges', in (2008) 8 *University of California, Berkeley Technical Report* No. UCB/EECS, available at <http://citeseerx.ist.-psu.edu/viewdoc/download?doi=10.1.1.156.9348&rep=rep1&type=pdf> accessed 8 April 2014.

answer to the increasing complexity of supply and communication systems.[23]

Smart grids are only the first steps in the future of cyberphysical systems. Classical computer systems separate physical and virtual worlds. Cyberphysical systems observe their physical environment by sensors, process their information and influence their environment with actuators according to communication devices. Thus, they integrate the analog signals of the physical world with digital information processing like organisms receiving analog signals through their sensory systems which are digitally processed by firing and non-firing neurons in their nervous systems and brains. A modern aircraft, for example, is a complex robot with sensors receiving analog signals of the external physical world which are processed digitally to generate AI-supported more or less autonomous decisions which are only supervised by humans. The aircraft system is embedded in a global communication network of air traffic. Another example is a modern hospital considered as technical infrastructure with patients and physicians coordinated by intelligent information systems which are embedded in a global communication system of health care. Thus, cyberphysical systems are complex systems of many self-organizing net components, leading to the emergence of intelligent problem solving procedures increasing the adaptability, autonomy, reliability, healthcare, manufacturing, transportation, and consumer appliances.

Cyberphysical systems initiate a new phase of industrial revolution. The 1st phase transition of industrial revolution ("industry 1.0") was the steam engine, followed by the 2nd phase transition ("industry 2.0") of Henry Ford's assembly line of production. In this case, production is divided in elementary tasks which are realized step by step according to the program of an algorithm on an assembly line. In a 3rd phase ("industry 3.0"), human activities are supported or, sometimes, replaced by industrial robots which are still fixed to certain positions and motor activities. In industry 4.0, the internet of things is realized in the industrial world: Internet of things means that objects (and not only humans) communicate by sensors and intelligent software interfaces. They organize themselves in steps of production with respect to changing constraints. Production on demand and "tailored" to the

---

[23] Cyber-Physical Systems, in 'The National Science Foundation, *Program Announcements & Information*, 30 September 2008.

individual demands of clients will become possible. Cloud manufacturing connects industry 4.0 and internet of things with cloud computing, supported by VR (virtual reality) technology in parallel and distributed computer networks. Cloud manufacturing leads to decentralized networks of production and sale. The working world is organizing itself with respect to flexible working time of employees and individual ("tailored") service delivery for clients. Centralized and standard mass production is overcome in industry 4.0 and typical for industry 2.0 and 3.0.

Another example of sociotechnical infrastructure is ubiquitous robotics. In analogy to ubiquitous computing, computer functions are not concentrated in a single system (e.g., a supercomputer or a humanoid robot), but they are distributed in objects according to special utilities and services. For example, IT-infrastructure with sensors and communication functions can be embedded into flats and houses, in order to improve the living conditions of elderly people. Robotic infrastructure is also applied in hospitals, traffic systems or households.

A robot society is a group of robots which has the ability to communicate, interact, and to solve problems jointly. By that, a robot society can generate intelligent behavior like interacting ants of a population or interacting neurons of brains. A society is defined by its information and control structure which make possible common task planning and execution. In this case, a robot is a locally active agent driven by a battery and low input signals which are amplified and transformed into complex patterns of behavior.

Most of the autonomous mobile robots are operating in neither stabile nor structured environments. Therefore, a major trend in robotics is going towards multi-robot systems. In many cases, the decomposing of a complex task into parallel subtasks is a possibility to speed up the performance. Sometimes, several robots work with the same subtask, increasing the redundancy of the system. Furthermore, there can be tasks where a successful completion of a task requires close cooperation among the robots. Such case is, for example, the carrying of a large object together. It requires some sort of interaction between robots, whether is a direct communication or some sort of indirect communication through sensing the forces in the object to be transported.

This kind of task as well as many other tasks normally related to multi-robot systems has clear analogy to biological systems.[24] A group of ants solve the problem through sensing the forces and torque in the object. Based on this information they change the direction of forces accordingly or needed some ants change the position of their hold. Numerous similar examples can be found from nature. Tests by evolution during millions of years are proven to be feasible in dynamic and hostile environments and can thus provide valuable information and inspiration for similar type of engineering tasks.

The number of distributed autonomous robotic system applications will increase as the technology and knowledge improve. Various robot societies will move from research laboratories into everyday life. Normal applications concern everyday tasks like cleaning, monitoring, caring people in households or hospitals, etc.. In the future, robot societies will be taken to distant planets, deep sea module collection missions, mining operations. Robots on the nano level will be sent into veins for search of tumors, which they will attack at close range. Just as in natural systems the intelligence of the collective system will emerge from the multiple interactions among the members and with the environment.

In first steps of development, natural populations, for example ant societies, were studied to find the key issues. Next steps were to design a physical society. It consists of two types of autonomous mobile robots, and the task for the society is classical, to gather stones from an unknown environment along with the mapping of the environment while operating. The society has been implemented both as a physical society and as a simulated one. A possible application is the use of a robot society inside industrial processes.

# 8. Societal, Ethical, and Legal Challenges

The paradigm shifts of systems and synthetic biology, embodied robotics, and cyberphysical systems are part of a general tendency of converging science, technology, and society. The traditional separation of "natural" and "artificial" objects (Aristotle) or "grown" and "the

---

[24] E. O. Wilson, *Sociobiology: The New Synthesis* (25th Anniversary Edition. Cambridge M.A.: Belknap Press, 2000).

made" is misleading, because they are all complex systems emerging with respect to laws of evolution under different conditions. Therefore, innovations in synthetic biology, embodied robotics, and cyberphysical systems need ethical and legal analysis, based on interdisciplinary research, including expertise in ethics, law, science, and technology. With respect to safety, risk of negative environmental impact may emerge from unintended side effects of nonlinear complex dynamics in more or less autonomous cyberphysical infrastructures. There is also the risk of genome pool contamination, when synthetic organisms transfer genes to already existing organisms. Finally, one must consider the run-off risks, when synthetic organisms replicate and evolve out of control.

The global ethical goal of research and technology must be a world of sustainable innovation considering all these side-effects. Biological evolution of life on Earth was "blind" and often suboptimal under random conditions. Human innovations are sometimes narrow-minded with respect to market profits, military or evil goals. Synthetic biology, embodied robotics, and smart socio-technical infrastructures should aim at sustainable innovations of health and human well-being with respect to the whole Earth system. That needs careful analysis of complex system dynamics to take care of the human and societal conditions (conditio humana) of 21st century technology.

Obviously, complex systems analysis demonstrates that there is not a determined future of technology, but a variety of "futures" under changing constraints. In short: the epistemic question "What can we know?" must be complemented by the second famous question of Kantian philosophy: "What should we do?" It is well-known that it was the science fiction writer Isaac Asimov who, at first, tried to systemize certain laws of roboethics:

1. A robot must not harm humans or, by omission, allow that humans are harmed.
2. A robot must follow the order of humans if the order is not in contradiction to law 1.
3. A robot must protect its own existence if its protection is not in contradiction to laws 1 and 2.

Asimov's first draft of roboethis leads to an ethical roadmap of humanoid robotics, e.g.:

1. Are Asimov's three laws sufficient for practical roboethics?
2. Should roboethics aim at an ethics for robots, engineers, or users of robots?
3. How far should we go with implementing (programming) ethical norms into robots?
4. How should we adjust the implementation of ethical norms to robotic autonomy?
5. May robots be equipped with emotions?
6. How should robots be valued from a legal point of view?
7. Like the Ten Commandments of the Bible, Asimov's laws are not sufficient to regulate the detailed ethical and legal praxis of everyday life.

With respect to recent technological standards, roboethics can be restricted to an ethics of engineers and users of robots. As long as robots do not suffer from pain or feelings, we do not need an ethics for robots like (human) slaves in antiquity. But, in the previous chapters, we argued that feeling robots cannot be excluded by technical and scientific reasons, in principle. It is a normative decision to exclude these developments in the future, because we do not like to enlarge pain in the world by constructing feeling robots.[25] But, with respect to man-machine interface, technical systems should become more sensible for human-machine interactions in the sense of assistance and service systems: In this case, robots have no emotions, but they simulate sensibility to improve human-machine interface. Further on, we need robots with certain degrees of autonomy, in order to solve complex problems under changing constraints, because we cannot determine any detail in our living world of increasing complexity. Increasing degrees of autonomy lead to legal questions. At which degree of autonomous decisions is a robot no longer a mere technical object like a bicycle? Again, it is a normative question how far we should go, and it is not a technical or scientific question: For example, autonomous systems of car driving are already in use. In the previous chapters, we argued that robots must become more and more autonomous to solve complex problems. In this case, we need new legal regulations of responsibilities.

---

[25] This position was violently defended by the pioneer of AI, J. Weizenbaum, *Computer Power and Human Reason. From Judgement to Calculation*, (San Francisco: W.A. Freeman, 1976).

The ethical question arises how far we should allow these technical developments.

While the technical development of humanoid robots is still in an early state, IT- and robotic infrastructures are already realized and distributed all over the world. Therefore, an ethical and legal roadmap of cyberphysical systems is necessary, e.g.:

1. Which ethical and legal norms should be considered for embedded systems (e.g., assistance systems of car drivers)?

2. Automation does not only depend on technical development, but human acceptance. Which ethical and legal norms must be considered?

3. Which ethical and legal norms must be demanded for the introduction of automation in the working world (e.g., cloud manufacturing, industry 4.0)?

4. Which ethical and legal norms must be considered with respect to the demographic change and the introduction of technical infrastructure for the elderly?

5. Which ethical and legal norms should be demanded for digital dignity in the age of Big Data?

The last question leads to the fundamental principles of human rights. In legal tradition, human dignity is defined as self-purpose, i.e. humans must not be exploited by technical, economic, or any other interests.[26] But, according to Kantian philosophy, self-purpose is not a scientific category which can be applied and confirmed by empirical research. It is a normative demand of human self-interest ("self-interest of practical reason") to save human self-purpose as fundamental principle of ethics and law. It is justified by the long history of human experience in terrible struggles and wars. Therefore, as highlight of European Enlightenment, Kant's practical philosophy tried to deduce all kinds of ethical and legal regulations from this fundamental "regulative idea". Thus, in the Kantian framework, even high-tech of autonomous robots, cyberphysical systems, and industry 4.0 must be service and assistance systems of human interest to improve human living conditions.

That is the hard core of European humanism contrary to a so-called transhumanism which is sometimes proclaimed by intellectuals in the

---

[26] K. Mainzer, „Die Würde des Menschen ist unantastbar." Zur Herausforderung von Artikel 1 des Grundgesetzes durch den technisch-wissenschaftlichen Fortschritt', in *Jahrbuch der Universität Augsburg* (Augsburg: Universitätsverlag 1990), 211-221.

US and Asia. Transhumanism assumes an evolutionary development converging to a singularity as distinguished point of technical evolution when human nature is overcome by technical species with optimized abilities and infrastructures. But, transhumanism forgets that the technical development of mankind is no determined process leading to future states like planetary orbits. We can and should influence the development of technology according to normative advices. Transhumanism is no scientific hypothesis, but its arguments can often be exposed as an ideology following certain interests of, for example, IT-industries to optimize profits disregarding human rights.

Digital dignity is an application of human self-purpose to the IT-world of Big Data.[27] How can the personal interests of people be protected against an overcrowding network of information systems with commercial, political, and military interests? But, it is not easy to save digital dignity even in countries with a common basis of democratic values. For example, the legal praxis of US-democracy is quite different to German tradition. German lawyers deduce digital dignity from the principles of human rights. Thus, the principle must be protected against possible violations by anticipating legal rules. In short: the legal system is deduced and justified from principles. By the way, in Kantian philosophy, moral and legal rules are also justified by "transcendental deduction" from the fundamental norm of human dignity ("categorical imperative"). In the US-tradition, legal decisions are not justified by deduction from principles, but by referring to specific decisions of courts and judges. Therefore, during the last US-German conflict on IT-spying, there was also a great misunderstanding between both countries because of different legal cultures: For US-lawyers, the German demand of "digital dignity" was too diffuse, because they need concrete legal cases and decisions of courts they can refer to. It is obvious that, behind the different legal cultures of both countries, there are also different philosophical traditions: continental thinking in principles and the pragmatic approach in British and American philosophy.

---

[27] An application to medical technology is discussed in J. C. Joerden, E. Hilgendorf, F. Thiele, 'Human Dignity and New Developments in Medical Technology – an Exploration of Problematic Issues', in (2011) *Menschenwürde und moderne Medizintechnik* II 17, 9-55.

The different legal traditions must also be considered with respect to responsibility in the high-tech world. In German law, responsibility is clearly referred to the human subject of law. For example, in German traffic regulations, the car driver must be responsible for all actions. This restriction is obviously a problem for the introduction of completely automated cars. Further on, how should we regulate responsibilities for more or less autonomous networks and cyberphysical systems? In the US legal system, institutions and companies are also legal subjects which can be punished. In this sense, they are responsible for their actions. In German law, only human persons can be responsible and punished. Responsibility depends on intentions. Can technical systems have intentions? In the previous chapters, it was shown that humanoid robots and even cyberphysical systems (e.g., smart grids, automated companies of industry 4.0) can have their own intentions to some well-defined degrees. But, obviously, they have no consciousness or emotions like humans. On the other side, emotions and diffuse intuitions may disturb clear and robust analysis and decisions which could be better realized by autonomous technical systems (e.g., in traffic systems). In that sense, it cannot be excluded that technical systems can better take care of human interests than humans themselves.

According to humanism (contrary to transhumanism), the crucial point is that technical systems, humanoid robots as well as cyberphysical systems, must remain assistance and service systems of human interests independent of their degrees of automation and autonomy. In complex systems, responsibility depends on the degrees of participation in common actions of agents and stakeholders.[28] Even surprisingly emerging ("synergetic") effects of nonlinear interactions have clear causalities and, by that, responsibilities of engaged agents. With increasing complexity of technical systems and living conditions, the ethical and legal scenarios will become more complex and need careful analysis. Nevertheless, we should be cautious to delegate responsibilities to technical systems. In the end, humans should remain responsible for the whole system, although parts and aspects may be completely automated following their own intentions. The final

---

[28] The concept of cooperative responsibility in human communities is discussed in J. Nida-Rümelin, *Verantwortung* (Stuttgart: Reclam 2011), § 49.

intention to introduce technical systems must be humanistic. The final responsibility of technical systems must be human.

# Agency and interagency in socio-technical systems

*Sabine Thürmel*

In order to understand agency and interagency in socio-technical systems a concept of multi-dimensional, gradual agency is introduced. It offers a classification framework for the observation and interpretation of scenarios where humans and nonhumans interact. It may be applied to the analysis of the potential of social computing systems and their virtual and real actualizations. The approach may also be used to describe situations where options to act are delegated to technical agents. Ethically relevant scenarios where solely humans act can be compared to test-bed simulations and hybrid constellations. The state of the art in proto-ethical behaviour, social interaction and social autonomy of current socio-technical systems is presented.

## 1. Introduction

In June 2012 "The Economist" suggested that methods of experimental ethics might be helpful to generate "robo-ethical" behaviour morally acceptable to most people[1]. This is more than most experimental ethicists intend. Their main goal is to explore humans' intuitions[2]. But such an endeavour would be totally symmetric to attempts to improve human behaviour based on computer experiments. The Leibniz Center for Law at the University of Amsterdam has been looking – so far in vain – for a specific Ph.D. candidate: he or she should be capable of developing new policies in tax evasion scenarios.

---

[1] 'Robots go to war – March of the Robots' in Economist Print Edition Morals and the Machine available at <http://www.economist.com/node/21556103> accessed 6 May 2013.

[2] J. Knobe, Sh. Nichols, 'An Experimental Philosophy Manifesto', in J. Knobe, Sh. Nichols (eds) *Experimental Philosophy*, (New York: Oxford University Press, 2008), 3-16.

They should be based on agent-based models[3]. Such a "social computing" approach does not only offer to model social behaviour. It may also suggest ways how to change it.

Such suggestions may only be fruitful if the insights gained in the laboratory via social computing systems are transferable to real world scenarios. In order to explore the possibility of such a transference an agency-specific level of abstraction is presented. On this basis (current) test-bed simulations may be compared to scenarios where solely humans act.

Ethically relevant behaviour may only be simulated, if the corresponding software agents themselves possess at least proto-ethical capabilities. Some suggestions are made if and when social computing systems offer possibilities of social evolution and possess ethical impact.

# 2. Potentiality and actuality of agent-based systems

## 2.1 *The evolution of software agents*

The degrees of freedom built into computational artefacts may materialize in individual acts, mandated actions or collaborative interaction. The starting point of this evolution was constituted by interface agents providing assistance for the user or acting on his or her behalf. As envisioned by Brenda Laurel[4] and Pattie Maes[5] they evolved into increasingly autonomous agents to which tasks can be delegated. Increasingly, they rely on information on the internet for completing their tasks. Software agents may do things for us such as finding bargains on the Internet or performing more sophisticated information queries: "Like an army commander sending a scout ahead . . . you will dispatch [software] agents to collect information on your behalf. Agents will dispatch agents. The process multiplies. But [this process] started at

---

[3] Leibnitzcenter Multiagent Systems PhD position available University of Amsterdam, <http://www.leibnizcenter.org/general/multi-agent-systems-phd-position-available> accessed 24 November 2012.

[4] B. Laurel, *Computers as theatre* (New York: Addison-Welsley, 1991).

[5] P. Maes, 'Agents that reduce work and information overload', (1994) in *Communications of the ACM* 37 (7), 30-40.

the interface where you delegated your desires"[6]. Today virtual agents are commonly deployed in online auctions or eNegociations[7]. In game worlds they were first seen in one person offline video games. Interacting pure software agents and avatars became prevalent in MMORPGs (massively multiplayer online role-playing games) as World of Warcraft®. Realized as interworking collaborative software agents embedded in nets of devices they provide support for "smart energy"-distribution based on so called "smart grids"[8] or for other variants of the "Internet of things"[9].The collaboration of humans and virtual caregivers in health-monitoring systems is experimentally explored[10]. Agent-based social and organisational aware assistive technology is under development e.g. by Gómez-Sebastià et al.[11]. These endeavours and similar research intend to support the vision of "smart health", i.e. patients' competent treatment to be offered by collaborating humans, robots and software agents at any location while constantly monitoring the patients' health. Last but not least software agents may coordinate emergency response services in disaster management systems[12]. Thus software agents have been promoted from assistants to virtual interaction partners.

The socio-technical fabric of our world has been augmented by these collaborative systems. Incidentally, already in 1992 Solum posed the question in the North Carolina Law Review whether virtual agents

---

[6] N. Negroponte, *Being Digital* (New York: Vintage Publishing (Random House), 1995), 158.

[7] M. Woolridge, *An Introduction to MultiAgent Systems* (New York: John Wiley & Sons, 2nd ed., 2009).

[8] K. Mainzer, *Leben als Maschine?: Von der Systembiologie zur Robotik und Künstlichen Intelligenz* (Paderborn: Mentis Verlag, 2010).

[9] F. Mattern, M. Langheinrich, ,Eingebettete, vernetzte und autonom handelnde Computersysteme: Szenarien und Visionen', in A. Kündig, D. Bütschi (eds), *Die Verselbständigung des Computers* (Zürich: vdf Verlag, 2008), 55-75.

[10] See e.g. M. Hossain, D. Ahmed, 'Virtual Caregiver: An Ambient-aware Elderly Monitoring System', in (2012) *IEEE transactions on information technology in biomedicine: a publication of the IEEE Engineering in Medicine and Biology Society*, 1024-1031.

[11] I. Gómez-Sebastià et al., 'Towards an implementation of a social electronic reminder for pills', in (2012) V. Conitzer, M. Winikoff, L. Padgham, W. van der Hoek (eds), *Proceedings of the 11th International Conference on Autonomous Agents and Multiagent Systems* (AA-MAS 2012), 61-70.

[12] N. Jennings ALADDIN End of Project Report available at <http://www.aladdinproject.org/wp-content/uploads/2011/02/finalreport.pdf> accessed 6 May 2013.

may be the basis for persons in the legal sense of the law[13]. This opened up a new research field doing justice to the increasing autonomy of the software agents.

## 2.2 Social computing based on multi-agent systems

Multi-Agent Systems (MAS) permit to model collective behaviour based on the local perspectives of individuals, their cognitive processes and their interaction with the environment. The project ALADDIN presents a case in point: It offers a "multi-agent toolbox" supporting decentralised resource allocation in environments where "control is distributed; uncertainty, ambiguity, and bias are endemic; multiple self-interested stakeholders with different aims and objectives are present; resources are limited and continually vary"[14]. As part of this project demonstrators for the coordination of emergency response services have been built. They are based on electronic market mechanisms. The allocation of ambulances was performed more efficiently by the system than by humans[15]. This might result from the fact that MAS model rational behaviour under uncertainty, whereas humans do not rely on a fixed utility function as guidance for their acts. They may be guided by other considerations and experiences than the ones fundamental to the MAS system.

The goal of the agent-oriented programming paradigm is the adequate and intuitive modelling and implementation of complex interactions and relationships. Software agents were introduced by Hewitt's Actor Model[16]. Today a whole variety of definitions for software agents exists but all of them include mechanisms to support persistence, autonomy, interactivity and flexibility. Bionic approaches, as swarm intelligence, or societal models are adapted to implement collaborative approaches to distributed problem solving: the starting point of any software agent-based approach is a bionic or societal

---

[13] L. Solum, 'Legal personhood for artificial intelligences', (1992) in *North Carolina Law Review*, 2, 1231-1283.

[14] N. Jennings, (fn. 12), 2.

[15] 'Artificial Intelligence – no command and control' in Economist Print Edition No Command, no control, available at <http://www.economist.com/node/17-572232?story_id=17572232>, accessed 6 May 2013.

[16] C. Hewitt, P. Bishop, R. Steiger, 'A Universal Modular Actor Formalism for Artificial Intelligence', (1973) in *Proceedings of the 3rd international joint conference on Artificial intelligence IJCAI*, 235-245.

metaphor for distributed problem solving. The resulting computer science concept is specified as a computer program modelling the interacting software agents. At compile-time the high level program is transformed in a machine-executable computer program to be run in a distributed environment. During runtime any (instance of) a software agent may be perceived as a distinct thread or process.

Computer-based simulations provide a link between theory and experiment. Social simulation systems are similar to numerical simulations but use different conceptual and software models. Numerical methods based on non-linear equation systems support the simulation of quantitative aspects of complex, discrete systems[17]. In contrast, multi-agent systems (MAS)[18] are focused on the adequate and intuitive modelling and implementation of complex interactions and relationships. Agent-based approaches are especially suited to modelling and implementing open systems based on dynamically interacting entities pursuing individual potentially conflicting goals without central control using sophisticated approaches to communication and cooperation. Both the numerical approach and the agent-based one may complement each other. They can even be integrated to simulate both numerical, quantitative and qualitative, logical aspects e.g. within one expressive temporal specification language[19]. Agent-based models (ABMs) may be better suited than conventional economic models to model the "herding" among investors. Early-warning systems for the next financial crisis could be built based on ABMs[20].

Multi-agent simulation comprises the modelling, the implementation and the validation of multi-agent systems. Technical problem solutions may be tested in experimental environments to be executed in real-world interaction spaces at a later stage. The demonstrator for the coordination of emergency response services may go live. Thus it may coordinate human and nonhuman actors in genuine disaster recovery

---

[17] K. Mainzer, *Thinking in Complexity. The Complex Dynamics of Matter, Mind, and Mankind*, (Berlin: Springer, 5th edition, 2007).

[18] See M. Woolridge, (fn. 7).

[19] T. Bosse, S. Tibor, J. Treur, Jan, 'Integrating Agent Models and Dynamical Systems', in M. Baldoni, T. Son, M. van Riemsdijk, M. Winikoff (eds), *Declarative Agent Languages and Technologies* V, LNCS 4897 (Heidelberg: Springer, 2008), 50-68.

[20] 'Economics focus – Agents of change' in Economist Print Edition Agents of Change <http://www.economist.com/node/16636121/print> accessed 6 May 2013.

scenarios. Concerning its impact on the physical environment it possesses a virtual actuality in the test-bed environment and a real actuality when employed in real-time in order to control processes in the natural word. The same is true of individual technical agents: their potential is mediated. It reveals itself in concrete situations: „A technical system constitutes a potentiality which only becomes a reality if and when the system is identified as relevant for agency and is embedded into concrete contexts of action"[21]. A software agent executed in a purely virtual space has a virtual actuality. In real-life material environments the real actuality of software agents and robots materializes.

In contrast to Latour who only focuses on actual systems and their modes of existence[22] one may and should clearly distinguish between agency (potentiality) and action (actuality) – especially if the investigations are led by techno-ethicists. Moreover virtual actuality does not equate with real actuality in most circumstances. A plane crash in reality is very different from one in a simulator.

Experiments may be conducted either in a purely virtual environment or in a hybrid one. In the latter case humans may be integrated for clarifying and/or deciding non-formalized conflicts in an ad-hoc manner. Automatic collaborative routines or new practises for ad-hoc collaboration can be established. Novel purely virtual or hybrid contexts materialize. They realize collective and distributed agency. Therefore it becomes vital to understand agency and interagency in virtual and hybrid constellations.

# 3. Agency in sociotechnical systems

## 3.1 The Actor Network Theory (ANT)

Bruno Latour was the first to attribute agency and action both to humans and non-human[23]. Together with colleagues as Michel Callon he developed a symmetric vocabulary which they deemed applicable

---

[21] Chr. Hubig, *Die Kunst des Möglichen I – Technikphilosophie als Reflexion der Medialität* (Bielefeld, Germany: Transcript Verlag, 2006), 3.

[22] See e.g. B. Latour, *Reassembling the Social – An Introduction to Actor-Network-Theory* (Oxford: Oxford University Press, 2005).

[23] B. Latour, 'Mixing Humans and Nonhumans together: The Sociology of a Door-Closer', (1988) in *Social Problems* 35, 298-310.

both to humans and non-humans[24]. This ontological symmetry led to a flat concept of agency where humans and nonhuman entities were declared equal. Technographic work was done in laboratories and field tests. Observations gained were described as so-called actor networks: heterogeneous collectives of humans and nonhuman entities, mediators and intermediaries. The Actor Network Theory regards innovation in technology and sciences as largely depending on whether the involved entities – may they be material or semiotic – succeed in forming (stable) associations. Such stabilizations can be inscribed in certain devices and thus demonstrate their power to influence the further scientific evolution[25]. Thus the ANT approach could more aptly be called "sociology of innovation"[26]. The central empirical goal of the actor network theory consists in reconstructively opening up black boxes, i.e. convergent and (temporarily) irreversible networks[27]. However, it should be noted that Latour has quite a conventional, tool-oriented notion of technology[28]. This may be due to the fact that smart technology and agent systems are nowhere to be found in his studies.

## 3.2 *Distributed agency and technology in action*

Werner Rammert is convinced that "it is not sufficient to only open up the black box of technology; it is also necessary and more informative to observe the different dimensions and levels of its performance"[29]. It is investigated under what conditions we can attribute agency and inter-agency to material entities and how to identify such entities as potential agents[30]. A gradual concept of agency

---

[24] M. Callon , B. Latour, 'Don't Throw the Baby Out with the Bath School! A Reply to Collins and Yearley', in A. Pickering (ed.) *Science as Practice and Culture* (Chicago: Chicago University Press, 1992), 343-368, 353.

[25] B. Latour, 'Drawing Things Together', in M. Lynch, St. Woolgar (eds.) *Representation in Scientific Practice* (Cambridge, MA: MIT Press, 1990), 19-68

[26] B. Latour, (fn. 22), 9

[27] I. Schulz-Schaeffer, 'Akteur-Netzwerk-Theorie. Zur Koevolution von Gesellschaft, Natur und Technik', in J.Weyer (ed.), *Soziale Netzwerke. Konzepte und Methoden der sozialwissenschaftlichen Netzwerkforschung,* (München/Wien: Oldenbourg Wissenschaftsverlag, 2000), 187-212, 205

[28] W. Rammert, *Distributed Agency and Advanced Technology Or: How to Analyse Constellations of Collective Inter-Agency* (Berlin: The Technical University Technology Studies, 2011)

[29] Ibid., 11

[30] W. Rammert, I. Schulz-Schäffer, ‚Technik und Handeln: Wenn soziales Handeln sich auf menschliches Verhalten und technische Abläufe verteilt', in W. Rammert, I.

is developed in order to categorize potential agents regardless of their ontological status as machines, animals or human beings. The model is inspired by Anthony Giddens' stratification model of action[31]. It distinguishes between three levels of agency:

- causality ranging from short-time irritation to permanent re-structuring,

- contingency, i.e. the additional ability "to do otherwise" – ranging from choosing preselected options to self-generated actions - and, in addition, on the highest level

- intentionality as a basis for rational and self-reflective behaviour[32,33].

The "reality of distributed and mediated agency" is demonstrated e.g. based on an intelligent air traffic system[34]. Hybrid constellations of interacting humans, machines and programs are identified. Moreover a pragmatic classification scheme of technical objects depending on their activity levels is developed. This permits to classify the different levels of "technology in action". It starts with passive artifacts, continuing with reactive ones, i.e. systems with feedback loops. Next come active ones, then proactive ones, i.e. systems with self-activating programs. It ranges further up to co-operative systems, i.e. distributed and self-coordinating systems[35]. The degrees of freedom in modern technologies are constantly increasing. Therefore the relationship between humans and technical artifacts evolves "from a fixed instrumental relation to a flexible partnership"[36]. Rammert identifies three types of inter-agency: "interaction between human actors, intra-activity between technical agents and interactivity between people and

Schulz-Schäffer (eds) *Können Maschinen handeln? Soziologische Beiträge zum Verhältnis von Mensch und Technik* (Frankfurt: Campus, 2002), 11-64, 9.

[31] A. Giddens, *The Constitution of Society, Outline of the Theory of Structuration* (Cambridge, UK: Polity Press, 1984).

[32] See W. Rammert, I. Schulz-Schäffer, (fn. 30), 26.

[33] See W. Rammert (2011), (fn. 28), 1 ff.

[34] Ibid., 15

[35] W. Rammert, 'Where the Action is: Distributed Agency between Humans, Machines and Programs', in U. Seifert, J. Kim, A. Moore (eds). *Paradoxes of Interactivity* (Bielefeld and New Brunswick, Germany and U.S: Transcript and Transaction Publishers, 2008), 62-91, 7.

[36] W. Rammert (2011), (fn. 28), 13.

objects"[37]. These capabilities do not unfold "ex nihilo" but "medias in res". "According to [this] concept of mediated and situated agency, agency arises in the context of interaction and can only be observed under conditions of interdependency"[38]. These reflections show how „technology in action" may be classified and how constellations of collective inter-agency can be evaluated using a gradual and multi-level approach. Similar to Latour these authors are convinced that artefacts are not just effective means, but must be constantly activated via practise (enactment)[39].

The gradual model of Rammert and Schulz-Schäffer[40] does not suffice for experiments in ethically relevant behaviour: its wide ranging levels do not allow for a clear-cut delineation. Since this approach focuses exclusively on „agency medias in res", i.e. on snapshots of distributed agency and action, the evolution of any individual capabilities, be they human or nonhuman, are not accounted for. Even relatively primitive cognitive activities as learning via trial and error, which many machines, animals and all humans are capable of, are not part of the methodical symmetry between human and technology. A clear distinction between human agency, i.e. intentional agents, and the technical agency, a mere "pragmatic fiction"[41], remains.

In Rammert's view technical agency "emerges in real situations and not in written sentences. It is a practical fiction that has real consequences, not only theoretical ones"[42]. In his somewhat vague view the agency of objects built by engineers "is a practical fiction that allows building, describing and understanding them adequately. It is not just an illusion, a metaphorical talk or a semiotic trick"[43].

### 3.3 *Designing agency in and for social computing systems*

In contrast to Rammert, in this paper the agency of technical artefacts is not judged as being a fiction. It is perceived but as a level of

---

[37] W. Rammert (2008), (fn. 35), 6.

[38] W. Rammert (2011), (fn. 28), 5.

[39] W. Rammert, *Die Techniken der Gesellschaft: in Aktion, in Interaktivität und in hybriden Konstellationen*, (Berlin: The Technical University Technology Studies Working Papers TUTS-WP-4-2007, 2007), 15.

[40] See W. Rammert, I. Schulz-Schäffer (2002), (fn. 30).

[41] W. Rammert (2011), (fn. 28), 8.

[42] Ibid., 5.

[43] Ibid., 8.

abstraction in the sense of Floridi's "methods of abstractions"[44]. By choosing a certain level of abstraction (LoA) a theory commits itself to a certain interpretation of the object types[45] and their instantiations, e.g. the software agent types and their realizations. Using a multi-dimensional gradual agency concept[46] this level of abstraction may be characterized in more detail. This approach is intended for the observation and interpretation of scenarios where humans and nonhumans interact. The classification scheme (see also chapter 4) may already be used in the design phase, when a system based on different agent types is to be modelled.

From the designer's point of view metaphors often serve as a starting point to develop e.g. novel heuristics to solve so-called NP-complete (optimization) problems. Such metaphors may be borrowed from biology, sociology or economics. Research areas as neural nets, swarm intelligence approaches and electronic auction procedures are products of such approaches. In the design phase ideas guiding the modelling phase are often quite vague at first. In due course their concretization results in a conceptual model47, which is then specified as a software system. From the user's or observer's point of view during runtime the more is known about the conceptual model the better its potential for (distributed) agency can be predicted and the better the hybrid constellations of (collective) action, emerging at runtime, may be analysed. Latour's snapshots are complemented by a perspective on the system model. The philosophical benefit of this approach does not only lie in a reconstructive approach as intended by Latour and Rammert but also in the conceptual engineering of the activity space. Under a LoA for agency and action, activities may be observed as they unfold. Moreover the system may be analysed and

---

[44] L. Floridi, *The Philosophy of Information* (Oxford: Oxford University Press, 2011), 44 ff.

[45] L. Floridi, 'The Method of Levels of Abstraction', in (2008) *Minds and Machines*, vol. 18 Issue 3, 303-329, 327.

[46] Introduced in S. Thürmel, 'A Multi-Dimensional Agency Concept for Social Computing Systems', in (2012) *Proceedings of the LACAP Conference 2012 "Symposium: The Social Turn - MAS"*, 87-91, and expanded in S. Thürmel, *Die partizipative Wende: Ein multidimensionales, graduelles Konzept der Handlungsfähigkeit menschlicher und nichtmenschlicher Akteure* (Munich: Dr. Hut Verlag, 2013).

[47] A. Ruß, D. Müller, W. Hesse, ,Metaphern für die Informatik und aus der Informatik', in M. Bölker, M. Gutmann, W. Hesse (eds), *Menschenbilder und Metaphern im Informationszeitalter*, (Berlin: LIT Verlag, 2010), 103-128, 107.

educated guesses about its future behaviour can be made. Both the specifics of distinct systems and their commonalities may be compiled.

# 4. Multidimensional gradual agency

*4.1 A classification scheme for agency in heterogeneous constellations*

The conceptual framework for agency and action, first introduced in Thürmel[48], is intended to provide a multidimensional gradual classification scheme for the observation and interpretation of scenarios where humans and nonhumans interact. It permits to define appropriate lenses, i.e. levels of abstraction, under which to observe, interpret, analyse and judge their activities. The starting point is Rammert's pragmatic classification of technical objects depending on their activity levels[49]. In order to demonstrate the potential for agency not only the activity levels of any entities but also their potential for adaptivity, interaction, personification of others, individual action and conjoint action has to be taken into account.

Based on activity levels and on being able to adapt in a "smart" way acting may be discerned from just behaving. The potential for interaction is a precondition to any collaborative performance. The potential of the personification of others enables agents to integrate predicted effects of their own and other actions. This capability may affect any tactically or strategically motivated individual action. Moreover it is prerequisite to any form of defining conjoint goals and conjoint (intentional) commitment.

The activity level permits to characterize individual behaviour depending on the degree of self-inducible activity potential. It starts with passive entities as Latour's well-known road bumpers. Reactivity, realized as simple feedback loops or other situated reactions, is the next level. Active entities permit individual selection between alternatives resulting in changes in the behaviour. Pro-active ones allow self-reflective individual selection. The next level corresponds to the capability of setting one's own goals and pursuing them. These capabilities depend on an entity-internal system for information processing linking input to output. In the case of humans it equals a cognitive system connecting perception and action. For material

---

[48] For details see (fn. 46).
[49] See W. Rammert (2008), (fn. 28), 7.

artefacts or software agents an artificial "cognitive" system couples (sensor) input with (actuator) output.

Based on such a system for (agent-internal) information processing the level of adaptivity may be defined. It characterizes the plasticity of the phenotype, i.e. the ability to change one's observable characteristics including any traits, which may be made visible by a technical procedure, in correspondence to changes in the environment. Models of adaptivity and their corresponding realizations range from totally rigid to simple conditioning up to impressive cognitive agency, i.e. the capability to learn from past experiences and to plan and act accordingly. A wide range of models co-exist allowing to study and experiment with artificial "cognition in action". This dimension is important to all who define agency as situation- appropriate behaviour and who deem the plasticity of the phenotype as an essential assumption of the conception of man.

The potential for interaction, i.e. the coordination by means of communications is the basis to most if not all social computing systems and approaches to distributed problem solving. It may range from uncommunicative to hard-wired cooperation mechanisms up to ad-hoc cooperation.

Alluding to Dennett's intentional stance[50] Rammert talks about as-if intentionality which humans must attribute to technical agents for goal-oriented interaction[51]. I deem it more appropriate to focus on the capability for personification of others. Behavioural patterns may be explained based on the respective ability to perceive another agent as such. Thus a level of abstraction is found which focuses on agency and interaction and not on the ontological statuses of the involved agents. The personification of others lays the foundation for interactive planning, sharing strategies and for adapting actions. This capability is non-existent in most material and software agents. Some agents have more or less crude models of others, e.g. realized as so-called minimal models of the mind. A next qualitative level may be found in great apes[52] which also have the potential for joint intentionality. This provides the basis for topic-focused group decision making based on egoistical behaviour. Understanding the other as an intentional agent

---

[50] D. Dennett, *The Intentional Stance* (Cambridge, MA: MIT Press, 1987).

[51] See W. Rammert (2011), (fn. 28), 10.

[52] J. Call, M. Tomasello, 'Does the chimpanzee have a theory of mind? 30 years later', in (2008) *Trends in Cognitive Sciences*, Volume 12, Issue 5, 187-192.

allows even infants to participate in so-called shared actions[53]. Understanding others as mental actors lays the basis for interacting intentionally and acting collectively[54]. Currently there is quite a gap between nonhuman actors and human ones concerning their ability to interact intentionally. This strongly limits the scope of social computing systems when it is used to predict human behaviour or if it is intended to engineer and simulate future environments.

Both the potential for individual action and for conjoint action may be defined based on the above mentioned capabilities for activity, adaptivity, interaction and personification of others. One option is the following: In order to stress the communalities between human and nonhuman agents, an agent counts as capable of acting (instead of just behaving), if the following conditions concerning its ontogenesis hold: "the individual actor [evolves] as a complex, adaptive system (CAS), which is capable of rule based information processing and based on that able to solve problems by way of adaptive behaviour in a dynamic process of constitution and emergence"[55]. Based on the actor's capability for joint intentionality resp. understanding the other as an intentional agent or even as a mental actor, the actor may be able of joint action, shared or collective action.

### 4.2 *Distributed and collective agency*

Constellations of distributed agency range from purely virtual systems like swam intelligence systems where the individual agents only possess rather primitive capabilities to flexible partnerships between humans and software agents up to loosely coupled complex adaptive systems. The latter include MAS-based systems for so diverse problem spaces as predator-prey relationships of natural ecologies, legal engineering scenarios or disaster recovery systems.

Current collaborative constellations between humans and technical agents are asymmetric. Their acts are based on different cognitive systems, different degrees of freedom and only partially overlapping spheres of experience. However, new capabilities may emerge over time on the individual level (e.g. emergent semantics, emergent

---

[53] M. Tomasello, *Origins of Human Communication* (Cambridge, MA: MIT Press, 2008).

[54] Ibid.

[55] P. Kappelhoff, ‚Emergenz und Konstitution in Mehrebenenselektionsmodellen‘, in J. Greve, A. Schnabel (eds) *Emergenz – Zur Analyse und Erklärung komplexer Strukturen* (Berlin: suhrkamp taschenbuch wissenschaft, 2011), 319-345, 320.

consciousness). Self-organisation and coalition forming on the group level can occur. New cultural practices and novel institutional policies may emerge.

The proposed conceptual framework for agency and action offers a multidimensional gradual classification scheme for the observation and interpretation of scenarios where humans and nonhumans interact. It may be applied to the analysis of the potential of social computing systems and their virtual and real actualizations. The above introduced approach may also be used to describe situations where options to act are delegated to technical agents. The corresponding variants of proto-ethical impact and social autonomy may be characterized.

# 5. Protoethical behaviour, social interaction and social autonomy

## 5.1 *Proto-ethical behaviour of software agents*

In order to clarify the state of the art in software agents' ethics Moor's distinctions between ethical-impact agents, implicit ethical agents, explicit ethical agents and full ethical agents may be used[56]. In social computing the three classes of lesser ethical agents may be found: software agents used as mere tools may have an ethical impact; electronic auctioning systems may be judged implicit ethical agents, if "its internal functions implicitly promote ethical behaviour—or at least avoid unethical behavior"[57]; disaster management systems based on MAS systems may be exemplary explicit ethical agents if they "represent ethics explicitly, and then operate effectively on the basis of this knowledge"[58]. It is open to discussion whether any software agent will ever be a full ethical agent which "can make explicit ethical judgments generally is competent to reasonably justify them"[59]. But the first variants of ethical (machine) behaviour, i.e. proto-ethical systems, are already in place.

---

[56] J. Moor, 'The Nature, Importance, and Difficulty of Machine Ethics', (2006) *in* IEEE INTELLIGENT SYSTEMS, 18-21.

[57] Ibid., 19.

[58] Ibid., 20.

[59] Ibid., 20.

## 5.2 *Social interaction in multi-agent systems*

In line with a well accepted approach in enaction research "social interaction" may be defined as follows: "two or more autonomous agents co-regulating their coupling with the effect that their autonomy is not destroyed and their relational dynamics acquire an autonomy of their own. Examples [include] conversations, collaborative work, arguments, collective action, dancing and so on"[60]. While pondering the question "Can social interaction constitute social cognition" these authors do not exclude cross-species interactions or interactions with robots[61]but they do not provide any examples or further elaborations of these constellations.

The most basic coupling is rigid, without any dynamics, based on predefined communication and collaboration patterns. This feature is often found in human-machine or machine-machine interaction. Incidentally, this form of social interaction may even be best realized by computers because they are able to actualize this type of purely rule-oriented social behaviour in true perfection which the institutionalized-bureaucratic environment aspires to but never reaches[62].

The coordination dynamics of interacting humans and nonhumans, the co-regulation of their coupling is often contextual. Examples include virtual assistants or robopets. In disaster management systems where the dispatch function may be interchangeably exercised by human and nonhuman agents (proto-)social interaction may be thought of as an as enabler of (proto-)social cognition. Social performance constituted by fully fledged social interaction lies in the future. However, participatory sense making e.g. between humans and robots is an active research field: The behavioural and cognitive processes that underlie human communication are studied in order to develop methods to synthesize such abilities in machines[63]. The dynamics of social interaction and learning might allow "to bootstrap the cognitive system" of technical systems as described e.g. in a "roadmap for

---

[60] H. De Jaegher, E. Di Paolo, Sh. Gallagher, 'Can social interaction constitute social cognition?', (2010) in *Trends in Cognitive Sciences*, Vol. 14, No. 10, 441-446, 441.

[61] Ibid., 441.

[62] H. Geser ‚Der PC als Interaktionspartner', in (1989) *Zeitschrift für Soziologie*, Jg. 18, 230-243, 234.

[63] Sociable Agents Group (2013) in Sociable Agents Center of Excellence Cognitive Interaction Technology, available at <http://www.techfak.uni-bielefeld.de/ags/soa/> accessed 25 April, 2013

developmental robotics"[64]. Dominey and Warneken intend to explore „the basis of shared intentions in human and robot cognition"[65]. They demonstrate how "computational neuroscience", robotics and developmental psychology influence each other in a very fertile way. Thus enacting conjoint agency in heterogeneous constellations is well past its embryonic stage.

### 5.3 *Social autonomy in multi-agent systems*

The fact that current technical agents "lack humans' consciousness, intentionality and free will"[66] does not mean that they do not possess a degree of "social autonomy in a collaborative relationship". This form of goal-autonomy was defined by Falcone and Castelfranchi as having to two components: "a) meta level autonomy that denotes how much the agent is able and in condition of negotiating about the delegation or of changing it; b) a realization autonomy that means that the agent has some discretion in finding a solution to an assigned problem, or a plan for an assigned goal"[67]. Even certain current software agents may possess this kind of social autonomy thus displaying a certain proto-social behavior. Such software agents need not necessarily be based in a Belief-Desire-Intention(BDI)-model[68]. However, if one intends to base a computational model of trust on BDI-agents, an elaborate approach is to be found in the trust theory of Castelfranchi and Falcone[69]. As an aside, it should be mentioned, that one cannot only model trust, but also implement "mischievous" software agents, agents who aim at spreading false information, if it suits them. Incidentally, in the biological world this domain is exclusively reserved for humans[70].

---

[64] A. Cangelosi et al., 'Integration of Action and Language Knowledge: A Roadmap for Developmental Robotics', in (2010) *IEEE Transactions on Autonomous Mental Development*, VOL. 2, NO. 3, 167-195.

[65] P. Dominey, F. Warneken, 'The Basis of shared intentions in human and robot cognition', in (2011) *New Ideas in Psychology* 29, 260-274

[66] See Moor 2006, (fn. 56), 20

[67] R. Falcone, Chr. Castelfranchi, 'The human in the Loop of a Delegated Agent: The Theory of Adjustable Social Autonomy', in (2001) *IEEE Transaction on Systems, Man, and Cybernetics – Part A: Systems and Humans*, Vol. 31, No 5, 406-418, 407.

[68] Ibid., 416.

[69] Chr. Castelfranchi, R. Falcone, *Trust Theory: A Socio-Cognitive and Computational Model* (Chichester: UK: Wiley Series in Agent Technology, 2010).

[70] D. Buttelmann, M. Carpenter, M. Tomasello, 'Eighteen-month-old infants show false belief understanding in an active helping paradigm', in (2008) *Cognition*, Volume 112, Issue 2, 337-342.

# Towards a philosophical defence of legal compatibilism

*Filippo Santoni de Sio*

Recent progress in the mind sciences has fuelled radical scepticism towards the foundation of legal responsibility. In order to neutralize radical scepticism, the autonomy of law as a normative enterprise is often invoked. However, this simple defensive strategy is not sufficient to overcome radical scepticism, and a more solid philosophical defence of legal compatibilism is required. In this chapter I offer a brief sketch of such a philosophical defence.

## 1. Science and legal responsibility

The progress of the sciences of mind in the last decades of the XX century has fuelled radical sceptical attitudes towards the metaphysical foundation of legal responsibility. According to radical scepticism, the progress in the mind sciences is in strong tension with our legal system of attribution of responsibility, insofar as this presupposes the freedom of human action, or "free will" and mind sciences seem to show that this freedom does not exist. Radical scepticism on responsibility has in turn triggered the reaction of those that we dub conservatives. Conservatives think that practices of attribution of legal responsibility are, taken as a whole, still justified, no matter what mind sciences have discovered so far or will discover in the future about the functioning of human brain.

Whereas I think that the attitude of conservatives is basically correct, and that the progress of the science of mind does not necessarily shake the foundation of the building of responsibility practices, I also think that the arguments that are put forward by conservatives are often not fully satisfying. A common strategy among conservatives is that which appeals to the autonomy of law. According to this line of argument, science and law are separate enterprises with different goals; whilst it is up to the science of mind to explain how (according to different versions of the argument) the brain or the mind work, *it is up to the law to establish how people should behave*. Unlike science, legal attributions of responsibility are basically norm-setting practices and it is thus up to the law not to the scientists to decide how responsibility practices should work[1].

I find this line of argument dissatisfying for two reasons. Firstly, the conservatives insistence on the autonomy of the law tends to push to the background the many ways in which the science of the mind has affected legal responsibility practices in the past, and the ways in which scientific progress may legitimately affect those practices in the future[2]. Conservative are right in insisting that the rules of responsibility essentially reflect moral and social norms of behaviour, but they are wrong insofar as they deny or downplay the fact rules of responsibility also reflect a certain conception of human action; and that whilst responsibility is in itself an essentially normative concept, some concepts *presupposed* by the system of attribution of responsibility – i.e. freedom, rationality, capacity – reflect also a certain view of what human agents and actions *are*.

Secondly and relatedly, the conservative strategy based on the autonomy of the law tends to ignore that there are also broader theoretical – non-purely-legal – reasons to be conservative about the foundation of responsibility practices. And it is in the interest of the law to spell out these reasons as clearly as possible, in order to convincingly address the sceptical concerns. By only appealing to the normativity of the law, conservatives may certainly save their legal citadel from the sceptical assaults; but unless they also find a way to defend the conceptual hill upon which the legal citadel stands, their citadel will sooner or later collapse. This chapter contains a sketch of some *theoretical* reasons in defence of legal practices of responsibility. After

---

[1] Cfr. W. Glannon, 'Neurobiology, Neuroimaging, and Free Will', in (2005) 29 *Midwest Studies in Philosophy* 68–82; M. S. Gazzaniga, 'Neuroscience in the Courtroom', in (2011) 304 *Scientific American* 54–9, S. J. Morse, 'The Non-problem of Free Will in Forensic Psychiatry and Psychology', in (2007) 25 *Behavioral Sciences and the Law* 203–20; and the discussion of this literature by N. A Vincent, 'Legal Responsibility Adjudication and the Normative Authority of the Mind Sciences', in (2011) *Philosophical Explorations*, 14(3) 316-321.

[2] Cfr. N. A. Vincent, (fn 1), 321-325.

briefly explaining how the law conceives of "free will", I will focus on the role played by the concepts of capacity and rationality in attributions of legal responsibility, and I will offer some theoretical arguments in defence of this use. I will close by offering one exemplification of a correct use of these concepts in legal attributions of responsibility.

Insofar as it aims to defend the idea that scientific causal explanations of the functioning of the human brain are compatible with morally justifiable legal practices of attribution of responsibility, this chapter aims to offer a defence of *legal compatibilism*. However, insofar as it aims to offer some philosophical arguments for this compatibility – in addition to the above-mentioned prevalently pragmatic or legal ones – the chapter also aims to pave the way for a *philosophical defence of "legal compatibilism"*.

## 2. Legal compatibilism

Radical scepticism on the foundation of legal responsibility *denies* the compatibility between causal explanations of human behaviour and (morally justified) practices of attribution of legal responsibility. Radical scepticism is thus one form of incompatibilism. Incompatibilism relies on two ideas about free will, namely: a) that free will is incompatible with causal explanations of human behaviour, and b) that attributions of legal responsibility are morally justified only if free will exists[3]. In the incompatiblist perspective, the progress of the sciences of the mind threatens the moral foundation of legal practices of responsibility because the mind sciences offer more and more rich causal explanation of human behaviour, and the richer the causal explanations the thinner the ground for free will and responsibility.

According to legal compatibilism, incompatibilism adopts a too narrow conception of "free will". Legal compatibilists distinguish between a narrow and a broad sense of free will. According to the narrow sense, free will designates a special power of the human mind to act independently or even

---

[3] Another form of incompatibilism is libertarianism, according to which statements a) and b) are true, *and* free will exists (so that responsibility practices are safe). For a recent defence of legal libertarianism see D. Hodgson, *Rationality + Consciousness = Free Will* (New York: Oxford University Press, 2013).

in contrast with the causal laws of the universe – this is the *contra-causal* conception of free will. According to the broad sense, "free will" designates the set of conditions under which it is reasonable to consider a subject as the author of their actions (capacity, voluntariness, intentionality, etc.); this set of conditions may also not include "free will" in the contra-causal sense. Indeed – compatibilists admit – scientific progress and a secularized view of man are in tension with the contra-causal conception of free will. But scientific progress and secularism are not necessarily in tension with the belief in the existence of free will in the broad sense. Legal compatibilists claim that the law *should not*, in principle, rely on a contra-causal view of free will; and that, as a matter of fact, western legal systems *do not* rely on it. The law should not rely on a contra-causal conception of free will because the law is a rational enterprise, and it should therefore not adopt a conception like the contra-causal conception of free will that seems to presuppose a dualistic view of man (the mind as a metaphysically independent soul), and a quasi-religious view of human faults and responsibility (actions as morally attributable because originated in the transcendent dimension of the mind)[4].

However, most importantly, no matter what incompatiblists think, as a matter of fact the law does not adopt a contra-causal conception of free will, and thus its foundation is not shaken by the progress of science and a secularized view of mind and man. Incompatiblists often seem to rely on the idea that existing legal exemptions and excuses work by identifying a causal mechanism underlying the wrong action. Therefore, they think that the more science will be able to say about the causal mechanisms underlying human actions, the more we will be able to plea for exemptions and excuse; in the long run we may have no responsible agents at all. But excuses do not rely on causation. In the legal debate on the foundation of legal excuse there is controversy about whether their common rationale is absence of intention[5], absence of choice[6], non-conformity of action to the agent's character[7], or a combination of these principles[8]. What is generally agreed upon is the

---

[4] Cfr. F. Santoni de Sio, N.A Vincent, 'Rationality + Consciousness = Free Will by David Hodgson', in (2014) *Criminal Law and Philosophy* DOI: 10.1007/s11572-013-9282-1.

[5] R. J. Wallace, *Responsibility and the Moral Sentiments* (Cambridge MA: Harvard University Press, 1994).

[6] M. S. Moore, 'Choice, Character, and Excuse', in (1990) 7 *Social Philosophy and Policy* 29-58.

[7] V. Tadros, 'The Character of Excuse', (2001) 21 *Oxford Journal of Legal Studies* 495-519.

[8] J. Horder, *Excusing Crime* (Oxford: Oxford University Press, 2004).

non-relevance of the causal origin of action for the evaluation of the agent's responsibility[9].

Still, incompatiblists may insist that whilst the law may have its own political, pragmatic or consequentialistic reasons to endorse certain principles and not others, these principles may still be not morally or philosophically well grounded. If this were the case, we should seriously consider a radical reform of our legal system. I think that legal compatibilists should take this philosophical challenge more seriously than they have done so far. In the next sections I will present a sketch of some philosophical arguments in defence of legal compatibilism.

# 3. Properties and capacities

The basic incompatiblist insight is that causal explanations are not compatible with alternate *possibilities*, so that once it is showed that a certain behaviour was (deterministically) caused by certain causal antecedents, it is not possible any more to describe that behaviour as the outcome of a *choice* made by the agent. A standard compatiblist reply to this challenge is to insist that morality and the law are justified in assuming that for an individual action x that they perform, there is a range of alternative actions that the agent has, in general, the *capacity* to do (y, z, n). So that when an agent (voluntary) does x, it is reasonable to assume (in the absence of abnormal circumstances) that she *could have done* y, z, n, and that its doing x was therefore a choice under her control[10]. I think that this line of argument does not seem to take the basic incompatiblist insight seriously enough. Capacity is a kind of possibility. And the basic incompatiblist insight challenges the idea of there being possibilities open in front of agents at the time t of their action x, given the sum of agent's mental states m and the sum of external circumstances c. In this perspective, that the agent has a capacity only means that the agent may have done y, z or n *at the different times* $t_0$ or $t_2$, and/or *under the slightly different mental circumstances* $m_0$ or $m_2$

---

[9] M. S. Moore, 'Causation and the Excuses', (1985) 73 *California Law Review* 1091-1149 85.

[10] Cfr. J. M. Fischer and M. Ravizza, *Responsibility and Control: A Theory of Moral Responsibility* (Cambridge: Cambridge University Press, 1998), and the critique by F. Santoni de Sio and N.A Vincent, (fn. 4).

and/or *under the slightly different external circumstances* $c_0$ or $c_2$. But this does not matter in the incompatiblist perspective. What matters is that *at time* t, *under mental circumstances* m *and external circumstances* c, the agent *could not* have done otherwise than she did.

In order to address the incompatiblist challenge, legal compatibilists should not simply insists that agents are the authors of their actions because they have general capacities to perform different actions *in different circumstances*. Capacity is a kind of possibility, and given that incompatiblists seem to have a good argument to deny the existence of real open possibilities in front of the agents under specific circumstances, legal compatibilists should at least try to explain *what kind* of possibility a capacity for action is, and how may *this* possibility resist the incompatiblist fury.

Legal compatibilists must and can accept this metaphysical challenge. The concepts of possibility and capacity are not ethical or legal inventions, specifically designed to give theoretical support to specific moral or legal practices. As Daniel Dennett has efficaciously explained[11], these categories are indispensable to describe and make sense of general features of objects in the world. As G.E. Moore had pointed out long before Dennett, a cat who is not actually climbing a tree in the garden because busy chasing a mouse indoors still has the capacity to climb trees, whereas a dog lacks this capacity[12]. Tony Honoré eventually concurred, explaining that in describing the world we can legitimately use two senses of "can"[13]; we may sometimes use the "can" *particular* (the incompatibilist can), according to which at any given time an individual subject or object can only do what is allowed to do by the complete sum of the particular material conditions that realize at that time; however, much more often, in order to give a more efficacious description of reality we need to use the *general* sense of "can". The general "can" refers to what subjects or objects may be expected to do given their *general nature*, or what we may I would call their *formal properties*. Admittedly, if things are looked at and described from the point of view of the *material conditions realizing at a given time*, such formal properties will disappear. And if we look at things from this particular perspective, we can do no other than joining

11 D. C. Dennett, *Freedom Evolves* (New York: Viking Press, 2003).
12 G. E. Moore, *Ethics* (Oxford: Oxford University Press, 1912).
13 A. M. Honoré, 'Can and Can't', in (1964) 73 *Mind* 463-479.

incompatiblists in saying that while busy chasing a mouse indoor a cat has not the capacity to climb the tree, any more than a dog has that capacity; or, according to an example by Alan White[14], that a car with a less-than-fully open throttle has not the capacity to run at 100 mph.

I think that legal compatiblist should shift the burden of proof upon incompatiblists and ask them the following question: What is gained by rejecting the common view of the world and assuming their perspective? Incompatiblists would probably say that by relying on their purely material description of the world we can get closer to a *true* description of things. However, this seems to beg the question. Why must a description of the world that does not make any room for the concepts of possibility and capacity, and thus prevent the attribution of formal properties to different subjects – for instance, in G.E. Moore's example, being a tree-climber animal – should be closer to the truth? Aren't formal properties one important way to *define, identify* and *distinguish* different kinds of objects – for instance, cats and dogs or cars with different horse powers? Incompatiblists seem to claim that if we have to take science seriously and to be loyal to the truth, we have to give up the general sense of "can", namely the concept of capacity. I think that a good defence of compatibilism should start from the simple consideration that it does not seem to be in the truth's interest to eliminate one interesting way to distinguish different kinds of objects in the world.

# 4. Human capacities and moral statuses

The distinction between material descriptions of states of affairs and formal properties of objects that we have just sketched is particularly relevant for the understanding of the relation between science and attribution of responsibility. In the past decades, a leading defender of legal compatibilism, Stephen Morse, has engaged in a passionate defense of the general principles for the attribution of responsibility embedded in the (Anglo-American) criminal law against the alleged threats coming from the progress of neuroscience. Morse has defended the existence of agency and responsibility against the radical skeptical

---

[14] A. White, *Modal Thinking* (Ithaca, NY: Cornell University Press, 1975), 41.

challenge by stressing the *explanatory force* and *practical necessity* of what he calls "folk-psychological explanation" for human behavior, i.e. explanation based on people's intentions, plans, desires, beliefs, choices, etc. As neuroscience – Morse rightly claims - hasn't (so far) demonstrates that we are mechanical puppets, we are still legitimated to see ourselves and others as "intentional creatures" who "can violate expectations of what they owe each other"[15].

Morse claims that what he calls the general capacity for practical rationality is "the primary responsibility condition". In line with the requests of incompatiblists, he endorses a *synchronic* view of capacity according to which in order for the attribution to be fair the relevant capacity must be possessed by the agent "*at the time* in question"[16]. Moreover, Morse correctly assumes that a capacity actually possessed may sometimes remain *not exercised*, and observes that in fact even generally rational people often act "irrationally and foolishly"[17]. However, Morse's doesn't clearly explain what these general capacities *are*, and how they should be attributed. On what basis should we for example distinguish between a subject that at time $t_1$ *possesses but does not exercise* the capacity for rationality, from one that at time $t_1$ *doesn't possess* that capacity, even if she possessed it at $t_0$, and will possess it again at $t_2$? Morse's only answer is that even when they fail to behave rationally it is a "usual legal *presumption* that most adults are so capable"[18]. As he doesn't clarify what the *philosophical ground* for this *legal presumption* is, one might think that the presumption in the end depends on the *epistemic limits* of the law, that is on the actual *impossibility of a legal inquiry* into the real mental conditions *of* agents at the time of their action. But in this way radical skeptics may finally get what Morse doesn't want to give them – the admission that the *presumption* of capacity is in the end only a *fiction* or an *illusion*.

To avoid the risk of turning general capacities into legal fictions, one should replace the idea of capacity as a legal presumption with a more solid philosophical conception of capacity. I have suggested elsewhere the idea of human capacity as a normative power deriving from a

---

15 S. J. Morse, 'Determinism and the Death of Folk Psychology: Two Challenges To Responsibility from Neuroscience', in (2008) 9 *Minnesota Journal of Law, Science & Technology* 1-36.
16 Ibid., 7.
17 Ibid.
18 Ibid.

status[19]. This view strongly relies on the general metaphysics of capacities as properties sketched in the previous section. According to my view, the past performance of rational behaviour, together with other formal and material conditions, allows the law to attribute the agent the *status* of a rational agent. Statuses are for human agents what formal properties are for non-human subjects and objects. Cats are tree-climbers, human are practical reasoners. The possession of the status gives the agent – among other things - *the capacity* to act rationally in a given set of circumstances. Therefore, if at time *t* the agent legitimately possesses the status of a rational agent, and the circumstances are of a kind that allow, in general, the exercise of that capacity, then *ipso facto* the agent possesses the capacity to behave rationally. If she acts irrationally, this counts as a *failed exercise* of a general capacity possessed by her. A closer analysis of the material conditions in which the failure happened – e.g. the observation of the agent's neurological states at the time of action – may certainly explain why the capacity has not been exercised. However, unless the material circumstances are such as to prevent the legitimate attribution of the status of a practical reasoner to the agent (e.g. the agent is seriously mentally ill), her behaviour will count as a failed exercise of a capacity at that moment possessed by the agent. Statuses, like other formal properties, do not appear and disappear with *any* change of material conditions.

However, also material conditions matter in the attribution of capacities. They matter less than incompatibilists think, but more than some legal conservatives think. In fact, which capacities a given subject possesses directly depend on which statuses she possesses. However, as there are also material restrictions to what statuses can be attributed to different individuals, these material restrictions will also indirectly influence the attribution of capacities in relation to specific actions in specific circumstances. The legislator should not, for example, attribute the status of a rational agent to a small toddler or to a seriously psychotic man. The general mental conditions of these subjects are such that it is not reasonable to impose on them any or very low expectations of rational behavior. Still, when the material (and formal) conditions for the attribution of the status are met by a given subject –

---

[19] F. Santoni de Sio, B. Jespersen, 'Function, Roles, and Human Capacity' in 2 *Methode: Analytic Perspectives* 58-66.

for instance, an adult, neurotypical subject may legitimately be considered as a rational subject – then what capacities that subject possesses at a given time depends on the features of her status, not on the material circumstance (including her neurological states) in which she finds herself to acts.

# 5. Responsibility and practical rationality

Before concluding, it may be useful to provide an example of how these concepts of capacity and practical rationality may work in the context of legal attribution of responsibility. Issues of free will and capacity have been recently debated in legal and forensic psychiatric literature, in relation to the question on the criminal responsibility of offenders affected by addictions and "personality disorders" involving compulsive behaviour such as kleptomania[20]. The legal debate is centered on the question whether the traditional insanity defence should sometimes be applied to cases of volitional disorders involving "loss of control", or the application of the insanity defence should rather be restricted to offenders affected with mental disorders affecting their basic cognitive capacity, such as schizophrenics. In my opinion, the interesting question is not *whether some* volitional defects should count as an exempting condition under the insanity law. I think they should. The interesting question is *how* to include such elements in the law without opening the door to the risks of abuse and confusion. Here a correct use of words and concepts may be decisive. In particular, I think that a good part of the practical problems raised by the recognition of a "volitional defect" as a (partial) exemption from legal responsibility lies in the use of the misleading language of

---

[20] For a pioneering discussion of the issue see J. Feinberg, 'What is So Special About Mental Illness?' in J. Feinberg, *Doing and Deserving: Essays in the Theory of Responsibility* (Princeton: Princeton University Press, 1970) 272–92; H. Fingarette, 'Addiction and Criminal Responsibility' in (1975) 84 *Yale Law Journal* 413. Among more recent works see S. J. Morse, 'Culpability and Control' in (1994) 142 *University of Pennsylvania Law Review* 1587; H. Fingarette, 'Uncontrollable Urges and Irrational People', in (2002) 88 *Virginia Law Review 1025*. On addiction and responsibility see also R. J. Wallace, 'Addiction as a Defect of the Will: Some Philosophical Reflections', in (1999) 18 *Law and Philosophy* 621.

"irresistible impulse", together with a confusing view of mind and capacity entailed by that language[21].

The 1957 English reform on *diminished responsibility* introduced among other things the possibility to offer a mitigation of punishment for offenders affected by volitional disorders, and allowed psychiatrists to be called to the stand to testify that the accused acted on an "irresistible impulse". Invited to comment on this reform, a Wittgensteinian philosopher expert in Aristotelian and Thomist studies like Anthony Kenny wrote, quite provocatively:

> The only remedy for this state of affairs will presumably be for the prosecution to call a philosopher to testify that there cannot be any such thing as an irresistible impulse, and therefore the accused cannot have acted on one, any more that he can have murdered a married bachelor or stolen a square circle[22].

Kenny wanted to highlight a conceptual confusion involved in the idea of a human action being the product of an irresistible impulse. On the one hand, a human *action* is by definition a behaviour that is controlled by the agent's psychological states – her desires, motives, intentions. On the other hand, the concept of an "irresistible impulse" evokes the idea of a purely mechanical *event*, a behaviour that cannot be attributed to the agent – a reflex, an electrically induced movement, etc. Therefore, the statement that a human action is the product of an irresistible impulse is a logical contradiction, because it amounts to the statement that the same behaviour is voluntary and involuntary at the same time.

Kenny's point should not be read as entailing that addictive and compulsive action are normal, paradigmatic, voluntary actions. Admittedly, there is something special in the psychological conditions of people affected by serious addiction and volitional disorders[23]. And this condition may require that we judge and treat these people according to different moral and legal standards. Moreover, the

---

[21] For a borader discussion of the topic of this section see F. Santoni de Sio, 'Irresistible Desires as an Excuse', in (2011) *22 King's Law Journal*, 289–307.

[22] A. P. J. Kenny, *The Ivory Tower* (Oxford: Blackwell, 1988) 56.

[23] J. Kennett, N. A Vincent, A. Snoek, 'Drug Addiction and Criminal Responsibility', in N. Levy, J. Clausen (eds.), *Handbook on Neuroethics* (Dordrecht: Springer, forthcoming).

expertise of a psychiatrist may sometimes certainly be helpful to have a better understanding of what these psychological conditions are, and to decide if and how the presence of these conditions should influence our responsibility judgement on these people's wrong actions. However, that of an addictive or compulsive actions as the product of an irresistible impulse is a poor and confusing metaphor. Poor insofar as it equates addictive and compulsive actions and the complex psychological structures associated with them with simple involuntary behaviour like reflex and physically induced movements. Confusing because it suggests the legitimacy of the reduction of these complex human actions to purely mechanical phenomena.

I think that the reason why seriously addictive and compulsive actions may be partially exempted from responsibility is that these are (voluntary) actions performed by agents who suffer from a (partial) inability to will. This explanation allows, in general, to shift the focus from what Kenny calls a "paramechanical" view of action to a view of action as the product of agents equipped with special linguistic, mental, and social – in one word: rational – capacities. However, in order to make sense of this claim, it must be explained what an *ability to will* is, and this is not a trivial task. We can easily decide whether someone has a given physical or intellectual ability, by wondering whether given certain conditions and given a sufficient motivation on her part, that agent will deliver a particular performance – for instance, a physical performance like lifting a weight or an intellectual performance like doing an arithmetical sum. However, there is no performance which stands to the ability to will in the relationship which the performance of doing sums stands to the correspondent intellectual ability, or the performance of lifting a certain weight to the correspondent physical ability. There are certainly "activities" which are typical for agents equipped with a will, but these are *motivational* states like deciding, choosing, and regretting, rather than performances like lifting weights or making arithmetic calculations. In fact, that which authorizes the attribution of a human will to a subject is its ability to perform actions *in a certain way* – namely intentionally, deliberately, rationally – not to perform particular *kinds of actions*[24]. Therefore, in order to make sense of volitional disorders as inabilities to will one cannot rely either on the

---

[24] Cfr. A. P. J. Kenny, *The Metaphysics of Mind* (Oxford: Clarendon, 1989), 80-81 and the discussion by F. Santoni de Sio, (fn 21).

poor metaphor of mechanical forces forcing the hand of the agent or on the simple application of the logic of physical or intellectual abilities. One must rely, once again, on the idea of a defect of that general, complex, partly cognitive and partly volitional *capacity* that is human practical rationality.

A legal case will serve as an illustration of the role that the concept of a capacity for practical rationality may play in deciding hard cases of responsibility for actions committed by subjects affected by volitional compulsive disorders. In *R v Byrne*, the court had to decide a case of murder in which the defendant was a sexual psychopath driven by violent and perverted sexual desires.[25] In his verdict, the judge Lord Parker explains that the point of the "diminished responsibility" defence in cases of compulsive disorders is recognising that some kinds of loss of control may lessen the defendant's culpability.[26] Sure, the judge admits, in diminished responsibility pleas some evidence of an 'abnormality of mind' on the part of the subject should also be presented. However, according to Lord Parker 'abnormality of mind' is a term 'wide enough to cover the mind's activities in all its aspects ... the ability to form a rational judgement as to whether an act is right or wrong, but also the ability to exercise will power to control physical acts in accordance with that rational judgement'[27].

By eschewing the terminology of "irresistible impulse" the court in *Byrne* has significantly reduced the risk of muddling the jurors up. Particularly fitting is its definition of willpower as an ability to *rationally* control one's physical acts. Indeed, the point is not whether physical acts are attributable to *the agent's mind*, or whether they are somehow controlled by it. Of course they are, because they are intentional, goal-directed and desire-based actions, made in the absence of external coercion and clearly under the mental guidance of the agent. The point is whether the agent is, in general, *rational* enough to be attributed the status of a responsible agent.

---

[25] R. v. Byrne, (1960) 2 QB 396.
[26] Ibid., 402.
[27] Ibid., 403.

# Robots and liability
# Justifying a change in perspective

*Andrea Bertolini*

Robots are most often deemed so innovative and peculiar that a radical change in the existing legal system is required, in particular with respect to liability rules. This 'exceptionalism' is often justified pursuant to the intrinsic technological characteristics of the machine, among which autonomy and the ability of the robot to learn. However, it is not always clear whether a similar claim is of an ontological or functional nature. Therefore, after demonstrating how robotic applications profoundly differ from one another and thus cannot be addressed unitarily, the analysis moves on to consider whether autonomy and the ability to learn suffice in justifying a change in perspective. While a strong form of autonomy may cause robots to be deemed beings – thus grounding an ontological argument for the changing of existing norms –, this option shall be disregarded as an extreme case, belonging more to science fiction than legal analysis. To the contrary functional arguments can be made – based on constitutional principles and policy considerations – in order to justify the adoption of different liability rules so as to favour those technologies that are deemed desirable, thus allowing us to pick the gifts of the evil deity we prefer.

## 1. Ontological v/s functional

When addressing the issue of the regulation of the – harmful – acts of robots, it is often claimed that, since they are so peculiar[1], existing

---

[1] R. Calo, *Robotics and the New Cyberlaw*, available at <http://www.roboticsbusiness-review.com/pdfs/roboticscyberlaw.pdf> accessed 4 April 2014, 120 ff, identifies the peculiarity of robots in their (i) embodiment, (ii) emergence, and (iii) social meaning, and thus promotes an idea of 'moderate exceptionalism', since «its introduction into the mainstream requires a systematic change to the law or legal institutions in order to re-

rules are insufficient and therefore new paradigms[2] are required to fill the ever-widening 'responsibility gap'[3] created by their development and increasing diffusion in society.

Robots, indeed, represent – in most cases at least[4] – a new kind of technology, yet this is not per se sufficient in forcing a change in the existing set of rules, nor in excluding it. In fact, while it is most common amongst lawyers to claim the need for a different legislative framework of the given subject matter time after time analyzed, decisive are rather the grounds used to support such a conclusion. Much less problematic is then a question of whether a change in the regulation of robotic technologies is needed, than the reason why such need is identified.

---

produce, or if necessary displace, an existing balance of values». The author takes an intermediate position in the debate, rejecting the reduction of the law of robots to the law of the horse – using the image sketched by Frank H. Easterbrook, 'Cyberspace and the Law of the Horse', University of Chicago Legal Forum, (1996), 207. Yet the consequences, which can indeed be shared, derived by author at the end of such analysis – for instance the need to rethink liability rules in terms of uncertainty management due to the impracticability of the unpacking of liability (see Calo, 140) – appear not to depend on a similar recognition of exceptionality. Robots are most certainly a special object of study, requiring specific solutions to be elaborated for their better development and diffusion in society – funditus infra §§7-8 – and to this purpose may exploit the knowledge acquired in other fields of the law (environmental law, product liability law, the laws on the circulation of vehicles and medical liability too) and even contribute to modify general beliefs and assumptions, as well as interpretation of general standards and principles of the law (including for instance torts). This though represents a typical phenomenon in the legal discourse, pursuant to which 'second law' becomes 'first law', thus shaping the overall legal system, allowing it to evolve C. Castronovo, 'Diritto Privato Generale E Diritti Secondi La Ripresa Di Un Tema' in Europa e diritto privato, (2006), 397 ff.

  [2] C. Leroux et al., 'Suggestion for a Green Paper on Legal Issues in Robotics' in (2012) *Suggestion for a green paper on legal issues in robotics – Contribution to Deliverable D3.2.1 on ELS issues in robotics*, available at <http://www.eurobotics-project.eu/cms/upload-/PDF/euRobotics_Deliverable_D.3.2.1_Annex_Suggestion_GreenPaper_ELS_Issues-InRobotics.pdf> accessed 4 April 2014.

  [3] A. Matthias, 'The Responsibility Gap: Ascribing Responsibility for the Actions of Learning Automata' in (2004) *Ethics and Information Technology*, 6 , 175; B - J. Koops, Hildebrandt-Mireille, D. Jaquet-Chiffelle, 'Bridging the Accountability Gap: Rights for New Entities in the Information Society?' in (2010) *Minnesota Journal of Law, Science & Technology*, 11(2), 497.

  [4] Industrial robots have in fact been long around, see for a discussion B. Siciliano, O. Khatib, 'Introduction', in B. Siciliano, O. Khatib (eds.), *Handbook of Robotics* (Heidelberg: Springer, 2008), 1 ff.

In particular two are the possible alternative perspectives: (i) a difference may be found in the way robots 'are', inducing us to conclude that they could amount to beings – at least within a certain degree –; or (ii) their peculiar functioning may suggest the adoption of a technically – in a legal dimension – different scheme. An argument grounded sub (i) may be deemed ontological, sub (ii) functional, the differences – even with respect to the outcomes – are substantial.

In a private law perspective, the ascription of liability fundamentally entails the shifting of a cost – namely of damages[5] – from one party to the other, when the damaging party is either deemed at fault[6] or held strictly liable[7], pursuant to a general provision[8] or – in some cases – a

---

[5] As a quick reference see G. Calabresi, D. A. Melamed, 'Property Rules, Liability Rules, and Inalienability: One View of the Cathedral' in (1972) *Harvard Law Review*, 85/6, 1089.; R. Posner, *Economic Analysis of Law* (New York: Wolters Kluwer, 2007).

[6] Fault rules are normally the common rule for the ascription of liability. See D. B. Dobbs, R. E. Keeton, D.G. Owen, *Prosser and Keeton on Torts* (St Paul, Minn.: West Publishing, 1995).; D. B. Dobbs, *The Law of Torts* (St. Paul, Minn.: West, 2004).; C. Castronovo, *La Nuova Responsabilità Civile* (Milano: Giuffrè, 2006); F. D. Busnelli, 'Voce «Illecito Civile»' in *Enciclopedia giuridica* (Rome: Treccani, 1989), 1.; G. Wagner, H. Kötz, *Deliktsrecht* (Munich: Vahlen, 2013).

[7] Strict liability differs from a fault based rule since the claimant is not required to demonstrate that the defendant was negligent or violated a specific norm specifying a standard of conduct to be held in similar circumstances. It suffices to establish the existence of a nexus between the harm suffered and the conduct (or defect). Such rules are normally deemed more favorable to the claimant, yet it is disputable whether it is not the causal nexus the most relevant burden to be fulfilled. At the same time the idea is challenged that strict liability rules provides additional deterrence incentives, see Posner, (fn 5 ), 182; M. A. Polinsky, S. Shavell, 'The Uneasy Case for Product Liability' in *Harvard Law Review*, 123 (2009-2010), 1437.

[8] General provisions in civil law countries set forth a fault based rule, so does art. 2043 of the Italian Civil Code stating that «Qualunque fatto doloso o colposo che cagiona ad altri un danno ingiusto, obbliga colui che ha commesso il fatto a risarcire il danno.»; art. 1384 of the French Civil Code «Tout fait quelconque de l'homme, qui cause à autrui un dommage, oblige celui par la faute duquel il est arrivé à le réparer»; and §823 German Bürgerliches Gesetzbuch (BGB) «(1) Wer vorsätzlich oder fahrlässig das Leben, den Körper, die Gesundheit, die Freiheit, das Eigentum oder ein sonstiges Recht eines anderen widerrechtlich verletzt, ist dem anderen zum Ersatz des daraus entstehenden Schadens verpflichtet.(2) Die gleiche Verpflichtung trifft denjenigen, welcher gegen ein den Schutz eines anderen bezweckendes Gesetz verstößt. Ist nach dem Inhalt des Gesetzes ein Verstoß gegen dieses auch ohne Verschulden möglich, so tritt die Ersatzpflicht nur im Falle des Verschuldens ein». But some open clauses for strict (or semi-strict) liability rules may also be set forth by the legislator, see for instance art. 2050 c.c. «Chiunque cagiona danno ad altri nello svolgimento di una attività pericolosa,

specific norm[9]. To this end – physical[10] – persons are held liable because (i) they can determine themselves and their actions towards a desired end, and (ii) they – both physical and legal – own assets, with which they can face the claims brought against them for the compensation of damages. In particular because of (i) liability rules may produce that deterrence effect so fundamental to the legal system as a whole, inducing a desirable behavior on the side of the subjects acting in society; because of (ii) victims may obtain due compensation and achieve – at least through a pecuniary equivalent – the redress of the negative consequences suffered.

Absent the capacity of the subject to determine itself towards a given end the attribution of liability may not serve its harm prevention function; absent autonomous assets – and the ability to earn such assets[11] – another subject needs to be identified in order to provide required compensation to the victim.

Things, as well as animals, do not satisfy neither the first nor the second requirement and cannot therefore be held liable, thus the person 'behind' them is[12]. Robots, until proven otherwise, are objects and thus such liability rules apply to them.

---

per sua natura o per la natura dei mezzi adoperati, è tenuto al risarcimento, se non prova di avere adottato tutte le misure idonee a evitare il danno».

[9] The most relevant example to the analysis here conducted is the one of the Directive 85/374/EEC - liability for defective products (henceforth the directive), enacted with specific legislative provisions in all European member states.

[10] Legal persons such as corporations do have a person or group of people deciding for them and the choices made by the internally competent organ are attributed to the entity itself, thus shifting the consequences of the decisions to it.

[11] If the subject being held liable is not earning the assets with which it is called to compensate, it is the person providing those assets, who is actually bearing the negative consequences of the subject's actions, and ultimately being held liable.

[12] Often specific rules expressly provide that the owner of the animal is held responsible for the harm caused by it, see art. 2052 of the Italian Civil Code «Il proprietario di un animale o chi se ne serve per il tempo in cui lo ha in uso, è responsabile dei danni cagionati dall'animale, sia che fosse sotto la sua custodia, sia che fosse smarrito o fuggito, salvo che provi il caso fortuito»; art. 1385 of the French Civil Code «Le propriétaire d'un animal, ou celui qui s'en sert, pendant qu'il est à son usage, est responsable du dommage que l'animal a causé, soit que l'animal fût sous sa garde, soit qu'il fût égaré ou échappé»; §833 BGB «Wird durch ein Tier ein Mensch getötet oder der Körper oder die Gesundheit eines Menschen verletzt oder eine Sache beschädigt, so ist derjenige, welcher das Tier hält, verpflichtet, dem Verletzten den daraus entstehenden Schaden zu ersetzen. Die Ersatzpflicht tritt nicht ein, wenn der Schaden durch ein Haustier verursacht wird, das dem Beruf, der Erwerbstätigkeit oder dem Unterhalt des

The inadequacy of existing norms may thus on the one hand be argued on an ontological basis suggesting that robots shall be deemed subjects, moving them from the realm of things to the one of beings; on the other hand on a merely functional basis it could be assessed that the incentives provided by existing rules lead to undesirable consequences either in terms of excessive harm being caused or not enough technology being developed and distributed into the market.

In order to support an ontological claim it shall be proved that robots satisfy the substantial requirement set forth under (i) above; for a functional claim to be successful instead policy arguments need to be found, stressing the social and constitutional relevance and desirability of the given application as opposed to others.

Most commonly the authors, who argue in favour of a change of paradigm, do not clearly state whether their claim is ontological or merely functional[13], rather they focus on some mainly technical aspects of robots, which are considered relevant for such a discussion, in particular the robot's autonomy and its ability to learn.

Those two aspects need then to be taken into account in order to determine whether – and under which conditions – they could ground an ontological argument for a shift in the rules for the ascription of liability, or rather be used in order to support a functional analysis, which will though prevalently rest on other normative considerations.

## 2. From 'robots' to robotic applications: the multiplicity of notions and the need for a distinctive trait

Before proceeding to analyze such technical traits and their relevance within a legal analysis of applicable liability rules, it is necessary to point out that in no way said traits are common to all robots, much less to the same – meaningful – degree.

---

Tierhalters zu dienen bestimmt ist, und entweder der Tierhalter bei der Beaufsichtigung des Tieres die im Verkehr erforderliche Sorgfalt beobachtet oder der Schaden auch bei Anwendung dieser Sorgfalt entstanden sein würde».

[13] A positive exception appears to be the one of R. Calo, 'Open Robotics' in *Maryland Law Rev.*, 70. 571 ff. in particular 603 ff., suggesting that exemptions such as those originally conceived for the American aviation industry could be used in order to foster the diffusion of robotic applications.

Indeed, it is impossible to isolate one or more traits, which are found in all applications, identified as robots[14], and the very term should rather be used for a purpose of synthesis, while a classification[15] may be better suited to describe what the object of the analysis is. The a-technical nature[16] of the word 'robot', cannot be successfully overcome by adopting either extremely broad[17] or – to the opposite – narrow[18] a definition, since, as it may be intuitively grasped, a driverless vehicle, a softbot, an automated vacuum cleaner, a humanoid robot, an industrial one or a prostheses have very little in common with one another.

The conclusion that can be driven, for the sake of the current analysis, is that we may not tackle the legal problems posed by robots unitarily; instead those distinctive traits – among which most certainly the ones mentioned above – are to be carefully considered, so as to point out the one(s), that may actually suggest – or in some cases force – a change in the existing paradigm.

Thus, since differences are more relevant than similarities, the analysis needs to be narrowly tailored, addressing single kinds of

---

14 The Oxford English Dictionary defines the entry 'robot' as «A machine capable of carrying out a complex series of actions automatically, especially one programmable by a computer [...]; (Especially in science fiction) a machine resembling a human being and able to replicate certain human movements and functions automatically [...]; A person who behaves in a mechanical or unemotional manner [...]; another term for crawler (in the computing sense) [...]; South African A set of automatic traffic lights [...]» The definition is clearly unsatisfactory and only closely resembles literary and science fiction depictions of robots more than existing or currently researched technology. Calo (fn 1), 120, identifies in the robot's embodiment and subsequent ability to interact with the environment a distinctive and thus qualifying trait. Yet despite it being a common characteristic not all robots do have a physical body allowing them to materially modify the external world, and yet may profoundly influence people lives. Softbots and expert systems are examples thereof, available at <http://researcher.ibm.com/researcher/view_project.php?id=2099> accessed 4 April 2014.

15 See P. Salvini, 'Taxonomy of Robotic Technologies' in (2013) *Robolaw Grant Agreement Number*. 289092, D4.1.

16 It is in fact derived by K. Capek, *Rossumovi Univerzální Roboti.*, available at < http://preprints.readingroo.ms/RUR/rur.pdf > and simply means enslaved labor; accessed 5 April 2014.

17 An example is the definition offered by A. Santosuosso, C. Boscarato, F. Caroleo, 'Robot E Diritto: Una Prima Ricognizione' in *La Nuova Giurisprudenza Commentata*, (2012), 494, 498 defining a robot as «una macchina che svolge autonomamente un lavoro».

18 Such are normally the definitions offered by engineers and scholars, particularly focusing on their specific field of interest, for a rich survey see Salvini, (fn 15).

applications or classes thereof, rather than attempting at creating an all-encompassing set of rules for 'robots'[19] as a whole.

## 3. Identifying the pivoting criteria: autonomy and the ability to learn

The most commonly cited criteria, when discussing the need for a change in existing legislation, are the so called robot's autonomy and ability to learn. The two are often not clearly distinguished from one another and most commonly the former is defined as depending – at least in part – on the latter[20].

Yet such promiscuity leads the analysis to be vague and ultimately unsatisfactory, not allowing to identify which characteristic would actually make said machines so peculiar as to justify a change in perspective for the ascription of liability; much less it would allow to determine whether such a difference shall be imputed to an ontological or rather a merely functional consideration.

Moreover not only should autonomy be kept separate and distinct from the ability to learn, since one machine could show a relevant degree of the former without any bit of the latter, but its very notion needs to be further specified at least in two different sub-concepts[21]: (i) self-awareness or self-consciousness, leading to free will and thus identifying a moral agent, and (ii) the ability to intelligently interact in the operating environment. The first corresponds to the ethical condition for the identification of an agent, and amounts to the requirement set forth in §1 to justify the ascription of liability to a subject. The second instead may only be used in order to ground a

---

[19] This instead was the approach of the Christophe Leroux et al.,(fn 2).

[20] Autonomy is often identified as the ability to act in a way which was not so clearly determined or programmed, the ability to learn, perceived as the ability of the machine to do something different (normally more) than what it was originally coded into the machine's software appears to go in the same direction, see for instance C. E. A. Karnow, 'The Application of Traditional Tort Theory to Embodied Machine Intelligence', WeRobot (2013), available at < http://conferences.law.stanford.edu/werobot/wp-content/uploads/sites/29/2013/03/Karnow_Curtis.pdf> accessed 5 April 2014.

[21] M. Gutman, B. Rathgeber, T. Syed, 'Action and Autonomy: A Hidden Dilemma in Artificial Autonomous Systems', in M. Decker, M. Gutman (eds.), *Robo- and Informationethics. Some Fundamentals* (Münster: Lit Verlag, 2012), 231 ff.

functional argument since it does not amount to requiring the machine to be able to decide according to its own intentions. Both notions need though to be discussed in greater detail.

# 4. Strong autonomy

The ability to decide freely and coordinate one's actions towards a chosen end, which we may label as 'strong autonomy'[22], amounts to the philosophical prerequisite defining a 'moral agent'[23] responsible for his own conduct[24]. The mere ability to produce functional states without any further intervention, instead qualifies as 'behaviour', typical of animals and fully explained by an 'as if relation'[25].

It is self-evident that current robots, conceived to complete a specific task identified by their user, do not show such form of autonomy; rather it is disputed in AI literature whether a similar complexity of the system could ever be achieved[26]. For the purpose of the current analysis it shall though suffice to state that should such a robot be created, displaying intention and capable of coordinating its

---

[22] Ibid., 245 ff.

[23] In brief, see T. Kapitan, 'Free Will Problem', in Robert Audi (ed.), *The Cambridge Dictionary of Philosophy* (Cambridge: Cambridge University Press, 1999), 326.

[24] Julian Nida-Rümelin, *Verantwortung* (Stuttgart: Reclam, 2011)., §6, 25 ff. where he states «Wir sind für alle unsere Handlungen verantwortlich. Wenn etwas als Handlung einer Person gilt, ist diese Person dafür verantwortlich». The author further specifies that in order for a behaviour (Verhalten) to be deemed an action (Handlung) an alternative is required among which to choose; yet external forceful pressure does not per se exclude that the action shall be imputed to the person. Instead the assessment of the nature of the conduct (reproachable and thus responsible or not) varies accordingly. More clearly stated §9, 32 «Wir haben Verantwortung für unser Verhalten, sofern wir Gründe haben, uns so und nicht anders zu verhalten.»

[25] Gutman, Rathgeber, Syed, see (fn 21), 237.

[26] Current studies tend to prefer a more limited approach, aiming at granting the machine a specific ability, rather than replicating the functioning of the human mind, see L. Floridi, *Philosophy and Computing: An Introduction* (London.: Routledge, 1999), pos. 2862 ff. distinguishing between GOFAI (Good Old Fashioned AI) and LAI (Light AI).

actions towards its own desired end[27], it ought to be deemed a full-fledged agent, thus 'Träger von Rechten'[28].

From the point of view of private law, a similar machine ought to be deemed a subject, not anymore an object of law, and liability ascribed directly to it, not to a human being behind it. Racial or slave laws[29] could be applied, creating a discrimination between robots and human beings, yet if equal treatment was denied, such a decision could be considered discriminatory[30].

Indeed, such form of autonomy would per se suffice in justifying an ontological change of perspective in the ascription of liability; much more questionable would rather be whether such kind of technology is desirable and should be actively pursued in the first place[31].

## 5. Weak autonomy

A much more limited concept is the one of weak autonomy[32], corresponding to all behaviours that are not determined by the intervention of an external agent, who though identifies the goal to be achieved. Such a machine may show the highest degree possible of 'heteronomous autonomy'[33] and yet not qualify as an agent[34]. From a

---

[27] A similar ability could be measured through an adjusted version of the Turing test – A. Turing, 'Computing Machinery and Intelligence', in (1950) *Mind*, 59, 433 ff. – where a robot would be asked to provide rational explanations for its actions.

[28] A. Matthias, *Automaten Als Träger Von Rechten* (Berlin: Logos Verlag, 2010). passim.

[29] See S. N. Lehman-Wilzig, 'Frankenstein Unbound', in (1981) *Futures*, 449. Agreeable considerations are then made by J. J Bryson, 'Robots should be Slaves', available at http://www.cs.bath.ac.uk/~jjb/ftp/Bryson-Slaves-Book09.html.

[30] For a discussion see R. Dworkin, *Taking Rights Seriously* (London: Duckworth, 1977), 225 ff.

[31] See Lehman-Wilzig, (fn 29), 445: "In sum one cannot give robots the Promethean fire-gift of intelligence and still hope to keep them sacked. One way or another, then, robot freedom must lead to some harmful behaviour even if well intentioned"; Koops, Hildebrandt-Mireille, and Jaquet-Chiffelle, (fn 3), 561, stating how, if such machines were created, they could decide to take control and decide for themselves what degree of freedom and rights to grant us.

[32] See G. Rathgeber, Syed (fn 21), 236.

[33] Ibid. 246-7.

[34] See ibid., 247: "[t]his determination of the functionality of an artificial system remains adequate eve if ends are realized via steps which are only determinable by their

moral perspective, the artefact would not be properly 'acting' since someone else is identifying the outcome the robot has to – attempt to – achieve.

This is the case of most existing and currently researched robotic applications (such as driverless vehicles to name a very well known example) since the ability to operate unattended certainly represents much of the purpose for developing robotic technologies in the first place, allowing humans to increase productivity and free up their time[35].

Despite it possibly appearing as an extreme and rather formal statement, it is deeply rooted in a rational understanding of society and its interactions[36]. A driverless vehicle, which is choosing the route to reach a given address, keeping traffic under control, looking out for jaywalking passersby, deciding on the speed to keep, while maybe controlling the cabin's internal temperature and radio broadcasting, is still performing tasks it was designed to perform, and specific identified by its owner or user; the same could be said about a robot-maid taking care of the house, irrespective of how many choices it had to make in order to fulfil the task it was put at.

Indeed, a similar principle is not foreign to legal theory, since the notion of agency precisely reflects the dual nature of a subject (an agent) that acts towards an end set by another (a principal), producing direct effects in his patrimonial sphere, so long as it is acting within his powers[37]. The choices of the agent are to a great extent free – but for the final objective, which instead was identified by the principal –, and show the greatest degree of autonomy, such as that typical of an adult human being.

The consequence for the sake of the current analysis is simply that the most sophisticated machine, capable of performing complex tasks without any intervention by a human being would still not amount to a

---

outcome and not by specific single steps. For example, if neural networks are used, which may be described as black-boxes considering the internal states of the net itself, the outcome has to be functionally equivalent to the determined ends".

[35] See Floridi, (fn 26), 4696 ff.

[36] See Nida-Rümelin, (fn 24), §10, 33 "Die Fähigkeit zur Deliberation, zur Abwägung von Gründen, macht uns zu rationale, freien und verantwortlichen Wesen. [...] Im abwägen von Gründen äußert sich der (rationale) Kern unserer personalen Identität".

[37] For a brief reference see B. A. Garner, *Black's Law Dictionary* 8th edn.(Minnesota: West Group, 2004), 67 ff.

subject, and could thus not be held personally liable, at least based on an ontological argument.

Yet the ability of the robot to perform complex tasks, implying numerous intermediate decisions, unattended and unsupervised induces some authors to acknowledge a substantial loss of control on the side of the producer or programmer. The programmer – it is said – does not necessarily – and actually could never – cover and anticipate every possible action the robot performs; rather, such machines evaluate the data and impulses received from the external world with such a degree of freedom, that the overall outcome appears to be unexpected and unforeseeable.

This claim though, despite appearing at a first glance plausible, cannot be shared: so long as the machine performs the tasks it was originally designed for (a driverless car drives, a ro-dog walks the blind[38], a mars rover wonders on an unknown distant planet[39]), what the machine does is precisely and by definition under the control of the producer or programmer, and them alone. Ultimately, but for its designer the robot would not have those actuators allowing it to physically interact with the surrounding world in the way it does, nor the software enabling it to process external inputs and decide on the preferable course of action.

Indeed, the complexity of its functioning and the diverse expertise required for assembling a similar machine, do not allow to easily identify the individual who may be blamed for the negative occurrence[40]; yet it may be disputed whether this actually represents a necessity, either for deterrence or for compensation purposes. In fact, it shall be noted that blame and the duty to compensate do not always correspond: a subject who cannot be deemed at fault – pursuant to a negligence standard – may still be bound to bear the negative consequences of an event – for instance pursuant to a strict or vicarious liability rule[41] – because of other kinds of – policy – considerations,

---

[38] The ro-dog example is set forth by Santosuosso, Boscarato, Caroleo, (fn 17), 508 ff.

[39] This is the example made by A. Matthias, (fn 3), 176.

[40] Most likely the cooperation of multiple factors will have lead to the accident, and liability may be deemed difficult to disentangle, see Calo, (fn 1), 140, thus suggesting the adoption of a risk management approach.

[41] The already mentioned defective products directive see (fn 9) sets forth a strict liability rule. Relevant examples of vicarious liability rules are those of the liability of par-

such as – to name a very specific example – his ability to better insure against the given event, or exploit economy of scale mechanisms[42]. This would at once grant compensation and allow to provide incentives on the party who may intervene along the decision line which starts with the design of a given application and ends with its distribution on the market.

Moreover it shall be stressed that not all damages are to be compensated. If the negative outcome corresponds to a level of risk, which is deemed desirable for society[43], then the damage shall stay with the victim, or be indemnified through alternative mechanisms – e.g. welfare state[44] –, not directly burdening the producer or programmer of the machine, since being the given activity overall beneficial to society it needs to be encouraged rather than opposed.

Ultimately tracing the line between the ascription or denial of liability appears to be an entirely technical problem, but in a private law perspective. Applying products liability rules to hold the producer liable – as it would probably be the straight forward solution pursuant to existing regulation – may prove a reasonable alternative among others, which still can be conceived. Which liability scheme to adopt though is a question that little has to do with the autonomous functioning of the machine, rather with other kind of arguments, functional and policy oriented, that indeed vary according to different kinds of applications.

---

ents for the acts of children, and of employers for their employees. For an wide comparative analysis see D3.1.

[42] See Calabresi, Melamed, (fn 5), 1096-7.

[43] This notion operates both under a normal tort law regime as well as under specific products liability provisions. As in a well known British tort law case, the judge Baron Bramwell stated 'For the convenience of mankind in carrying on the affairs of life, people as they go along roads must expect, or put up with, such mischief as reasonable care on the part of others cannot avoid.' (emphasis added), Holmes v. Mather, 10 L.R.-Ex. 261, 267.

[44] The question may be asked why should the gain for society be entirely borne by the victim, see G. Calabresi, *Il Dono Dello Spirito Maligno. Gli Ideali, Le Convinzioni, I Modi Di Pensare, Nei Loro Rapporti Col Diritto* (Milano: Giuffrè, 1996), 23-24 and 87, or alternative compensation mechanisms shall be conceived to spread the loss as well as the gain, once it materialized on one single individual.

# 6. The ability of the robot to learn

The notion of learning is itself quite general and needs to be further specified before it can be assessed whether it actually forces a change in the existing paradigm for the ascription of liability. Most certainly not every learning capacity induces the same kind of consideration, in particular with respect to the problem of (un)foreseeability of the tortious outcome.

In the first place, we need to distinguish what may be considered the mere appearance of learning, when instead the machine is merely executing a program it has, for instance, downloaded from a cloud database (we may call it an app)[45].

A different form of learning derives instead from the interactions with the external environment: the more complex the robot, the more sensors and actuators it has, the more it will be able to derive information and inputs from the surroundings in which it operates. According to some authors, a robot's ability to acquire and elaborate data in order to complete its tasks constitutes actual learning:

> Presently there are machines in development or already in use which are able to decide on a course of action and to act without human intervention. The rules by which they act are not fixed during the production process, but can be changed during the operation of the machine by the machine itself. This is what we call machine learning[46].

Such a notion of learning is, however, extremely wide and needs to be narrowed down, isolating those forms of self-modification of the machine and of its functioning that may increase the level of unforeseeability of the output.

There are two technical approaches to artificial intelligence which need to be taken into account: neural nets and genetic algorithms. The

---

[45] In such a case the machine would actually be executing a program it was originally designed for it. Not differently from a computer a similar machine would not be actively learning but rather applying new software designed for that specific purpose. In such a case it is safe to assume that any malfunctioning of the program could be ascribed alternatively to the programmer or producer of the hardware–in particular to the latter if the former conformed to the standards identified by the latter for the design of software to operate on the machine, or maybe even expressly authorized its release as an aftermarket product or service meant to be used on its apparatus.

[46] See Matthias, (fn 3), 177.

former is the attempt to emulate the functioning of the neural network[47] in a living system, the process of storing information modifies the system itself, and thus data cannot be accessed and controlled or modified at a later moment.

A machine so conceived would learn by functioning, as if it was trained through a process of trial and error. In such a perspective, more than the programming phase, the subsequent exploration provides the actual design of the system and cannot be distinguished from it[48].

The latter instead entails a very high degree of self-modification of the machine. In evolutionary robotics techniques the machine, which is created to accomplish a given task, is the product of a 'repeated process of selective reproduction, random mutation and genetic recombination[49]. Here, instead of programming a robot with detailed instructions on how to complete a specific task,

> [a]n initial population of different artificial chromosomes, each encoding the control system ... of a robot is randomly created. Each of these chromosomes is then decoded into a corresponding controller ... and downloaded into the processor of the robot. The robot is then let free to act ... according to a genetically specified controller while its performance of a given task is automatically evaluated ... The fittest individuals are allowed to reproduce by generating copies of their chromosomes ... the newly obtained population is tested again on the same robot. This process is repeated for a number of generations until an individual is born which satisfies the fitness function set by the user.[50]

According to Matthias[51], the circumstance that the information stored in an artificial neural network cannot be accessed and controlled at any given moment in time, and the absolute absence of influence in the output obtained through genetic programming methods, cause a fundamental loss of control on the part of the programmer, which makes the attribution of liability unjustified. Such circumstances would therefore highlight the existence of a so-called 'responsibility gap'.

---

[47] See J. Hertzberg, R. Chatila, 'Ai Reasoning Methods for Robotics', in Bruno Siciliano and Oussama Khatib (eds.), *Handbook of Robotics* (Berlin: Springer, 2008), 220.

[48] Ibid., 220.

[49] See D. Floreano, P. Husbands, S. Nolfi, 'Evolutionary Robotics', in ibid., 1423 ff.

[50] Ibid., 1424.

[51] See Matthias, (fn 3), 181 ff.; in a rather similar fashion see Karnow, (fn 20), 4 ff.

The supposed loss of control is though more apparent than real, being mostly restrained to the design phase. Despite allowing a greater degree of unpredictability of the machine's behaviour, such programming techniques mostly influence the conception of the robot more than its day to day operation. Therefore, if a neural network requires training in order to perfect its skills and accomplish a given task the development phase of the machine ought to include that very training. Once released onto the market the product is supposed to have learnt or perfected a sufficient skill to interact safely, at least as safely as the existing non robotic – or even non-learning robotic – application would. This is the case, for instance, with the walking-dog for the blind. Until its training is complete and the dog can perform the tasks for which it is required, it cannot be sold or employed for the assistance of the disabled, and no different kind of reasoning should apply to a robot performing the same task.

Such a perspective is even more evident when one comes to evolutionary robotics. First, the technique is most often confined to laboratory experiments, frequently software simulations of interactions which in reality never occur[52]. Secondly the purpose of said technique is to develop otherwise unconceived solutions for the functioning of a machine, whose performance is measured against a fitness function: the outcome pursued is the best possible 'individual' for the task, thus not an ever changing or self modifying application.

In nature, in fact, the genetic sequence of a being does not modify itself over time (unless pathologies occur); similarly the algorithm of the single machine, which is a part of an evolutionary robotics study, is given and does not change during the experiment, but is modified through (re)production of a new specimen. Then, once the desired outcome is obtained, the evolutions process is deemed complete. In both cases the ability of a robot to modify itself is indeed limited or can be actively limited after the completion of the design phase and before it is released onto the market and commercialized. Therefore, even if designing such applications does not entail coding complex lines of software into a specific language, but rather requires the use of alternative – and to some extent more sophisticated – methods of production, this does not per se influence the final consideration that it is the programmer – or creator if we want to call it that – who has control over the general/global outcome. It is in fact the producer's

---

[52] See Floreano, Husbands, Nolfi, (fn 49), 1428-9.

decision as to what kind of technique to use in order to achieve the best result possible, both in terms of sophistication and functionality of the robot as well as safety; only the producer could in fact devise and conceive possible methods aimed at preventing damage arising from the proper – or even improper – use of his product.

In other words, if foreseeability is a matter of experience, and thus of the repetition of interactions between the environment and the machine, great insight can be gained during the testing and development phase by the producer of a robot, as of any other kind of technological application[53].

Finally, even if we assumed that an ability to modify itself was granted to the robot after the moment it was introduced into the market, we still need to consider that this would be the active decision of the producer or programmer to provide his machine with a given capacity. It is clear, though, that such a possibility should only be allowed when it is sufficiently safe to do so, in light of the devices or measures that could be built in (according to existing knowledge) so as to prevent undesired consequences.

To better explain such a concept we may resort to the example of an adaptive elevator using 'artificial neural networks and reinforcement learning algorithms'[54] in order to better assess traffic patterns and minimize waiting periods. Such a robot is not learning to complete an additional task than the one it was conceived for, yet it is improving its effectiveness and efficiency over time. In this example, the robot 'leaves an important executive waiting for half an hour on the 34th floor, so that he cannot attend a business meeting'[55] and therefore damage results as a consequence thereof. Yet, holding the producer liable in such cases appears to be a satisfactory and straightforward solution, at least based on two different considerations. First, it is foreseeable that the patterns of use of an elevator in a large building with different kinds of offices and business hours, as well as with different kinds of users pursuing various occupations, may vary over time. Therefore, the program that allows the elevator to learn should enable it to identify potential outliers (say, for instance, a conference attracting a vast number of individuals to a particular floor for a limited number of

---

[53] See Karnow, (fn 20), 18.
[54] Matthias, (fn 3), 176.
[55] Ibid., 176.

days) and not base its decisions entirely on them; that is to say, that the elevator ought not to be made an 'inductive turkey'[56]. Secondly, the producer ought to have assumed that exceptional circumstances may occur where it is necessary to be able to quickly and safely override the program and call the elevator at need. Such a 'safety device' should be embedded in the application and the producer ought to be held liable for not having conceived it.

From a philosophical perspective, we may say that the ability to learn is a choice the agent made for the machine; the subsequent behaviour is therefore heteronomously determined by the 'creator' who caused the robot to be what it is, and have those abilities, which were originally allowed or conceived, irrespective of how they have evolved. From an ontological perspective therefore, the ability of the robot to learn and modify itself does not make it an individual, since it is still not free or exerting that degree of self-determination which allows to acknowledge the existence of a – truly autonomous and independent – being. It is clear, instead, that should a robot show a strong form of autonomy and – because of that – be free to chose what it is learning, as a human would, then it would amount to a being, not anymore to a thing. Such would ultimately be the consequence of the machine being strongly autonomous, and not simply capable of learning, thus imposing its acknowledgment as a person and not anymore as a thing.

From a merely functional point of view instead, it was shown that the ability to learn does not suffice per se in justifying a change in the rules for the ascription of liability: the different forms in which control may be exerted by its 'creator' do not invalidate existing liability mechanisms. In the end, in fact, but for the human who designed and produced the robot in a given fashion, the robot would not have had those capacities, which in hypothesis later led to the tortious outcome. In which cases the producer ought to be held liable does thus not – entirely – depend on the peculiar functioning of the machine, rather on multiple policy considerations, that indeed vary according to the kinds of applications and classes thereof.

---

[56] This is the typical example derived from B. Russell, *The Problems of Philosophy* (Oxford.: OUP Oxford, 2001), pos. 879, who used a chicken to criticise inductivism. The turkey, having been fed on a daily basis, infers that it will continue to be fed in the future, yet the day comes for it to be butchered. The sample of data the turkey bases its judgment upon is in fact limited and does not take into account the possibility of unexpected events, also known as black swans: see N. N. Taleb, *The Black Swan* (New York: Random House 2007), 40 ff.

# 7. Developing a functional approach: the gifts of the evil deity

If an evil deity offered mankind a gift, that made people's life substantially better and even more enjoyable, yet demanding a sacrifice of a given number of – innocent – human lives every year, despite said offer may appear to many outrageous, others in society would voice for its acceptance, and would probably be right doing so.

This powerful example was originally conceived by Guido Calabresi for his tort law classes, in order to address traffic accidents, the use of automobiles in modern society, and the policy choices associated therewith[57]. The immediately shocking result – namely that the choice of allowing the use of motor vehicles corresponds to knowingly sacrifice a given number of human lives – although, is not the single most important consideration, which can be derived from such narrative. Modern society is today much better prepared in accepting the brutal conclusion that not even human life represents an uncompromisable value, and the allocation of scarce resources often forces a trade-off between interests, which only at a first glance may appear immeasurable with one another[58].

In fact, further elaborating the example, Calabresi points out that even if the evil deity allowed those who totally and completely refused the benefits of the gift – even in an indirect fashion – to be safe and free from any of its possible negative consequences, such a choice may be so expensive as being totally unrealistic[59]. When a vast number of individuals makes a choice, the cost of non-conforming may be so relevant as to place the person outside of society[60], and the alternative narratives, which can be thought of, so as to justify the acceptance of the gift, most often serve a mere conscience-soothing purpose, rather than providing an accurate rational explanation.

---

[57] See Calabresi, (fn 44). The narrative here summarized begins at 10.

[58] Quality of life together with amusement may be considered relevant as much as human life itself, and people constantly decide to trade the length of their lives for a greater level of pleasure, see ibid., 22.

[59] Ibid., 12

[60] As it is for instance today the choice not to use internet and its applications in order to attempt to preserve one's privacy.

If we generalize the example, though, we may conclude that the gift of the evil deity corresponds to any form of technological progress[61], which brings new and unconceived opportunities to society, and yet demands a cost, even to those who may decide not to make a direct or even indirect use of it. Although, once the veil is pierced, and the terms of the choice to be made are understood – including the partiality of the information available at the moment the decision has to be made – alternatives can be conceived in order to determine the desired outcome, also in terms of distribution[62].

This is to say that progress is neither uniform nor inevitable and society, when it is aware of what is scarifying may well decide to pick and choose the gift(s) of the evil deity, deemed desirable, and the conditions, that time after time make it so.

Robotics as one of the most relevant forms of technological progress perfectly fits this briefly sketched narrative, and thus allows us to ponder, which kinds of applications are to be encouraged, and what level of risk – not just in terms of lives but also of other rights, such a s privacy, that are valued and protected by existing legal systems – we are willing to trade for the great potentials to be gained[63].

As already shown, because robotic applications are extremely diverse from one another, the answers to such questions may be not easily generalized, and the arguments to justify a given policy, in favor or against a specific technology, may not be automatically transposed to another.

In order to sketch a simple example of such kind of analysis robotic limbs may be taken into account. In the short and medium run prostheses are going to become an ever more appealing tool for the disabled to reduce their impairment in every-day life. To this purpose constitutional law arguments can be found[64], which suggest, if not

---

[61] See Calabresi, (fn 44), 22-23.

[62] Ibid. 23.

[63] The exact assessment of what is desirable may be hard to determine since technology shapes men and their preferences, in a way that cannot be fully foreseen, for a discussion of this aspect see M. Coeckelbergh, *Human Being @ Risk* (Berlin: Springer, 2013), 103 ff.

[64] Such as art. 4(g) of United Nation Convention on the Rights of Persons with Disabilities, stating that member states undertake

«To undertake or promote research and development of, and to promote the availability and use of new technologies, including information and communications technologies, mobility aids, devices and assistive technologies, suitable for persons with di-

impose, the adoption of specific measures in order to favor their development, despite such a decision may entail the acceptance of a higher level of risk, in terms of number of accidents we are willing to accept[65]. A robotic prostheses in fact, because of the complex interactions between the machine (and its artificial intelligence) and the nervous system of the human, has a level of error which can hardly be eliminated[66]. Yet because of the limitless ways in which the single prostheses may be used (consider for instance a hand), and the different environments in which the same movements may be required, leaving the entire cost of all potential damage on the producer – through the application of a strict liability rule, such as the one set forth by the EU Defective Products Directive – may radically impair their development and diffusion onto the market, in particular given the limited number of potential users[67]. At the same time if their development and use was favored through the adoption of a different liability scheme, and therefore a higher degree of risk was overall accepted – for instance allowing someone with an implanted robotic arm to drive, despite knowing that in a given percentage of cases the malfunctioning of the

---

sabilities, giving priority to technologies at an affordable cost.» For a discussion see M. Schulze, *Understanding the Un Convention on the Rights of Persons with Disabilities* (New York: Handicap International, 2010), 50 ff., available at <http://www.equalityhuman-rights.com/uploaded_files/humanrights/unconventionhradisabilities.pdf> accessed 5 April 2014.

[65] A similar example is made by Calabresi when discussing the participation of the young and the elderly to traffic, typically categories of individuals which are much more inclined to cause or be involved in a traffic accident, see Calabresi, (fn 44), 50.

[66] The ability of a decoder to assess what the meaning of the biological signal received actually was varies as a function of the duration of the signal itself. If the incoming signal lasts 900 ms (milliseconds) the accuracy can be much greater than if it lasts only 300 ms. Yet such a duration is incompatible with a practical use in everyday's life. The experimental studies conducted on monkey show that an average accuracy of about 85% can be achieved, while in other cases there could be false positive signals. For the discussion of such data see M. Controzzi et al., 'Decoding Grasp Types from the Monkey Motor Cortex and on-Line Control of a Dexterous Artificial Hand' in *Converging Clinical and Engineering Research on Neurorehabilitation Biosystems & Biorobotics* Volume 1, 2013, pp 67-71.

[67] There are fortunately fewer than two million amputees in the US, and not all of them would qualify for the use of robotic prostheses: Information available at <www.amputee-coalition.org/fact_sheets/amp_stats_cause.html> accessed 5 April 2014.

prostheses may lead to a crash[68] – so as to encourage the active participation of implantees in society, it is not said that the innocent victim ought to bare all the negative consequences arising therefrom[69]. Thus, for instance, a no fault plan[70] could be conceived, providing the harmed party with immediate – even automatic – compensation, and through the different financing schemes of a similar fund, different redistributive polices could be pursued, spreading the cost more or less on society as a whole, as well as on producers, at the same time pursuing ever greater quality and safety standards for such kinds of products.

Later, in a long-run scenario it may even be conceived that a robotic prosthesis becomes more sophisticated than a natural limb, allowing a higher number of degrees of freedom, being stronger, more flexible, and possibly faster in reacting than a natural body part[71]. Non-amputees may develop an interest towards such kind of devices in order to keep up with a race towards improved skills, where the disabled could all at once find themselves at an advantage over the normally-able.

Such a more futuristic scenario is the one depicted in post-human accounts, triggering entirely different problems, such as the issue of whether a line can be traced between recuperation and enhancement[72] and whether the second at all should be allowed, or criteria developed in order to regulate similar practices.

This is most likely one of those fields where compensation rules would most certainly fail in making the looser – harmed party – whole[73], since the recognition of a full right to self-modification[74]

---

[68] A similar case occurred with C. Kandlbauer, a man whose both arms had been replaced by technologically advanced prostheses, and died in a car crash, see <http://www.theguardian.com/world/2010/oct/22/christian-kandlbauer-arm-dies-crash> accessed 5 April 2014. From the information available it is not possible to establish whether the accident derived from a malfunctioing of the prostheses or other independent cause.

[69] See Calabresi, (fn 44), 51 and 89.

[70] See ibid. 31 ff.

[71] Paradigmatic in this respect the Pistorius' case, on which see G. Wolbring, 'Oscar Pistorius and the Future Nature of Olympic, Paralympic and Other Sports', in (2008) *SCRIPTed,* 5/1, 139. ff.

[72] See N. Agar, *Humanity's End* (Bingley: Bradford, 2010); see Coeckelbergh, (fn 63); F. Lucivero, A. Vedder (eds.), 'Beyond Therapy V. Enhancement? Multidisciplinary Analyses of a Heated Debate' in *The Robolaw Series, vol. II* (Pisa: Pisa University Press, 2013).

[73] See Calabresi, (fn 44), 113 ff.

would entail rejecting the opposed principle of a sacred nature of the human body[75], which some may adhere to.

Composing such a clash is a complex task, to be tackled through the tools of philosophy as well as – and in particular – constitutional law, as the fundamental norm regulating human interactions in society. Moreover the choices made could prove to a great extent irreversible, contributing to make something look normal, which otherwise would have not[76]; finally, the choice to reject this specific gift of the evil deity may later on prove to be an unbearable cost for those who still are against it, but would otherwise find themselves at a substantial disadvantage, not being able to compete or participate in society, without enhancing – in a way or another – their own bodies.

The two briefly sketched issues here raised are clearly independent despite being connected. Fear for the latter scenario should not necessarily lead to adopt measures which would impair the former, at least for a fact, that post-humanist accounts refer to scenarios that are certainly more distant in time, and by then – legal and philosophical – tools could be conceived, that would allow to handle such a technological development effectively. Although policy decisions relating to the development of prostheses will need to discount – in some ways – potential dual uses of the same technologies, in particular when deciding who should bear the negative consequences of their malfunctioning. Policy decisions, together with constitutional arguments do play a central role to this end, and may suggest a – functional – change in perspective even in the ascription of liability.

---

[74] See *The Transhumanist Declaration* available at <http://humanityplus.org/philo-sophy/transhumanist-declaration> accessed 5 April 2014., in particular point 8.

[75] See Paul, Letter to the Corinthians, 6:19, available at <http://www.vati-can.va/archive/ENG0839/__PZB.HTM> accessed 5 April 2014.

[76] See Calabresi, (fn 44), 105 ff. discussing practices such as the use of pornography and the exhibition of naked bodies on public broadcasts.

# 8. Conclusion

It was shown that despite robots being an extremely innovative technology, it is not their technical peculiarities, that require a change in perspective for the ascription of liability.

Only the sort of full-fledged autonomy, similar to the one of an adult human being, would force us to consider them beings, rather than objects. Yet such kind of technology is far from being achieved today and should therefore only be considered as the upper limit where an ontological argument would actually suffice in justifying the adoption of an entirely different set of rules for the damage caused by robots.

Short of that neither a weak form of autonomy, amounting to the greatest degree of freedom in determining the way to perform the most sophisticated task, nor the ability to learn would per se suffice in grounding an ontological argument. Robots would still be objects, more precisely products, to which existing laws could apply.

Such a conclusion does not entail stating that existing liability rules should not be changed in order to favour – in some cases at least – the development of specific applications. Yet the kind of arguments to be investigated are never technical, depending on the very functioning of a specific application or set of applications. It is not their 'autonomous nature' that renders existing schemes less than optimal or even inadequate.

Rather, other sort of considerations matter, for robots as for any other sort of gift of the evil deity: social considerations, policy considerations and constitutional law principles more than everything else provide the required arguments to policy makers for undertaking a choice.

A robotic prostheses is neither autonomous, being directly attached to the human body and directly controlled by it, nor capable of learning; rather it is the wearer who may learn new ways to use it. According to most scholars though it does not show any of those essential technical traits, which would appear to justify a change in perspective in order to fill that ever widening liability gap identified by similar technologies. Nonetheless a constitutional law argument may suggest the adoption of a favourable liability scheme so as to incentivise their development.

To the contrary a fully autonomous house maid is not so substantially different from any other household product. But for its creator the machine would not have those actuators, or sensors allowing it to interact with the external world. Assessing what the desirable level of safety for a similar machine is itself entirely a matter of fact, which does not entail a substantially different kind of analysis – on the side of the policy maker, be it a legislator or judge – than that of other non robotic applications. At the same time, if considering existing legislation the argument was to be made to justify a change in the applicable rules for the ascription of liability, it is not at its technological characteristics that one should – mainly – look.

The absence of ontological reasons forcing a change in perspective when regulating – the harmful acts of – robots, simply entails that man is empowered with a free choice; moreover the choice being functional, it fundamentally comes down to a well argued – and sufficiently – informed decision on what kind of technology – and future – appears to be desirable.

# Dealing with the diffusion of legal responsibility: the case of robotics

*Susanne Beck*

Robotics is, without doubt, one of the most important technologies of our time. In more and more areas of life – traffic, elderly care, education, production of goods, military, etc. – the usage of „autonomous"[1] machines is regarded as advantageous. Not only are these machines meant to disburden humans of specific tasks and decisions; sometimes one can even read the argument that machines might, for some tasks, even be more suitable[2] because they are not hindered by forgetfulness, fatigue or aggression.

Until now, the best way for legislator and jurisprudence to react to these new developments still has to be found. The legal[3] system is, traditionally, oriented towards individual responsibility.[4] In the case of

---

[1] In the following, "autonomous" is used in a broad sense, meaning nothing more than a certain space for decision-making for the machine. For a project working on different understandings of autonomy and their changes because of human-technology interactions see information available at <http://www.isi.fraunhofer.de/isi-de/v/projekte/WAK-MTI.php.> accessed 10 May 2014.

[2] "Fortunately, these potential failings of man [*passion for inflicting harm, cruel thirst for vengeance, unpacific and relentless spirit, fever of revolt, lust of power, etc.*] need not be replicated in autonomous battlefield robots" (R. Arkin, 'Governing Lethal Behavior: Embedding Ethics in a Hybrid Deliberative/Reactive Robot Architecture', in *GIT-GVU-07-11*, available at <https://smartech.gatech.edu/jspui/bitstream/1853/22715/1/formalizationv35.pdf> accessed 8 May 2014, 2).

[3] The concept 'responsibility' is, at the moment, mainly discussed in moral contexts, thus many of the following aspects are connected to the ethical debate. But not just is the concept also important for the legal system, it originally stems from this context, see K. Bayertz, 'Herkunft der Verantwortung', in K. Bayertz (ed.), *Verantwortung – Prinzip oder Problem?* (Darmstadt: Wissenschaftliche Buchgesellschaft 1995), 17.

[4] I. Kant, 'Metaphysik der Sitten' (1797), in W. Weischedel (ed.) *I. Kant. Werke in zehn Bänden* (Bd. 7, Frankfurt a.M.: suhrkamp, 1994), 337 (AA 6, 230). For the relevance of individualism as early as in Roman Law see O. Behrends, 'Der Römische Weg zur Subjektivität: Vom Siedlungsgenossen zu Person und Persönlichkeit', in R. L. Fetz, R. Hagenbüchle, P. Schulz (eds.), *Geschichte und Vorgeschichte der modernen Subjektivität* (de Gruyter: Berlin / New York, 1998), 204 et seqq. See also K. Bayertz (fn. 3), 7. He also

robotics, this orientation faces difficulties, as will be discussed in the following. After analysing the current situation of robotics and its legal problems, it also will be asked which consequences changes of the legal concept „responsibility" could have.

# 1. The current development of robotics

Without being able to describe the whole variety of new research and products in the area of robotics, here I want to give an overview over the changes in the development of contemporary AI and robots which are relevant for the following considerations. Form the legal point of view, especially the 'autonomy' of machines is important.

Compared to traditional machines, modern AI and robots are said to approximate human thought patterns,[5] making robots having awareness of themselves and themselves in space, for example, of vital importance. By this, robots shall become able to adapt to complicated, unstructered environments and to complete varying tasks (partly cooperating with humans, partly by themselves). Self-activity of machines is growing permanently, passing through different 'activity niveaus'. At least from the niveau of (not directly controlled) interaction with human beings, behaviour and relationships of robots are differing from traditional machines[6] which have been regarded as epitome of determination.[7] Relevant differences can also be found in interactions of machines with machines: Multi-agent-systems are solving problems collectively – and are therefore, hardly predictable. Thus the actions of these kinds of autonomous machines are less controllable and predictable than the ones of traditional machines.

---

describes the development of responsiblity from a legal term to a widely discussed moral concept (16 et seqq.).

[5] Y. - H. Weng, C. - H. Chen, C.-T. Sun, 'Toward the Human Robot Co-Existence Society: On Safety Intelligence for Next Generation Robots', in (2009) 1 *International Journal of Social Robots*, 267-282.

[6] T. Christaller, 'Autonome intelligente Systeme', in T. Christaller (ed.), *Robotik - Perspektiven für menschliches Handeln in der zukünftigen Gesellschaft* (Berlin: Springer, 2001), 72.

[7] W. Rammert, 'Technik in Aktion: Verteiltes Handeln in soziotechnischen Konstellationen', in T. Christaller, J. Wehner (eds.), *Autonome Maschinen* (Wiesbaden: Westdeutscher Verlag, 2003), 293.

Autonomous machines are planned to be established in different areas of life - traffic[8], production of goods, household[9]. These machines cannot just facilitate everyday life but care-robots[10] and „ambient assisted living"-systems[11] could also extend the time span of living at home for the elderly, e.g. by alarming the doctor on call in cases of emergency. It is thinkable that robots or computer systems might even replace, to a certain extent, social contacts and fulfil emotional needs[12], give advice or remind of everyday obligations (for some social groups or even for society as such). These are just some examples of everyday life areas in which autonomous machines could find their way into. Another area in which the potential usage of autonomous machines is intensively discussed is the military (lethal autonomous robots – LARs).[13]

Despite the wide range, the common denominator of all these potential applications is the function of disburdening humans not just of performing certain mechanical tasks and gaining information as preparation for decision making, but even of making these decisions. Thus,

---

[8] For some information about prototypes of autonomous cars examples available at <http://www.nytimes.com/2010/10/10/science/10google.html?_r=1>; <http://jalopnik.com/5828101/this-is-googles-first-self+driving-car-crash> accessed 8 May 2014.

[9] Although the prognosis of Bill Gates (B. Gates, 'A Robot in Every Home', in (2007) *Scientific American*, 58–65) has not come into reality yet and might not for some time, it still cannot be doubted that service robots already have and will be of more and more relevance in households.

[10] Information available at <http://www.care-o-bot.de/de/care-o-bot-3.html> accessed 8 May 2014; M. Butter et al., 'Robotics for Healthcare', in (2008) *European Comission, DG Information Society.*

[11] T. Kleinberger et al., 'Ambient Intelligence in Assisted Living: Enable Elderly People to Handle Future Interfaces', in C. Stephanidis (ed.), *Universal Access in HCI, Part II* (Berlin/Heidelberg: Springer 2007), 103–112.

[12] Basic approaches are already recognisable in PARO, a robot animal used to comfort sick and elderly people (further information available at <http://www.paro-robots.com/> accessed 8 May 2014).

[13] Some exemplary contributions to the debate: H. - Y. Liu, 'Categorization and Legality of Autonomous and Remote Weapons Systems', in (2012) 94 *International Review of the Red Cross* 630–634; M. Schmitt, J. Thurner, '"Out of the Loop": Autonomous Weapon Systems and the Law of Armed Conflict', in (2013) 4 *Harvard National Security Journal* 231, 238; Human Rights Watch, 'Losing Humanity: The Case Against Killer Robots', in (2012) 19 *Human Rights Watch and International Human Rights Clinic*, 3–20; US Department of Defense, 'Unmanned Systems Roadmap 2007-2032'. (Washington 2007), available at <http://www.dtic.mil/cgi-bin/GetTRDoc?Location=U2&doc==GetTRDoc.pdf &AD=ADA475002> accessed 8 May 2014.

humans might only decide beforehand where to use autonomous machines and give them some guidelines for their decisions but leave the assessment of the situation to the machines, sometimes even giving them the ability to learn from former situations and experiences to advance their decision making process. At this point, it is important to note that transferring the decision making onto machines is not just a side effect, but the main idea of this development.

Research, production and practical usage of such machines bear various risks.[14] The most obvious one is the violation of rights or goods of third parties because of malfunctions or mistakes in the decision making process[15], be it a misinterpretation of a very deep and long sleep of the monitored elderly as emergency or of a child with a toy gun as enemy. But even without malfunctioning the decisions made might lead to damages; if, for example, a car has learned to draw aside in case of a potential collision and in one situation acts according to this experience, avoids a big empty plastic bag but thereby collides with another car or pedestrians, the decision could be "right" from the point of view of the machine but still morally questionable.

Besides these obvious directly damaging risks, one also discusses the potential influences of decreasing human contact for society.[16] The main contact of an elderly person being a robot, children being educated by computers, work places being shaped by cooperation of humans and machines and even war being conducted by "killing machines" – all this might change society deeply in a way we cannot even foresee yet. Although every new technology has been accompanied by fears about

---

[14] For an overview, see: P. Lin, K. Abney, G. A. Bekey (eds.), *Robot Ethics - The Ethical and Social Implication of robotics* (Cambridge, USA: The MIT press 2012); P. Lin, K. Abney, G. A. Bekey 'Robot ethics: Mapping the issues for a mechanized world', in (2011) 175 *Artificial Intelligence*, 5-6.

[15] For an overview of this and other legal problems see M. de Cock Buning, L. P. C. Belder, R. W. de Bruin, 'Mapping the legal and normative framework for the sustainable development of Autonomous Intelligent Systems in Society', in S. Muller et al. (eds.), *The Law of the Future and the Future of Law Series* (Den Haag: Hilll 2012), 195-210.

[16] See, for example, A. Sharkey, N. Sharkey, 'Granny and the robots: Ethical issues in robot care for the elderly', available at <http://staffwww.dcs.shef.ac.uk/people/A.Sharkey/sharkey-granny.pdf> accessed 8 May 2014, with further references. The authors ask for some restrictions of the usage of robots because of the problems caused by decreasing human contact: "For example, guidelines could be drawn up about the amount of time that a person could be left alone with a robot without human company" (34).

its changing society and leading to unpredictable challenges, it still is plausible that machines interacting socially like it is planned at the moment does lead to concerns. One of these concerns is that humans might lose their relevance in certain fields, maybe leading to unemployment or decreasing valuation of human actors.

Public debates on the development in robotics have only just begun, at the moment apparently dominated by the fear of unemployment because of increasing usage of machines[17] or by the thread caused by killing machines.[18] Also the question if one wants to – if sick or in need of care – be cared for by machines instead of human beings is posed.[19]

Despite it not being my main topic, I want to mention the similar development in technological enhancement of humans because it raises comparable questions concerning responsibility. Technologically influencing the human brain is not the only, but maybe the most drastic example for these techniques' potential of changing the concept of responsibility. Again, their function is to compensate for human deficiencies and again, risks for society are not only caused by potential malfunctioning but also by the possible effects on self-awareness and perception by third parties of the person being "partly machine" as responsible participant in social interaction. These developments challenge the traditional dualism between indetermined humans and determined machines in many ways.[20]

---

[17] This was already discussed in the case of industrial robots (and at least a clear causal link was doubted, e.g. by K. H. Ebel, 'The Impact of Industrial Robots on the World of Work', in (1986) 125 *International Labor Review* 39; S. A. Levitan, C. M. Johnson, 'The future of work: does it belong to us or to the robots?', in (1982) *Monthly Labor Review*, 10-14) For a glimpse on the current debate see, e.g., M. Ford, 'Could Artificial Intelligence Create an Unemployment Crisis?', in (2013) 56 *communications of the acm*, 37-39.

[18] See, for example, H. - Y. Liu (fn. 13).

[19] For example by N. Sharkey A. Sharkey, 'Living with robots: ethical tradeoffs in eldercare', in Wilks, Y. *Close Engagements with Artificial Companions: Key psychological, social, ethical and design issues* (Amsterdam: John Benjamins 2010) 245-256; R. Sparrow, L. Sparrow, 'In the hands of machines? The future of aged care.', in (2006) 16 *Mind and Machine*, 141-161.

[20] W. Rammert, 'Technik in Aktion: Verteiltes Handeln in soziotechnischen Konstellationen', in T. Christaller, J. Wehner (eds.), *Autonome Maschinen* (Wiesbaden: Westdeutscher Verlag 2003) 289-315.

# 2. Questions from the legal perspective

Some of the questions one has to ask as observer of this development from a legal perspective are discussed in other contributions in
this volume; thus I just want to give a short overview over the ones relevant for the following analysis because of their relations with the concept of responsibility; afterwards I will focus on this concept and how it
is challenged at the moment, inter alia by robotics.

The topics most often mentioned in legal debates about robotics
are[21]: liability for damages (civil and criminal); data protection; correla-
tion between private norms (ISO) and law; finally intellectual property
rights and labour law. Sometimes it is discussed if certain (international)
laws restrict the usage of autonomous machines in specific areas of life
in general, especially in the context of armed machines[22].

Some of these debates around data protection or intellectual property rights resemble the discussions of law having to be adapted to other
new technologies[23] (e.g. internet or biotechnology); also the questions
arising from the actions of autonomous machines being unpredictable
and dangerous are not new, because this is the case for (maybe too)
many new technologies and actually the reason for calling modern society "risk society".[24] The same accounts for problems caused by modern
risks normally not produced by individuals but by collectives.[25] Especially the last two points have already led to challenges for traditional
legal concepts such as responsibility: First of all, society – and thus, law
– had to find ways to deal with risks which are inherently unpredictable
and could, in theory, endanger human life on earth as such (esp. nuclear

---

[21] For an overview over different legal discussions, see exemplary C. Leroux, R.
Labruto (eds.), 'Suggestion for a green paper on legal issues in robotics', available at
<http://www.eu-robotics.net/cms/upload/PDF/euRobotics_Deliverable_D.3.2.1_-
ELS_IssuesInRobotics.pdf.> accessed 8 May 2014; See M. de Cock Buning, L. P. C.
Belder, R.W. de Bruin (fn. 15).

[22] See H. - Y. Liu (fn. 13).

[23] For some debates around new technologies and law see, e.g., the contributions in
the journal *Law, Innovation and Technology*; for an insight from a political perspective see,
e.g., P. J. Leahy, 'New Laws for New Technologies: Current Issues Facing the Sub-
committee on Technology and the Law', in (1991-92) 5 *Harvard Journal Law & Technology* 1.

[24] U. Beck, *Risikogesellschaft* (Frankfurt a.M.: Suhrkamp 1986).

[25] See, for example, W. Lübbe, *Kausalität und Zurechnung – über Verantwortung in kom-
plexen kulturellen Prozessen* (Berlin: de Gruyter 1994).

energy) but still are necessary and therefore have to be integrated into social life. Secondly, the importance of collective integration of individuals for evaluating their actions has increased. One consequence of the focus on collectives has been the development of "legal persons" as new addressees of responsibility.[26] Thus, the development of robotics ties in with a changed responsibility concept.

In the following, though, I want to focus on the unique aspects which stem from these machines actually being planned to function "autonomously": The concept of responsibility is not only challenged – as it is by other new technologies – if the machines do not function as planned, but also if they do. The changes affect not just the situations in which risks realise themselves but even the situations in which the machines work fully as intended, because that actually means to overtake, at least to some extent, human responsibility.

## 3. Responsibility and its current challenges

The moral or legal basis of "traditional" responsibility – if there is such a thing – is important for my considerations in that way that, combining Christian as well as Humanistic elements, the traditional understanding is bound to individuals.[27] There is no doubt that, historically, one can find social constructions without an understanding of individual responsibility, such as legal concepts of collective or institutional liability.[28] Also, one can find different concepts of responsibility in different nations[29] and of course, responsibility in public law has a differ-

---

[26] For a legal history of the concept „person" and „personhood", which are closely connected not just to rights but also to (legal) responsibility see S. Beck, B. Zabel, 'Person, Persönlichkeit, Autonomie - Juristische Perspektiven', in O. Friedrich, M. Zichy (eds.), *Persönlichkeit – Neurowissenschaftliche und neurophilosophische Fragestellungen* (tbp).

[27] See (fn. 4). For the relevance of personal identity for the concept see J. Nida-Rümelin, *Verantwortung* (Stuttgart: reclam 2011), 75 et seqq.

[28] See S. Beck, B. Zabel (fn. 26).

[29] For an analysis of the social-moral development in different cultures see M. Keller et al., 'Denken über moralische Verpflichtung und interpersonale Verantwortung im Zusammenhang unterschiedlicher Kulturen', in W. Edelstein, G. Nunner-Winkler (eds.), *Moral im sozialen Kontext* (Frankfurt am Main: Suhrkamp 2000) 375–406.

ent meaning than in criminal law[30]. All these facets are important to fully grasp "the" concept of responsibility. But I want to focus on what I think are some least common denominators and also on what is changing about the concept, especially its legal anchorage.

Besides the debates and differences about what legal responsibility is based upon, what it means in the different legal areas and what its consequences are – I am quite sure we can agree on the importance of the aspect of "response"[31]. Also in the German translation one finds this element of "responding" ("antworten") of someone to someone about something. Someone does not necessarily mean individual person, but it does mean an entity which is considered to have some kind of legal personality. The person is made responsible for actions (retrospective as well as prospective) by his counterparts on the base that he was or is "free" – at least from outer determinants – to act in a certain way.[32] And although we all now agree that legal responsibility is not comprehensive with moral responsibility, it also cannot be doubted that it is infused by morality in many ways.[33] Maybe the legal area in which these aspects become most visible is criminal law (at least in English the notions guilt, culpability, responsibility and liability all are used in the context of criminal law), but they are relevant in all other areas, too.

In the last decades, some challenges for the traditional understanding of the individual offender being responsible for his former action have occurred. As commonly known one of these challenges was the introduction of collectives as legal persons, which, in some countries, are liable even under criminal law.[34] This already has led to some diffu-

---

[30] For an overview over different meanings of responsibility in different legal contexts see H. Dreier, 'Verantwortung als Rechtsbegriff', in U. Neumann, L. Schulz (eds.), *Verantwortung in Recht und Moral* (Stuttgart: Franz Steiner 2003), 9-38.

[31] See K. Bayertz (fn.3), 16.

[32] For an overview over the debate see the contributions in: G. Roth, S. Hubig, H. G. Bamberger (eds.), *Schuld und Strafe* (München: C. H. Beck 2012); R. - D. Herzberg, *Willensunfreiheit und Schuldvorwurf* (Tübingen: Mohr Siebeck 2010); T. Hörnle, *Kriminalstrafe ohne Schuldvorwurf* (Baden-Baden: Nomos 2013); C. Jäger, 'Willensfreiheit, Kausalität und Determination', in (2013) *Goltdammer's Archiv*, 3-14; E. - J. Lampe, G. Roth, M. Pauen (eds.), *Willensfreiheit und rechtliche Ordnung* (Frankfurt a.M.: suhrkamp 2008); R. Merkel, *Willensfreiheit und rechtliche Schuld* (Baden-Baden: Nomos 2008).

[33] About the relationship see, e.g., E. Hilgendorf, 'Recht und Moral', in (2001) *Aufklärung und Kritik*, 72 ff.

[34] For an overview see S. Beck, 'Corporate Criminal Liability', in M. Dubber, T. Hörnle, *Oxford Handbook of Criminal Law* (tbp); J. Gobert, A. - M. Pascal (eds.), *European*

sion of the concept of responsibility, especially taking into account that such concepts can also serve as hide-out for the responsible individuals.[35] This is intensified by modern theories about social interactions, such as the system theory, which sometimes tend to divert the attention from the individual actor.[36]

Actually, the debate about modern risk society in many ways seems to circle around the question what the individual is actually (still?) responsible for, which constraints have to be considered when discussing responsibility, how one can be responsible in the context of modern risks.[37] Fitting quite smoothly into this diffusion is the current reactivation of the determinism-indeterminism-debate.[38] Not only the content, but also the timing of this neuro-science evoked debate is interesting: It seems to mirror the current doubts about individual responsibility of other contexts.

Thus one can state that the ideal of individual legal responsibility has, to some extent, found its limits over the last decades, in a way that exceeds the typical limits of every "ideal" concept. The diffusion has led to adaptions of the law in many ways – just to give an example, besides the already mentioned introduction of the legal person: In German criminal law (and I suppose it to be similar in other countries) nowadays one speaks about "risk criminal law"[39] which in many ways is trying to adapt to the changing circumstances and thereby leaves traditional categories on all stages of criminal liability (objective and subjec-

---

*Developments in Corporate Criminal Liability* (Oxon / New York: Routledge 2011); Pinto/Evans, Corporate Criminal Liability, 3rd ed., 2013.

[35] "When everyone is responsible, then no one is responsible, and the ethic of responsibility itself is imperilled" (J. S. Parker, 'Doctrine of Destruction: The Case of Corporate Criminal Liability', in (1996) 17 *Managerial and Decision Econ*, 393; see also S. Beck (fn. 34), E.I.

[36] J. J. M. van der Ven, 'Verantwortung und Verantwortlichkeit – Versuch einer rechtsphilosophischen Standortbestimmung', in H. M. Baumgartner, A. Eser (eds.), *Schuld und Verantwortung* (Tübingen: Mohr Siebeck 1983), 31-50.

[37] See K. Bayertz (fn. 3) 24 et seqq.; F. - X. Kaufmann, 'Risiko, Verantwortung und gesellschaftliche Komplexität, in K. Bayertz (ed.), *Verantwortung – Prinzip oder Problem?* (Darmstadt: Wissenschaftliche Buchgesellschaft 1995), 72-97. To different kinds of responsibility which are debated at the moment (r. for consequences, cooperative r., corporate r., political .r, scientific r.) see J. Nida-Rümelin (fn. 27), 108 et seqq.

[38] See (fn. 32).

[39] E. Hilgendorf, *Strafrechtliche Produzentenhaftung in der „Risikogesellschaft"* (Berlin: Duncker & Humblot 1993); C. Prittwitz, *Strafrecht und Risiko* (Frankfurt a.M.: Vittorio Klostermann 1993).

tive elements of the offence, justifications, individual culpability) as well as by introduction of new offences directed more towards prevention of risks in general than the ascription of individual responsibility.

Some of the reasons for these developments have already been mentioned, especially the complexity of modern risks. Individuals seem to surrender to these risks, the complexity of decisions has led to a situation that is sometimes even called the "tyranny of choice"[40]; the feeling of not being able to influence the course of modern risks as individual and being determined in many ways has become overwhelming; no one does seem to feel able to "respond" about these risks to society. Actually, society seems more interested in preventing or at least controlling specific risks as such than in such a response, inter alia because if some of these risks are realised it is impossible to re-establish the situation beforehand. Thus, not just individual responsibility has vanished in many contexts, but also concepts such as "precaution-ethics"[41] or "preventive criminal law"[42] have been developed.

In general, law is able to adapt to these new developments and construct specific concepts of legal responsibility which consider the circumstances of the situation in question.[43] These changes of legal concepts is not necessarily problematic; to the contrary, it is better to create limited, but realistic responsibility concepts than to overburden the individual by making him responsible although external restrictions to his potential actions have been strong and his potential to avoid future harm has been limited. To the extent that law, including criminal law, is able to include new kinds of responsibilities without sacrificing its fundamental principles, the adaptions seem to be of some advantage because they are more realistic and probably more feasible.

On the other hand, one has to be aware that reducing individual responsibility too much can have negative consequences, for both, actors and counterparts[44]: For actors, because they lose not only self-esteem but also the feeling of actually being able to influence certain

---

[40] B. Schwartz, 'The Tyranny of Choice', in (2004) _Scientific American_, 71-75.

[41] H. Jonas, _Das Prinzip Verantwortung_ (Frankfurt a.M.: Suhrkamp 1979).

[42] See, exemplary, W. Hassemer, 'Sicherheit durch Strafrecht', in (2006), _Höchstrichterliche Rechtsprechung im Strafrecht_, 130-143.

[43] See, e.g., the contributions of J. Schuhr, E. Hilgendorf in S. Beck (ed.), _Jenseits von Mensch und Maschine. Ethische und rechtliche Fragen zum Umgang mit Robotern, Künstlicher Intelligenz und Cyborgs_ (Baden-Baden: Nomos 2012).

[44] See J. J. M. van der Ven (fn. 36).

developments, to act responsible, to control certain risks – and this feeling of one's owns actions being almost irrelevant can be quite problematic. For counterparts, because there is no one there to "respond" either preventively or retrospectively – no one might feel the need to create developments in a way that reduces harm beforehand and even after the harmful event no one might be addressable for the need for response.

This does not only concern the financial aspects because most of the time the reimbursement of financial losses does not by itself fulfil the need for compensation of the damaged person. In many cases the feeling that someone actually responds personally to the damage, either voluntarily by regretting one's former action or – at the least – forced by (criminal) law, is also important for communicating the wrongness of the action to the victim as well as to society.

# 4. Responsibility – challenged by robotics?

In this situation of already diffused legal responsibility, we are building machines for the purpose of taking over responsibilities even on the stage of decision making. Overwhelmed by the so called "tyranny of choice" in over complex situations, by everyday life entailing endless risks of damaging third parties, by unforeseeability of the consequences of already small decisions, we react technologically: We are building machines not just to decide how to best find our way in traffic or to get our car into a parking spot, not just to remind us about our medicine or buying food as soon as the fridge is empty – we are building machines to decide about life and death of other human beings.

It could be interesting to reflect which is hen and which is egg here: Is this social development only possible because the idea of individual responsibility has already faded away or do we just live in a society where no other concept of responsibility is possible anymore? Is a more diffused, broader concept of responsibility maybe generally more adequate and thus we just have to adapt to the changes?

### 4.1. *Responsibility for mistakes*

In the following I will focus on the complexity of the responsibility question posed by robotics[45], starting with the – in this context mainly discussed – question of what happens if an autonomous robot makes a mistake and thereby damages a third party. From a legal point of view, this conflict can, inter alia, be solved in the following ways:

- One of the human parties is regarded as generally liable, e.g. the user. This is how, for example, the law handles park distance control systems at the moment.[46]

- Only the human party is liable who, provably, made a mistake. This would put the burden of proof onto the third party, thus posing a strong hindrance to his possibility of receiving damages.

- All human parties "behind" the robot (researcher, programmer, producer, user) can be transformed to a new legal entity (electronic person). This does not, per se, solve all problems and not necessarily exclude the other solutions but gives the third party a kind of addressee, at least for its financial claims.[47]

- One could even, e.g. for social useful robots (garbage collecting robots), think about transferring part of the damages onto society itself, meaning having the tax payer filling in for the cases in which the origin of the mistake cannot be proven.

Here one can already get a glimpse of the complexity: All of these solutions are based on premises about who is profiting from the usage of robots, who should be "punished" financially for its mistake, who is thought to be in control or stay in control even if the machine overtakes some of the originally human decision-making.

### 4.2. *Responsibility for risks and side effects*

But this is only the question of a specific damage. Before that, one has to decide in which areas of life one actually can accept robots with a certain damaging-potential, because even if one can solve the problem

---

[45] For the problem of ascribing responsibility generally A. Matthias, 'The Responsibility Gap: Ascribing Responsibility for the Actions of Learning Automata', in (2004) 6 *Ethics and Information Technology* 175-183.

[46] District Court Munich (trans.: Amtsgericht München), Urteil vom 19.7.2007 – Az.: 275 C 15658/07, NJW RR 2008, 40.

[47] S. Wettig, E. Zehendner, 'The Electronic Agent: A Legal Personality under German Law?', in (2003) *2nd Workshop on the Law and Electronic Agents* (LEA), 97-112.

of financial compensation, not all damages can be fully recovered. In certain areas it might be regarded as inadequate to actually put third parties to risk, if the social usage of the robot is not high enough.

In my opinion, this is, besides many other aspects, a strong argument against the usage of robots with the potential to kill human beings. The risk of their making a mistake could simply be too high to bear it socially.

Risks in this context do not only include damages or mistakes but also unwanted side effects. Of course, every new technology is accompanied by discussions about slippery slopes, dehumanisation of society, irreversible negative consequences.[48] The intense debate in the case of robotics is not surprising: The imagination of robots nursing the elderly or baby-sitting, taking over our communication, giving psychological advice or waging our wars obviously threatens our accustomed social interactions. Without using these potential changes as reason to restrict or even forbid specific research or production in robotics, I mainly want to underline that deciding for their usage also includes responsibility for these potential side effects.

### 4.3. Responsibility-transfer

This view onto responsibility problems in the context of robotics shall be concluded by focussing on the already mentioned aspect of the responsibility transfer onto machines. When machines overtake decisions, new questions will arise not just if something goes wrong, but for each decision made by machines: Who is the responding entity? Can the machine respond in a way that is necessary for the social and legal construct of responsibility?

For example, it seems much harder to forgive a machine if it makes a decision which affects one's own life – as said, not just if this decision was wrong, but also, if a robot tells an employee that because of his calculation he loses his job or – coming back to the drastic but because of that demonstrative example of the military, if the robot decides that a human life has to end.

---

[48] For an analysis of this kind of argumentation see, e.g., W. van der Burg, 'The Slippery Slope Argument', in (1991) 102 *Ethics* 42-65.

It therefore is actually debated if it is a violation of human dignity to let a machine make this life-or-death decision[49] because human dignity could include the right that a human being decides about the end of human lives, that this other human being has to live with his decision, that someone "responds" to the consequences of this decision.

The necessity of human response could also lead to the exclusion of autonomously deciding robots in other areas of life than the military, even if factually possible and sometimes even if the machine might make less mistakes than human being, just because a human response is a social condition, at least at the moment. It is not impossible that this necessity decreases with the changes of various social concepts but for now, one has to respect the current situation.

# 5. Potential legal solutions and their consequences for concepts

From an inner perspective, it does not pose a big problem to the legal system to reduce individual responsibility in the cases of robots making decisions, to create new legal entities with specific legal responsibilities[50] and to support these changes by strengthening of institutional responsibility in the background, because institutions will decide about the direction of robotics – by financing research, giving out licences, insuring under conditions, etc.

Making these decisions one will have to bear in mind that the direction of robotics will probably have influence on basic social concepts. By intentionally constructing machines which make decisions for us, we give away part of our (social) identity – or maybe better, we reconstruct our identity in a way that includes machines because we have beforehand decided to use them for a specific part of our autonomy-space. We change our understanding of autonomy[51] by reducing human decision making potential in specific situations – the focus will lie on the

---

[49] P. Asaro, 'On banning autonomous weapon systems: human rights, automation and the dehumanization of lethal decision making', in (2012) 94 *International Review of the Red Cross* 687-709; C. Heyns, *Report of the Special Rapporteur on extrajudicial, summary or arbitrary executions* (UNGA 13 April 2013) para 31, 92.

[50] See, e.g., the contributions of J. Schuhr, E. Hilgendorf in S. Beck (fn. 43).

[51] See S. Beck, B. Zabel (fn. 26).

decision to use the machine in a specific context as such. We change our understanding of personhood[52] – it is questionable if we still can be taken seriously as responsible actor if we hand over decisions or even social contacts (by, e.g., letting computers handle our email communication) and thus, we will change our social relations. To not always having a human counterpart as someone who can respond will change social interactions.

Between these changes and the legal solutions, there will be interdependence – the way law reacts to social changes can strengthen or weaken some of these constructs, can foster or hinder their changes, and again, the new concepts will change the legal system. This does not mean that the law should not consider the introduction of electronic personhood or cannot reduce individual responsibility in certain contexts – but it has to be understood that this does have repercussions onto identity, personhood, autonomy, etc.

# 6. Concluding remarks

Discussing responsibility in the context of robotics means more than asking the question "Who is liable if something goes wrong". It means to understand what happens if we intentionally hand over decision making onto machines. It means to legally react on changing fundamental concepts and consciously create the space for these changes. It means to leave room for decisions against machines taking over responsibility in specific contexts and it means to strengthen the awareness of the relevant institutions who will decide about the development of robotics: They do not only decide about the future of one new technology – in my opinion, they also decide about the future of our very basic social concepts, of our understanding of ourselves.

---

[52] See S. Beck, B. Zabel (fn. 26).

# Foundations and limits of an "ethicalization" of law

*Silja Vöneky*


## 1. Introduction – the "ethicalization" of law

Even though the concept of *ethicalization of law* is still new in the jurisprudential and legal-philosophical debate, it can be meaningfully understood as the increasing and intensified amending of legal norms by ethical, extralegal standards. This can be especially seen in three areas:

Firstly, there is an increasing amount of so-called "opening clauses" in acts and legal norms that concede normative relevance in national, supranational, and international legal systems to ethical standards. Such opening clauses for ethical benchmarks are found for example in the regulation of the European Union's Framework Programs for Research and Technological Development, which tie the allocation of research funds to ethical research requirements. Opening clauses also exist in biomedical law, like in the German Stem Cell Act (Stammzellgesetz, StZG)[1] and typically in the area of human subject research: for example various professional laws for physicians reference the Helsinki Declaration of the World Medical Association.[2]

---

[1] Gesetz zur Sicherstellung des Embryonenschutzes im Zusammenhang mit Einfuhr und Verwendung menschlicher embryonaler Stammzellen (trans.: Law for Protecting the Embryo in Relation to the Entry and Usage of Human Embryonic Stem Cells) of 28 June 2002 (Bürgerliches Gesetzblatt (BGBl.) I, 2277), available at < http://www.gesetze-im-internet.de/bundesrecht/stzg/gesamt.pdf> accessed 5 May 2014.

[2] World Medical Association (WMA) Declaration of Helsinki, Ethical Principles for Medical Research Involving Human Subjects adopted in June 1964 (18th General Assembly, Helsinki), last amendment in October 2013 (64th WMA General Assembly, Fortaleza); available at http://www.wma.net/en/30publications/10policies/b3/, accessed 5 January 2014.

Secondly, the ethicalization of research law can be seen by the still continuing institutionalization of ethics through ethics commissions. Today, the use of ethics commissions is largely legally set down, even in acts by parliaments, especially in the well-known area of human subject research, but also in further areas of biomedical law. For instance, according to the stipulations of the German Act for the Protection of Embryos (Embryonenschutzgesetz), the legislator deemed that the vote of an ethics commission is a mandatory prerequisite for a valid preimplantation genetic diagnosis (PGD).[3]

The third area of an ethicalization of law is that of generally non-binding – and therefore non-legal – codes, which obligate researchers to undertake „ethical" research.

Such ethical research-governing codes are created by research organizations, like the Max Planck Society, but also within the area of the European Union by for instance the EU-Commission on Nanotechnology.[4]

All three developments overlap and reinforce one another: In legal norms that contain opening clauses, like the German Stem Cell Act or the professional laws for physicians, or in codes of ethics, the use of an ethics commission, which shall determine what ethical and unethical research is in concrete cases, is often also provided for.

# 2. The relationship between ethics and law

Before it will be examined if and how opening clauses, ethics commissions, and codes of ethics can be justifiedly employed in a legal system to achieve ethical conduct, let me first address the relationship between ethics and law, as well as clarify the terminology:

---

[3] Section 3a of Gesetz zur Regelung der Präimplantationsdiagnostik zur Änderung des Embryonenschutzgesetzes of 7 July 2011 (BGBl. I, 2746), available at < http://www.parlament-berlin.de/ados/17/IIIPlen/vorgang/d17-1517.pdf> accessed 5 May 2014.

[4] Commission Recommendation of a code of conduct for responsible nano-sciences and nanotechnologies research of 7 February 2008 (C (2008) 424); available at http://ec.europa.eu/nanotechnology/pdf/nanocode-rec_pe0894c_en.pdf, accessed 5 January 2014.

## 2.1. *Ethical standards and legal norms*

At first, the distinction between ethical standards and law only makes sense if the term ethical standards denote all those standards, which have not been enshrined into law by a legislative body.

One can only sensibly talk about ethical and thus non-legal standards if these are either not set down by a legislative organ that is generally allowed to do so, like for example through a private research organization, a private association etc., or if they are explicitly set down as non-law, i.e. designated as non-binding, by a legislative organ that has generally the competence to legislate (like the EU-Commission's Nano-Code for example).

However, ethical standards need not only to be distinguished from law, but must also be classified based on their contents - especially two types. As normative ethics, ethics provides the reasons for the justification of and legitimacy of conduct; it is a "justificatory discipline," as Dietmar von der Pfordten writes in his book Rechtsethik (Ethics of Law).[5] As normative standards, ethical standards are therefore those that seek to answer the two fundamental ethical and moral questions with a view to what is right, generally independent of the prevailing morality and of the positive law: "How should I act?" and "Why is this action right or wrong?". Unethical actions are thus those, which cannot be justified by supra-legal reasons of justice.[6]

## 2.2. *Ethical minimum standards of science versus ethical responsibility standards of science*

If the (justified) goal of science is to gain knowledge or even truth, then all those standards that methodically ensure this gain of knowledge, this search for truth, are justified as ethical standards.[7] It is

---

[5] D. von der Pfordten, *Rechtsethik* (München: Beck, 2001), 54.

[6] For a deontological ethics see W. D. Ross, *The Right and The Good* (Oxford: Clarendon Press, 1930); for Ross' intuitionistic theory see R. Alexy, *Theorie der juristischen Argumentation* (Frankfurt am Main: Suhrkamp, 1983), 58 et seq.

[7] When answering the question of what concept of science should sensibly be used, it is most important to acknowledge that theories, this includes theories of natural science, are accepted since and until they provide a plausible explication for a certain amount of data or certain experiences and since alternative theories are either falsified or plainly unplausible within the scope of our daily experiences (H. Putnam, *Reason, Truth and History,* (trans.: Vernunft, Wahrheit und Geschichte) (Frankfurt am Main: Suhrkamp, 1990), 262 et seq.). This is even true when the explication is not highly

thereby unproblematic to state, that non-legal rules that want to prevent malpractice in research constitute ethical standards in this sense. Since the fulfillment of these standards is a necessary requirement for ethical scientific research, they will be referred to in the following as ethical minimum standards of science.

However, the ethical standards, which I will analyze with respect to their eligibility and admissibility, extend much further:

An example is the already mentioned code of ethics of the Max-Planck-Society from 2010.[8] According to this code, research within the Max-Planck-Society shall be committed to the well-being of mankind and to environmental protection, and risks for human dignity, freedom, property, and environment stemming from the work of Max-Planck researchers are to be minimized as much as possible.[9]

Another example is the also mentioned recommendation by the EU-Commission for a code of conduct for responsible nanosciences and nanotechnologies research from 2008 (in the following: Nano-Code):[10]

This code seeked to commit nano-research to ethical tenability.[11] For instance, the general principle that researchers and research institutions should be held accountable and liable for the possible

---

falsifiable (in contrast K. Popper, *Logik der Forschung* (Tübingen: Mohr, 3rd ed., 1969)). Thus, general requirements for the attainment of scientific knowledge are consistency, disambiguation and coherence, as well as instrumental efficiency and functional simplicity (see S. E. Toulmin, *An Examination of the Place of Reason in Ethics* (Cambridge: Cambridge Univ. Press, 1950), 88, 95). Scientific theories should not only be true, but also relevant; they have to be clear and adequate (H. Putnam, *Vernunft, Wahrheit und Geschichte* (Frankfurt am Main: Suhrkamp, 1990), 185 et seq.). Finally, all theories have to cope with the daily experiences of a man (according to Nida-Rümelin, this is the reason why the heliocentric view established itself; it did not question daily experiences, but was a new, plausible interpretation of these experiences, see J. Nida-Rümelin, 'Theoretische und angewandte Ethik: Paradigmen, Begründungen, Bereiche', in *Angewandte Ethik* (Stuttgart: Kröner, 2nd ed. 2005), 2 et seq., 38).

   8 Hinweise und Regeln der Max-Planck-Gesellschaft zum verantwortlichen Umgang mit Forschungsfreiheit und Forschungsrisiken; available at http://www.-mpg.de/200127/Regeln_Forschungsfreiheit.pdf, accessed 5 January 2014.

   9 C.1. and C.3. code of conduct of the Max-Planck-Society, available at < http://www.mpg.de/232129/researchFreedomRisks.pdf> accessed 5 May 2014

   10 See (fn 4).

   11 See 13th regard, 4th recommendation, Annex 1, 3.2 and 4.1.5 of the Nano-Code (fn 4).

social, ecological and health-related consequences of their research for current and future generations is contained in the code.[12]

If one looks at these codes, it is obvious that they are not about ethical minimum standards of research, but – which must be differentiated – are an embodiment of the ethos of scientific responsibility. The goal is to set down for researchers such non-legal, behavioral norms that are no longer only intended to serve science itself, but society as well.

For this ethos of scientific responsibility, one must recall the program, brought forward by Jürgen Habermas and Carl Friedrich von Weizsäcker in the 1970s, for the "finalization of science": according to this program, science should be devoted to the progress of human society.

Naturally, this program was radical and considerably more extensive than the above-mentioned ethical standards – Max-Planck-Code or the Nano-Code. The aim of these new codes is only a science, which neither harms the fundamental values and principles of the rest of society (human rights, environmental protection etc.) nor the basic rights of the those not involved but directly affected by the research, and which also is aware of the possible dangers of misuse of research results and seeks to reduce them. According to these new ethical standards, research, which indeed complies to scientific standards in the sense of scientific methods of cognition but conflicts with other ethical values and principles of society, is unethical. Distinct from the previously mentioned ethical minimum standards of science (internal ethical standards), I would like to denote these ethical standards as ethical responsibility standards of science (external ethical standards).

The following analysis of ethical standards in the law of research shall be limited to these previously mentioned responsibility standards, the external standards, because a special area of tension is revealed using them. Scientific freedom, as an ethical value and as a constitutionally ensured basic right that is even guaranteed without reservations by Art. 5 Para. 3 of the Basic Law of the Federal Republic of Germany, seems to be exposed to special dangers if scientific conduct is constrained by external ethical standards. While the conflict between scientific freedom and the minimum standards of research –

---

[12] See 3.7 Nano-Code (fn 4).

that is, the internal ethical standards of research – can be easily resolved, this is different for responsibility standards:

To observe external ethical responsibility standards of research often contradicts the acquisition of knowledge. A physician, who conducts research on human subjects by administering more placebos than are permitted by the standards of the Helsinki Declaration,[13] can under certain circumstances gain scientific insights more quickly and in greater quantity than if he or she adheres to the requirements of the declaration. A researcher, who conducts research on pox viruses without considering the consequences for society as a whole, can under certain circumstances contribute much more to the advancement of science with respect to knowledge than a researcher, who destroys these viruses because of the danger of misuse, as is demanded by the World Health Organisation (WHO). Whenever ethical responsibility standards are prescribed for scientific research through norms, the special danger of an intrusion into scientific freedom arises. And the investigation of whether these conflicts between science and ethics – more precisely: between the legally, also constitutionally, secured basic right and human right of scientific freedom and the external ethical standards – can be gently resolved for both sides through an ethicalization of the law of science still remains.

### 2.3. Necessity and limits of justification and justifiability of ethical standards

Since the following I will speak of ethical standards, the here-argued metaethical position must be presented; it is a reasonable question, whether today, given the (also) pluralistic states and a pluralistic world community, one can meaningfully speak about ethical standards or whether each recourse to such standards is a recourse to arbitrary, relative values and principles:

Here, my thesis is a cognitive and non-relative one: according to it, the aim of ethical reasoning is to get from opinions to knowledge.[14]

---

13 See Declaration of Helsinki, (fn 2), C. 32.

14 Therefore, there is no categorical difference between ethics and natural science. However, S. E. Toulmin, (fn 8), 127, has the opinion that the aim of moral reasoning is to modify unreflected, stated moral feelings; he sees a categorical difference between ethics and natural science: "Ethics is concerned with the harmonious satisfaction of desires and interests."; Ibid.,. 137, 223. This categorical separation contrasts with the criteria for all scientific research, given in (fn 7). See for a critical discussion of Toulmin's theses R. Alexy, (fn 7), 117 et seq.

Ethical attempts of reasoning – which are separated from causal explanations – thus allow for rational beings to accept ethical claims as legitimate or to reject them. If one assumes the Enlightenment's idea of man, then good reasons, i.e. rational justifications that are not causal explanations, are required to legitimize ethical claims to others.[15]

That ethical statements are statements capable of reason and truth, not only feigned statements or emotional expressions, recommendations or imperatives, has already been shown elsewhere and would go beyond the frame of this paper. It follows from my positions on the aim and character of science that convincing benchmarks for rational acceptability also exist for ethical positions and standards.[16]

---

[15] M. Quante, *Einführung in die allgemeine Ethik* (Darmstadt: Wissenschaftliche Buchgesellschaft, 2003), 145. Moreover, it is an "ought implying fact" that something is rational, see H. Putnam, 'Pragmatism and Moral Objectivity', in J. Conant (ed.) *Words and Life*, (Cambridge, Mass. et al.: Harvard Univ. Press, 1994), 151, 167 et seq.

[16] The community of natural scientists has a shared paradigmatic core and an established method. In ethics there is a multitude of theories, but there is no shared paradigmatic core. In fact, there are different paradigms like the utilitarian, the deontological, the contractualistic one etc. This is the reason why in philosophical ethics there will necessarily be some cases of dissensus with no possibility of reaching consensus, R. Posner, *The Problematics of Moral and Legal Theory* (Cambridge, Mass. et al.: Belknap Press of Harvard University Press, 1999) 62 et seq.; H. Putnam, (fn 8), 218. From that, it follows that policy advising in fields of ethics has to respect other rules than policy advising in fields of natural sciences. But there is no difference between ethics and natural science with regard to the phenomenon that there are questions that cannot be answered definitely – for example, in the case where both possible ways of conduct are that bad that no rational man can recognize definitely on which one to decide (B. Williams, *Der Begriff der Moral, Eine Einführung in die Ethik* (Stuttgart: Reclam, 1978)). Moreover, the relativity of contexts plays an important role, so that a certain behaviour may depend on a certain social context. But this is not a unique feature of ethics, but it occurs in natural scientific questions as well (Putnam, (fn 8), 199 et seq.). Furthermore, I want to point out that there is no categorical difference between ethics and natural sciences because ethics deals with "values", whereas natural sciences deal with "facts". Max Weber's thesis on the absolute dichotomy between facts and values, which means that what is called "good" or "bad" does not depend on facts, was convincingly refuted by the philosopher Hilary Putnam. Putnam has proved that both statements about facts and the practice of scientific research, which allows us to decide what has to be regarded as "fact", depend on values. (Ibid., 173 et seq.). According to this, there is no absolute dichotomy between facts and values, in fact we have to assume that facts are connected with values. This becomes clear when we think about the concept of science: the objective of all sciences is "truth". But what sensibly can be called "truth" depends on our criteria of rational acceptability (see (fn 7)). These criteria

From this it follows in turn that on the basis of reasons, better ethical positions can be differentiated from worse ethical positions.[17] Accordingly, the thesis, that all ethical assumptions are equally right or wrong and that ethical attitudes are thus arbitrary or random, is thus not maintainable.

However, one must distinguish between various grades of justification of ethical positions: The strongest form of justification would not be good reasons, but unquestionable reasons. If unquestionable reasons were necessary for a sufficient justification of an ethical position, then the project to justify ethical positions would have failed.[18] Generally, all reasons for ethical positions are questionable, an unquestionable, final justification is impossible. However, to demand such an unfulfillable standard for ethical justification would contradict our daily experiences, where we, even though there is no final justification, nevertheless distinguish between good and bad ethical theories and arguments on the basis of general benchmarks of rational acceptability, like instrumental efficiency, freedom from contradiction, coherency, completeness and functional simplicity. That thereby the possibility to reconcile all differences in opinions, i.e. reach a consensus, on ethical issues or – if a consensus cannot be reached – to at least convince a majority, does not exist, does not contradict the existence of better and worse reasons. Therefore, it cannot be convincing if one demands unquestionable reasons or – since and if this fails – completely dismisses ethical justifications as pointless. Rather, it is convincing if one develops reasonable standards for ethical justifications. Firstly, this entails that ethical claims of knowledge cannot be considered unjustified only because they in principle could turn out to be incorrect. Secondly, this entails that if there is dissent concerning ethical principles and values, then this is not a metaphysical, i.e. not an epistemological problem, but a political task.[19]

---

are cognitive values. Thus, the empiric world depends on our values. Putnam, ibid., 181 f.

[17] See Putnam, ibid, 280.

[18] Birnbacher, 'Für was ist der „Ethik-Experte" Experte?', in K.P. Rippe (ed.), *Angewandte Ethik in der pluralistischen Gesellschaft* (Fribourg, Switzerland: Univ.-Verl., 1999), 267, 273 et seq.; H. Putnam, (fn 16) 151 et seq., 152; see also Aristoteles, 'Nikomachische Ethik', in F. Dirlmeier (ed.) *Book* I, (Stuttgart: Reclam, 1969), 7.

[19] Explicitly John Dewey, see H. Putnam, (fn 16), 155. Richard Rorty also points out that the existence or non-existence of a consensus must be interpreted rather as a sociological than an epistemological problem: "To explain the absence of consensus by

# 3. Ethical standards in the law of research

Whether the ethicalization of law can resolve the conflicts between the human right of freedom of research and freedom-limiting external ethical standards shall be analyzed in the following with the help of three examples – (1.) opening clauses, (2.) the use of ethics commissions and (3.) the formulation of so-called non-binding ethics codes.

## 3.1. *Admissibility of ethical opening clauses*

Here, the question of when a legal system – more specifically: when a legal norm in a legal system – can justifiedly refer to extralegal responsibility standards in the area of regulation of scientific conduct arises.

Such an opening clause for ethical standards is for instance contained in the professional code of conduct of the state physicians' chambers:

"Physicians [shall] adhere to the ethical principles for medical human subject research laid down in the Helsinki Declaration by the World Medical Association".[20]

The Declaration of Helsinki is a declaration of the World Medical Association (WMA) regarding ethical principles for medical human subject research. It was first adopted by the World Medical Association in Helsinki in 1964; up until today it has been revised many times.[21] The 2000 Declaration of Edinburgh was for example revised because of the too extensive permission to use placebo-controlled experiments. The WMA is an organisation of national medical associations founded in 1947, which represents 95 national associations (the German member is the German Medical Association). The WMA is therefore a private association (a Non-Governmental Organisation, NGO) and not a

---

"lack of cognitive status" is like explaining a substance's failure to put you to sleep by its lack of dormitive power", R. Rorty, 'Dewey and Posner on Pragmatism and Moral Progress', *University of Chicago Law Review* 74 (2007), 915 et seq. 921. Against this view Posner, (fn 17), 62 et seq.

[20] See for example Section 15 subsection 4 Berufsordnung der Landesärztekammer Baden-Württemberg.

[21] See (fn 2).

subject of international law (not an International Organisation, IO), and does not have the competence to set down international law.

In this quality, the WMA differs from International Organizations like the United Nations or the United Nations Educational, Scientific and Cultural Organization (UNESCO). The WMA is also not representatively assembled: It lacks a balanced geographical representation of members on the one hand, since there is clear predominance of representatives from western cultural circles; on the other hand, voting like for the adoption of the Helsinki Declaration, is determined by majority rule.[22]

It is unclear and disputed whether such private rule-making can be justifiedly incorporated as an ethical standard in a legal order: Is the reference to expert legitimacy enough here, i.e. that those people, who are experts in certain areas can best set sensible rules for these areas, with the consequence that these rules possess a so-called output-legitimacy?[23] To accept such output-legitimacy already seems – disregarding fundamental theoretical objections – unconvincing because physicians are experts in medical questions, but not – at least not solely – in questions of research ethics. On the contrary: The danger that standards of professional morale will be declared as ethical principles exists. It is precisely necessary to prevent the development of a professional morale, which could lead to a moral particularism as described by Émile Durkheim.[24]

In order to determine general criteria for the justified use of opening clauses for ethical standards, the following principles therefore have to be observed:

Firstly, these extralegal ethical standards must be able to be justified as ethical standards with respect to their contents, i.e. with respect to values and principles of justice.

---

[22] See M. Chang, *Ethische und rechtliche Herausforderungen einer globalisierten Arzneimittelprüfung – Die Problematik klinischer Versuche an Menschen in Entwicklungsländern*, 2014 (in press); S. Mehring, *The Intersection of Medical Ethics and International Humanitarian Law*, 2014 (in press).

[23] For the concept and its theoretical foundation see F. Scharpf, *Demokratietheorie zwischen Utopie und Anpassung* (Kronberg/Ts.: Scriptor Verl., 1975); Ibid., *Regieren in Europa, Effektiv und demokratisch?* (Frankfurt/Main et al.: Campus-Verl., 1999).

[24] For the dangers of a particularisation of morals because of the specific morals of some professionals, see E. Durkheim, 'Physik der Sitten und des Rechts – Vorlesungen zur Soziologie der Moral', in H.-P. Müller (ed.) (Frankfurt am Main: Suhrkamp, reprint 1999) 14 et seq.

Only then can one at all speak of ethical standards in differentiation from rules of professional morale and only this sort of quality with regard to contents can counterbalance deficits in the procedural basis of legitimacy. An uncritical recourse to the Helsinki Declaration is thus to be rejected, if these rules have been significantly shaped by the physicians' professional morale and cannot be ethically justified.

Further, each legal system determines the limits of the justified incorporation of ethical standards; this means: If opening clauses in international law exist, then the incorporated ethical standards must not contradict international law; if they exist in European Union law, then there must not be a contradiction with European Union law. In the federal German legal system, ethical standards that are incorporated into the legal system through opening clauses are not allowed to contradict higher-ranking law, especially the Basic Law and basic rights, but also other constitutional principles, like the democracy principle, the dictate of the rule of law (Rechtsstaatsprinzip) etc.

If one looks at the example of the opening clause for the Helsinki Declaration in German legal norms, it is the case that: If the 2000 version of the Helsinki Declaration too extensively permits the employment of placebos, so that a violation of human dignity and of the protection of physical integrity according to the German Basic Law is existent, then its incorporation would not be admissible. Therefore, the consequence is an obligation to interpret these extralegal norms in compliance with the constitution or, if such an interpretation is not possible, to not apply them.

Interesting with a view to the legal system of Germany is the question of whether a dictate to interpret in compliance with international law also exists when interpreting extralegal, international standards like the Helsinki Declaration, should these be incorporated into the German legal system through opening clauses. In my opinion, this is not the case because this is precisely not a matter of international law. It is different, however, if ethical standards are referred to and thus simultaneously represent so-called international soft law, since they were passed by a subject of international law, like UNESCO's 2005 Universal Declaration on Bioethics and Human Rights.[25] In the case of

---

[25] International Declaration on Human Genetic Data of 16 October 2003 available at<http://portal.unesco.org/en/ev.phpURL_ID=17720&URL_DO=DO_TOPIC&URL_SECTION=201.html> accessed 5 May 2014 and Universal Declaration on Bioethics and Human Rights of 19 October 2005 available at < http://portal.unesco.o-

the latter, the dictate of interpretation in compliance with international law is to be adhered to, since (and whenever) Germany participated as a State in these declarations and is thus bound by them – although in a weaker normative degree than through hard law.

The so-called Wesentlichkeitstheorie of the Federal Constitutional Court of Germany, which as an effusion of the democracy principle and an embodiment of the parliamentary reservation proclaims that fundamental issues, especially those with interfere with basic rights, must be sufficiently clearly set down by the democratic legislator.[26] This is also be taken into account as a limit to the incorporation of extralegal, ethical standards into the legal system of Germany.

With a view to the benchmark of – in terms of content – democratic legitimacy, it already follows that the parliamentary law is the decisive agent of "democratic legitimacy": The parliamentary reservation of the Basic Law therefore demands that in fundamental normative areas, especially in the area of the exercise of basic rights, but overall in all issues that are of significant importance for the community insofar as these are accessible by state regulation, the fundamental decisions must be made by the parliamentary legislator.

Therefore, the core of the parliamentary reservation is the embodiment of an area of decision that exclusively lies in the competence of the parliament. Precisely with a view to the democracy principle[27] – next to the rule of law principle – the parliament must itself also decide on normatively fundamental issues and is not allowed to allocate these to sub-legal (or foreign) norm-setting authorities. The obligation of the parliamentary legislator to address issues and set norms affects not only whether a legal regulation should be undertaken, but also specifically determines their regulatory density.[28] This significance of the parliament is thereby not solely substantiated through its direct election by the people, but precisely also by the fact

---

rg/en/ev.php-URL_ID=31058&URL_DO=DO_TOPIC&URL_SECTION=201.html> accessed 5 May 2014

[26] See F. Ossenbühl, 'Vorrang und Vorbehalt des Gesetzes', in J. Isensee/ P. Kirchhof (eds), *Handbuch des Staatsrechts*, Band V (Heidelberg: Müller, 3rd ed.,, 2007, § 101, recital 46 et seq., 52; see for the historical background in detail C. Seiler, *Der einheitliche Parlamentsvorbehalt* (Berlin: Duncker & Humblot, 2000, 40 et seq., 51 et seq.) for the adjudication of the Federal Constitutional Court, ibid.., 64 et seq.

[27] See Federal Constitutional Court of Germany (BVerfGE) 49, 89, 126; E 58, 257, 268 et seq.; E 86, 90, 106; E 123, 39, 77 et seq.

[28] BVerfGE 101, 1, 34; E 123, 39, 78.

that a public discussion and debate concerning the subject of a regulation or decision is only enabled by the frame of a parliamentary proceeding. This once again emphasizes the principle of accountability of the state decision-making process to the people between elections and the therefore required transparency and publicity as essential parts of the democracy principle. Thus, if the central issue is the demand for public traceability, then it becomes evident that the criteria of transparency of state exercise of power not only appear as elements of the rule of law, but also as necessary conditions of the democracy principle of the Basic Law. Not only this democratic emphasis and support of the idea of transparency, but also its justification, which is tightly connected with the empirical-descriptive concept of legitimacy, are significant. Niklas Luhmann assumes that a (legislative) process is (only then) legitimate, if it is actually capable of generating a consensus and obtaining the trust of the observing audience.[29] Ernst-Wolfgang Böckenförde argues accordingly when he warns of the dangers of an expertocracy: If the representatives are decreasingly capable of making decisions through their own knowledge and judgment, then the parliaments dependency on expert knowledge does not remain secret from the represented and impairs their belief that the representatives are ready and capable to responsibly act and decide for the citizens collectively.[30]

It must be pointed out that it also follows from the democracy principle that only the normatively fundamental must be regulated by the parliament. Even with a view to the constitutionally-secured and democratically-legitimated executive, especially also the government, this precisely does not mean a general responsibility of the parliament, but – provided that the question of whether to regulate is not disputed – only the requirement that the regulation be sufficiently defined in order to guarantee an adequate flexibility for the administration or the political capacity of the government to act, if it is appropriate and necessary.

---

[29] A similiar concept of legitimation can be found in P. Badura, 'Die parlamentarische Demokratie', in J. Isensee/P. Kirchhof (eds), *Handbuch des Staatsrechts*, Band II (Heidelberg: Müller, 3rd ed., 2004), § 25, recital 30.

[30] See E. - W. Böckenförde, 'Demokratische Willensbildung und Repräsentation', in J. Isensee, P. Kirchhof (eds.), *Handbuch des Staatsrechts*, Band III (Heidelberg: Müller, 3rd ed., 2005), § 34, recital 38.

However, when this sufficient definition is reached in specific cases and in different areas of regulation is disputed. Controversy also exists especially when the generation of new knowledge and the incorporation of external expertise is concerned. Generally, however, from what has been said, it can be recorded that in normatively fundamental areas - if as much as possible a precisely composed conditional program in the area of legislation should not be necessary, possible or appropriate - generally at least procedural rules in the area of application of the parliamentary reservation must be established, which guide the insertion of external expertise and organize the interests of the parties, by the parliamentary legislator. Thus, a formal statute must determine the process and the organization, and thereby provide for the task-appropriate – i.e. usually well balanced and capable – composition of the respective commissions and committees.[31]

What follows from these general principles when applied to the present questions?

If one looks at the theory of legislative reservation and the concept of transparency as part of the democracy principle, the legislator must determine the balance between the basic rights of those involved, especially in human subject research – the scientific freedom of the researchers and the basic rights of the participating patients – like has generally been done for instance in the German Medicinal Products Law (Arzneimittelgesetz, AMG).[32]

Already from this a prohibition of dynamic references to ethical standards follows: It is not admissible to dynamically refer to the Helsinki Declaration "in its respective version", since the legislator cannot foresee which material standards are thereby incorporated into the law. Even static legal references to ethical, external standards – for example to a certain version of the WMA's Helsinki Declaration – are in any case questionable with respect to the democracy principle, if due to such references a substantial debate regarding the thereby incorporated material regulations is completely absent in parliament and no debate takes place concerning the thus factually legislating

---

[31] H. Dreier, in ibid. (ed.), *Grundgesetz Kommentar*, Band II (Tübingen: Mohr Siebeck, 2nd ed., 2006, Art. 20 (Demokratie), recital 122); A. Voßkuhle, 'Sachverständige Beratung des Staates', in J. Isensee, P. Kirchhof (eds), *Handbuch des Staatsrechts*, Band III (Heidelberg: Müller, 3rd ed., 2005), recital 68 et seq., 72.

[32] Gesetz über den Verkehr mit Arzneimitteln of 12 December 2005 (BGBl I 2005, 3394), last amendment on 19 July 2011 (BGBl I 2011, 1398).

NGO or committee, namely the WMA, its composition and its voting system.

### 3.2. *Admissibility of ethics commissions*

The second aspect of the ethicalization of research law is the increased institutionalization of ethics through the employment of ethics commissions.

Ethics commissions are interdisciplinary composed, independent commissions that preventively review the ethical tenability of certain research projects. Their employment is today even legally demanded as a means of preventive control of the conduct of researchers: On the one hand in the professional codes of conduct of the state physicians' chambers, but also in federal law and European Union Law in the area of human subject research, and in the area of biomedical law in the German Stem Cell Act and for the admissibility of preimplantation genetic diagnosis.

If legally a vote – or even a positive vote – by an ethics commission is a prerequisite for the admissibility of a research project, then this always constitutes an intrusion into the right of freedom of science, which must be justified.[33]

With a view to the right of scientific freedom that is guaranteed by Art. 5 Para. 3 of the Basic Law of Germany and the state's obligation to protect human dignity and physical integrity enshrined in Art. 1 Para. 1 Basic Law and Art. 2 Para. 2 Basic Law, it is valid for the Federal Republic of Germany that the limits of the law and of ethics must already be identified before potentially severe human subject research that endangers basic rights is commenced. This not only protects the research participants, but also the researchers themselves since they are restrained from unethical research and are safeguarded against external criticism by the positive vote of the ethics commission.

Thus, in the area of studies on medicinal products, but also in the area of remaining research on born humans, the necessity of preventive judgment of research through the activation of ethics commissions is justified from the perspective of balancing colliding basic rights. Yet, this also means that with respect to stem cell research, the question of

---

[33] M. Fehling, in R. Dolzer, K. Vogel, K. Graßhof (eds), *Bonner Kommentar zum Grundgesetz* (München: Vahlen), August 2011, Art. 5 Abs. 3 GG, recital 153.

whether the precursory inclusion of an ethics commission is constitutional can be hotly debated.

However, highly problematic and no longer constitutional is that the composition of overall over 50 research ethics commissions in Germany and their internal procedural regimes are usually allocated by bylaw solely to chambers of physicians and medical faculties of universities. Generally, it is only regulated by the parliamentary law of the German legislator that these ethics commissions must be independently and interdisciplinarily composed;[34] the state legislator also does not set further requirements. What is left over – that is, the number of members, the number of represented disciplines, the quantitative relationship of the disciplines to one another, the participation of so-called laymen and representatives of patients etc. – is exempted by the legislator. It is not surprising that here a considerable difference between the legal arrangement of the different bylaws and the composition of the commissions exists, as can be exemplarily shown by the comparison of the ethics commissions of the University of Bonn and the University of Heidelberg.[35] It should also not surprise one if a type of forum shopping occurs during the selection of ethics commissions by those who depend on the vote of the commissions. Thereby it is the method of the composition of these commissions that is significant. It is not astonishing if differently composed commissions reach different conclusions with respect to the same research project.

Hence in the area of human subject research that is relevant to basic rights, the parliamentary legislator must especially, by parliamentary act, determine the number of members of ethic commissions and specify in what quantity the various disciplines should be represented. The parliamentary legislator must, by parliamentary act, specify the main features of the process, the transparency and the organization of the ethics commissions according to the guidelines of the democracy principle of the Basic Law.

---

[34] See Section 42 subsection 1, sentence 1-3 Arzneimittelgesetz (see (fn 33)).
[35] See for a comparison S. Vöneky, *Recht, Moral und Ethik* (Tübingen: Mohr Siebeck, 2010), 600 et seq.

## 3.3. *Admissibility of codes of ethics*

The third concrete object of analysis is the ethicalization of the law of research through codes of ethics.

Here, I want to take a look the European Nano-Code, which was quite problematic with respect to scientific freedom:[36] The Nano-Code, which was based on a recommendation of the EU-Commission, contained a series of norms, which are not sufficiently precise and whose implementation could have a factually negative effect on research and science. With respect to the aspect of the guarantee of scientific freedom, three stipulations were especially significant: Firstly, the recommendation to make a balancing of risk a necessary part of applications for the sponsorship of research (4.2.3 Nano-Code); secondly, the recommendation to align nano-research towards the greatest possible public benefit and to give priority to publicly-beneficial research during the allocation of research grants (4.1.13 Nano-Code) and finally, the recommendation of an obligation of accountability of researchers for the social, ecological and health-related consequences of their nano-research (3.7 Nano-Code).

Overall, the code bound nano-research to ethical tenability, without however specifying what is ethically tenable or what the mentioned fundamental ethical principles are. Especially the general principle that researchers and research institutions should "be held accountable for the current and for future generations" for the "possible social, ecological and health-related consequences of their research" (3.7 Nano-Code) was too imprecise and too extensive.

Furthermore, the Nano-Code was only prima facie not legally binding, since it was an annex to a legally non-binding recommendation. It could rather be qualified as European soft law, since it unfolds a not insignificant factual, normative binding effect. The principles and concrete guidelines of the Nano-Code claimed to be a benchmark for ethical, i.e. responsible, nano-research.

Consequently, every non-observance of the code could be qualified as "unethical conduct". This, however, did not formally entail legal

---

[36] See for the following S. Vöneky, J. von Achenbach, 'Stellungnahme zu der Empfehlung der Kommission für einen Verhaltenskodex für verantwortungsvolle Forschung im Bereich der Nanowissenschaften und –technologien', in S. Vöneky (ed.), *Informationspapiere der Max-Planck-Forschungsgruppe „Demokratische Legitimation ethischer Entscheidungen"*, 6/2008, available at <www.fiponline.de> accessed 5 May 2014

binding force of the code, but lead to an especially strong factual binding force. To per se exclude these regulations from the basic rights safeguard and not qualify them as intrusions but as insignificant disturbances, which do not need to be justified, would misjudge their normative shaping power.

As a legal act of the EU – and in accordance with the principles mentioned above – the code had to be generally reviewed against the benchmark of the European basic rights. The European basic right of scientific freedom is so far not strongly developed despite being enshrined in Art. 13 of the Charter of Fundamental Rights of the European Union (CRCh).[37] This results from the interpretation of Art. 13 CRCh with a view to the not explicitly mentioned enshrinement of scientific freedom in the European Convention of Human Rights and with a view to the constitutional traditions of the various member states, of which the large majority – different than Germany – do not explicitly or at least not without reservation protect scientific freedom. A violation of the European basic right of scientific freedom, which offers a lesser protection against intrusions, by the Nano-Code can hence not be assumed.

However, the issue of German state organs being bound to the constitution when implementing EU law is to be viewed differently. Since the implementation of and adherence to the code by the member states occured voluntarily, the shaping leeway of the member states encompasses the entire code, so that the implementation by German public authorities can only occur within the framework of the Basic Law. In any event, the previously cited obligation of accountability of researchers for the social, ecological and health-related consequences of their nano-research can be viewed as a violation of scientific freedom (3.7 Code). A responsibility of the researchers for consequences of their research, like is established by § 7 of the Hessian University Law,[38] represents an intrusion into scientific freedom from the perspective of the safeguard of the basic right of scientific freedom. Such an intrusion can only be justified if it is clearly limited to the safeguard of constitutionally protected goods like health and life.[39] Thus, it seems obvious that the obligation of accountability of the Nano-Code violated

---

[37] Charter of Fundamental Rights of the European Union of 12 December 2007 (2010/C 83/02) (Journal of the EU C 83/389).

[38] Hessisches Hochschulgesetz of 21 December 2010 (GVBl. I, 617, 618).

[39] BVerfGE 47, 327, 1st key statement of the ruling.

the scientific freedom of the Basic Law: The code refered – as shown above – too vaguely to the possible social, ecological and health-related consequences, for which the researcher was hold accountable.

# 4. Conclusion

Sociologically understood, it is typical for social control in modern communities that de facto the ethical-moral accusation – i.e.: the accusation: "You act immorally!" – is being replaced through reference to the applicable law, i.e. through: "You act illegally". According to Niklas Luhmann, a gain in freedom and a peaceful function of a society lie precisely in this reference to the rule of law.[40] This peaceful function could be limited if increasingly an ethicalization of law and especially an ethicalization of the law of research take place, and if in this process it becomes necessary to adapt and also ethically judge research projects according to ethical guidelines.

Nevertheless, an opening of the law for ethical values does not contradict the character of the German legal system, which wants to be a system of justice in the widest sense. The Basic Law presents itself, despite its contribution to the legalization of basic and human rights and the general separation of positive law from ethics, as a system of justice that raises the claim to be the keystone of an ethical, positive-legal system. Despite the separation of law and ethics, it must be assumed that a system-immanent coherence of law, that is a coherence that is solely directed towards the positive system in the framework of this legal system, does not suffice according to its own claim.[41]

---

[40] N. Luhmann, 'Soziologie der Moral', in ibid. S. Pfürtner (eds), *Theorietechnik und Moral* (Frankfurt am Main: Suhrkamp, 1978, 8 et seq.; see also ibid, *Das Recht der Gesellschaft* (Frankfurt am Main: Suhrkamp, 1993), 124 et seq.

[41] Such an interpretation of a democratic constitution is not new: it can be found in the writings of the German antipositivist Rudolf Smend, who wrote about the Weimar Constitution. According to Smend, it is not only the task of the state to guarantee freedom, but to realize justice, see R. Smend, 'Verfassung und Verfassungsrecht', in ibid., *Staatsrechtliche Abhandlungen und andere Aufsätze* (Berlin: Duncker und Humblot, 3rd ed. 1994) 119 et seq. For the ideal of democracy, Nida-Rümelin states today:„Eine Demokratie unterscheidet sich von anderen Staatsformen darin, dass sie eine Brücke schlägt, ohne die eine Demokratie im Gegensatz zu anderen Staatsformen nicht lebensfähig ist: eine Brücke zwischen der Lebenswelt und der in diese eingelassenen

However, what the here stated requirement of supra-legal coherence can today mean and what is necessary for it is questionable, since a supra-legal system of norms or values that all agree to does not exist. If the system at hand refers to an ethical system and supra-legal conceptions of justice, without itself be able to state or guarantee them, then today this can only mean that thus generally – next to legality and constitutionality – a reflex of legal norms and decisions to reasoned, justified values is being targeted.[42]

However, in conclusion it is essential that should ethical standards justifiedly be incorporated in the legal system, they must be ethical standards in the normative sense. Thus, they must be justified with respect to content, namely through their convincing justifiability with supra-legal values or principles; and certainly not through recourse to a factually existing professional morale.

Furthermore, ethical principles are not allowed – should they be able to be effectively incorporated into the legal system of Germany – to violate the fundamental principles of the constitution. Ethical standards, which for example can be justified as utilitarian standards, nevertheless are not allowed to violate legally anchored basic and human rights. In Germany, scientific freedom is also part of these basic and human rights. If ethical standards infringe on this freedom, then this intrusion must be justified; if a justification does not exist, then the incorporation of ethical standards must not happen or be limited. Thus, in a legal system that is shaped by the freedoms of basic rights, ethics that limits basic rights must be pursued in a proportional and moderate way.

---

normativen und deskriptiven Überzeugungen einerseits und dem politischen System und der politischen Praxis andererseits." (J. Nida-Rümelin, *Demokratie und Wahrheit* (München: Beck, 2006) 26.

[42] This does not mean that unjust law is not law at all. On the contrary, I want to point out that a close connection between ethics and law is an aim of the political order of the Federal Republic of Germany. This connection requires neither a natural-rights thinking nor the assumption of a dependence of legal validity to ethical truths or values.

# When HAL kills, who is to blame? Computer ethics

*Daniel C. Dennett*

The first robot homicide was committed in 1981, according to my files. I have a yellowed clipping dated December 9, 1981, from the Philadelphia Inquirer - not the National Enquirer – with the headline "Robot killed repairman, Japan reports".

The story was an anticlimax. At the Kawasaki Heavy Industries plant in Akashi, a malfunctioning robotic arm pushed a repairman against a gearwheel-milling machine, which crushed him to death. The repairman had failed to follow instructions for shutting down the arm before he entered the workspace. Why, indeed, was this industrial accident in Japan reported in a Philadelphia newspaper? Every day somewhere in the world a human worker is killed by one machine or another. The difference, of course, was that – in the public imagination at least – this was no ordinary machine. This was a robot, a machine that might have a mind, might have evil intentions, might be capable, not just of homicide, but of murder. Anglo- American jurisprudence speaks of mens rea – literally, the guilty mind:

To have performed a legally prohibited action, such as killing another human being; one must have done so with a culpable state of mind, or mens rea. Such culpable mental states are of three kinds: they are either motivational states of purpose, cognitive states of belief, or the nonmental state of negligence.[1]

The legal concept has no requirement that the agent be capable of feeling guilt or remorse or any other emotion; so-called cold-blooded murderers are not in the slightest degree exculpated by their flat

---

[1] R. Audi (ed.), *Cambridge Dictionary of Philosophy* (Cambridge: Cambridge University Press, 1995), 482.

affective state. Star Trek's Spock would fully satisfy the mens rea requirement in spite of his fabled lack of emotions. Drab, colorless – but oh so effective –"motivational states of purpose" and "cognitive states of belief" are enough to get the fictional Spock through the day quite handily. And they are well-established features of many existing computer programs.

When IBM's computer Deep Blue beat world chess champion Garry Kasparov in the first game of their 1996 championship match, it did so by discovering and executing, with exquisite timing, a withering attack, the purposes of which were all too evident in retrospect to Kasparov and his handlers. It was Deep Blue's sensitivity to those purposes and a cognitive capacity to recognize and exploit a subtle flaw in Kasparov's game that ex plain Deep Blue's success. Murray Campbell, Feng-hsiung Hsu, and the other designers of Deep Blue, didn't beat Kasparov; Deep Blue did. Neither Campbell nor Hsu discovered the winning sequence of moves; Deep Blue did. At one point, while Kasparov was mounting a ferocious attack on Deep Blue's king, nobody but Deep Blue figured out that it had the time and security it needed to knock off a pesky pawn of Kasparov's that was out of the actor: but almost invisibly vulnerable. Campbell, like the human grandmaster watching the game, would never have dared consider such a calm mopping-up operation under pressure.

Deep Blue, like many other computers equipped with artificial intelligence (AI) programs, is what I call an intentional system: its behavior is predictable and explainable if we attribute to it beliefs and desires – "cognitive states" and "motivational states" – and the rationality required to figure out what it ought to do in the light of those beliefs and desires. Are these skeletal versions of human beliefs and desires sufficient to meet the mens rea requirement of legal culpability? Not quite, but, if we restrict our gaze to the limited world of the chess board, it is hard to see what is missing. Since cheating is literally unthinkable to a computer like Deep Blue, and since there are really no other culpable actions available to an agent restricted to playing chess, nothing it could do would be a misdeed deserving of blame, let alone a crime of which we might convict it. But we also assign responsibility to agents in order to praise or honor the appropriate agent. Who or what, then, deserves the credit for beating Kasparov? Deep Blue is clearly the best candidate. Yes, we may join in congratulating Campbell, Hsu and the IBM team on the success of their handiwork; but in the same spirit we might congratulate Kasparov's teachers, handlers, and even his parents. And, no matter how assiduously they may have trained him, drumming into his head the importance of one strategic principle or another, they didn't beat Deep Blue in the series: Kasparov did.

Deep Blue is the best candidate for the role of responsible opponent of Kasparov, but this is not good enough, surely, for full moral responsibility. If we expanded Deep Blue's horizons somewhat, it could move out into the arenas of injury and benefit that we human beings operate in. It's not hard to imagine a touching scenario in which a grandmaster deliberately (but oh so subtly) throws game to an opponent, in order to save a life, avoid humiliating a loved one, keep a promise, or … (make up your own O'Henry story here). Failure to rise to such an occasion might well be grounds for blaming a human chess player. Winning or throwing a chess match might even amount to commission of a heinous crime (make up your own Agatha Christie story here). Could Deep Blue's horizons be so widened?

Deep Blue is an intentional system, with beliefs and desires about its activities and predicaments on the chessboard; but in order to expand its horizons to the wider world of which chess is a relatively trivial part, it would have to be given vastly richer sources of "perceptual" input – and the means of coping with this barrage in real time. Time pressure is, of course, already a familiar feature of Deep Blue's world. As it hustles through the multidimensional search tree of chess, it has to keep one eye on the clock. Nonetheless, the problems of optimizing its use of time would increase by several orders of magnitude if it had to juggle all these new concurrent projects (of simple perception and self-maintenance in the world, to say nothing of more devious schemes and opportunities). For this hugely expanded task of resource management, it would need extra layers of control above and below its chess-playing software. Below, just to keep its perceptuo-locomotor projects in basic coordination, it would need to have a set of rigid traffic-control policies embedded in its underlying operating system. Above, it would have to be able to pay more attention to features of its own expanded resources, being always on the lookout for inefficient habits of thought, one of Douglas Hofstadter's "strange loops," obsessive ruts, oversights, and deadends.[2] In other words, it would have to become a higher-order

---

[2] See D. R. Hofstadter, *Gödel, Escher, Bach: An Eternal Golden Braid* (New York: Basic Books, 1979).

intentional system, capable of framing beliefs about its own beliefs, desires about its desires, beliefs about its fears about its thoughts about its hopes, and so on.

Higher-order intentionality is a necessary precondition for moral responsibility, and Deep Blue exhibits little sign of possessing such a capability. There is, of course, some self-monitoring implicated in any well-controlled search: Deep Blue doesn't make the mistake of reexploring branches it has already explored, for instance; but this is an innate policy designed into the underlying computational architecture, not something under flexible control. Deep Blue can't converse with you – or with itself – about the themes discernible in its own play; it's not equipped to notice – and analyze, criticize, analyze, and manipulate – the fundamental parameters that determine its policies of heuristic search or evaluation. Adding the layers of software that would permit Deep Blue to become self-monitoring and self-critical, and hence teachable, in all these ways would dwarf the already huge Deep Blue programming project – and turn Deep Blue into a radically different sort of agent.

HAL purports to be just such a higher-order intentional system – and he even plays a game of chess with Frank. HAL is, in essence, an enhancement of Deep Blue equipped with eyes and ears and a large array of sensors and effectors distributed around Discovery 1. HAL is not at all garrulous or self-absorbed; but in a few speeches he does express an interesting variety of higher-order intentional states, from the most simple to the most devious.

HAL: Yes, it's puzzling. I don't think I've ever seen anything quite like this before.

HAL doesn't just respond to novelty with a novel reaction; he notices that he is encountering novelty, a feat that requires his memory to have an organization far beyond that required for simple conditioning to novel stimuli.

HAL: I can't rid myself of the suspicion that there are some extremely odd things about this mission.

HAL: I never gave these stories much credence, but particularly in view of some of the other things that have happened, I find them difficult to put out of my mind.

HAL has problems of resource management not unlike our own.

Obtrusive thoughts can get in the way of other activities. The price we pay for adding layers of flexible monitoring, to keep better track of our own mental activities, is ... more mental activities to keep track of!

HAL: I've still got the greatest enthusiasm and confidence in the mission. I want to help you.

Another price we pay for higher-order intentionality is the opportunity for duplicity, which comes in two flavors: self-deception and other-deception. Friedrich Nietzsche recognizes this layering of the mind as the key ingredient of the moral animal; in his overheated prose it becomes the "priestly" form of life:

For with the priests everything becomes more dangerous, not only cures and remedies, but also arrogance, revenge, acuteness, profligacy, love, lust to rule, virtue, disease – but it is only fair to add that it was on the soil of this essentially dangerous form of human existence, the priestly form, that man first became an interesting animal, that only here did the human soul in a higher sense acquire depth and become evil – and these are the two basic respects in which man has hitherto been superior to other beasts![3]

HAL's declaration of enthusiasm is nicely poised somewhere between sincerity and cheap, desperate, canned ploy – just like some of the most important declarations we make to each other. Does HAL mean it? Could he mean it? The cost of being the sort of being that could mean it is the chance that he might not mean it. HAL is indeed an "interesting animal."

But is HAL even remotely possible? In the book 2001, Clarke has Dave reflect on the fact that HAL, whom he is disconnecting, "is the only conscious creature in my universe." From the omniscient-author perspective, Clarke writes about what it is like to be HAL.

He was only aware of the conflict that was slowly destroying his integrity – the conflict between truth, and concealment of truth. He had begun to make mistakes, al- though, like a neurotic who could not observe his own symptoms, he would have denied it (p. 148).

---

[3] F. Nietzsche, *The Genealogy of Morals*, in W. Kaufmann, R. J. Hollingdale,. (New York: Random House, 1967), First Essay.

Is Clarke helping himself here to more than we should allow him? Could something like HAL – a conscious, computer-bodied intelligent agent – be brought into existence by any history of design, construction, training, learning, and activity? The different possibilities have been explored in familiar fiction and can be nested neatly in order of their descending "humanness."

1. The Wizard of Oz. HAL isn't a computer at all. He is actually an ordinary flesh-and-blood man hiding behind a techno-façade – the ultimate homunculus, pushing buttons with ordinary fingers, pulling levers with ordinary hands, looking at internal screens and listening to internal alarm buzzers. (A variation on this theme is John Searle's busy-fingered hand-simulation of the Chinese Room by following billions of instructions written on slips of paper.[4])

2. William (from "William and Mary")[5]. HAL is a human brain kept alive in a "vat" by a life-support system and detached from its former body, in which it acquired a lifetime of human memory, hankerings, attitudes, and so forth. It is now harnessed to huge banks of prosthetic sense organs and effectors. (A variation on this theme is poor Yorick, the brain in a vat in the story, "Where Am I?" in my Brainstorms.)[6]

3. Robocop, disembodied and living in a "vat." Robocop is part-human brain, part computer. After a gruesome accident, the brain part (vehicle of some of the memory and personal identity, one gathers, of the flesh-and-blood cop who was Robocop's youth) was reembodied with robotic arms and legs, but also (apparently) partly replaced or enhanced with special-purpose software and computer hardware. We can imagine that HAL spent some transitional time as Robocop before becoming a limbless agent.

4. Max Headroom, a virtual machine, a software duplicate of a real person's brain (or mind) that has somehow been created by a brilliant hacker. It has the memories and personality traits acquired in a normally embodied human lifetime but has been off-loaded from all-carbon-based hardware into a silicon-chip implementation. (A variation

---

    [4] John Searle. "Minds, Brains and Programs," in (1980) Behavioral and Brain Sciences 3, 417-58.

    [5] R. Dahl, Kiss, Kiss. (New York: Knopf, 1959).

    [6] D. Dennett. Brainstorms: Philosophical Essays on Mind and Psychology. in Montgomery, Vt.: Bradford Books and Hassocks, (Sussex: Harvester, 1978).

on this theme is poor Hubert, the software duplicate of Yorick, in "Where Am I?")

5. The real-life but still-in-the-future – and hence still strictly science-fictional – Cog, the humanoid robot being constructed by Rodney Brooks, Lynn Stein, and the Cog team at MIT.[7] Cog's brain is all silicon chips from the outset, and its body parts are inorganic artifacts. Yet it is designed to go through an embodied infancy and childhood, reacting to people that it sees with its video eyes, making friends, learning about the world by playing with real things with its real hands, and acquiring memory. If Cog ever grows up, it could surely abandon its body and make the transition described in the fictional cases. It would be easier for Cog, who has always been a silicon-based, digitally encoded intelligence, to move into a silicon-based vat than it would be for Max Headroom or Robocop, who spent their early years in wetware. Many important details of Cog's degree of humanoidness (humanoidity?) have not yet been settled, but the scope is wide. For instance, the team now plans to give Cog a virtual neuroendocrine system, with virtual hormones spreading and dissipating through its logical spaces.

6. Blade Runner in a vat has never had a real humanoid body, but has hallucinatory memories of having had one. This entirely bogus past life has been constructed by some preposterously complex and detailed programming.

7. Clarke's own scenario, as best it can be extrapolated from the book and the movie. HAL has never bad a body and has no illusions about his past. What he knows of human life he knows as either part of his innate heritage (coded, one gathers, by the labors of many programmers, after the fashion of the real-world CYC project of Douglas Lenat or a result of his subsequent training – a sort of bed-ridden infancy, one gathers, in which he was both observer and, eventually, participant. (In the book, Clarke speaks of "the perfect idiomatic English he had learned during the fleeting weeks of his electronic childhood.")

The extreme cases at both poles are impossible, for relatively boring reasons. At one end, neither the Wizard of Oz nor John Searle could do

---

[7] R. Brooks and L. A. Stein. "Building Brains for Bodies." in (1994) *Autonomous Robots* 1, 7-25.

the necessary handwork fast enough to sustain HAL's quick-witted round of activities. At the other end, hand-coding enough world knowledge into a disembodied agent to create HAL's dazzlingly humanoid competence and getting it to the point where it could benefit from an electronic childhood is a programming task to be measured in hundreds of efficiently organized person-centuries. In other words, the daunting difficulties observable at both ends of this spectrum highlight the fact that there is a colossal design job to be done; the only practical way of doing it is one version or another of Mother Nature's way – years of embodied learning. The trade-offs between various combinations of flesh-and-blood and silicon-and-metal bodies are any-body's guess. I'm putting my bet on Cog as the most likely develop-mental platform for a future HAL.

Notice that requiring HAL to have a humanoid body and live concretely in the human world for a time is a practical but not a metaphysical requirement. Once all the R & D is accomplished in the prototype, by the odyssey of a single embodied agent, the standard duplicating techniques of the computer industry could clone HALs by the thousands as readily as they do compact discs. The finished product could thus be captured in some number of terabytes of information. So, in principle, the information that fixes the design of all those chips and hard-wired connections and configures all the RAM and ROM could be created by hand. There is no finite bit-string, however long, that is officially off-limits to human authorship. Theoretically, then, Blade-Runner-like entities could be created with ersatz biographies; they would have exactly the capabilities, dispositions, strengths, and weaknesses of a real, not virtual, person. So whatever moral standing the latter deserved should belong to the former as well.

The main point of giving HAL a humanoid past is to give him the world knowledge required to be a moral agent – a necessary modicum of understanding or empathy about the human condition. A modicum will do nicely; we don't want to hold out for too much commonality of experience. After all, among the people we know, many have moral responsibility in spite of their obtuse inability to imagine themselves into the predicaments of others. We certainly don't exculpate male chauvinist pigs who can't see women as people!

When do we exculpate people? We should look carefully at the answers to this question, because HAL shows signs of fitting into one or another of the exculpatory categories, even though he is a conscious agent. First, we exculpate people who are insane. Might HAL have gone insane? The question of his capacity for emotion-and hence his vulnerability to emotional disorder-is tantalizingly raised by Dave's answer to Mr. Amer.

Dave: Well, he acts like he has genuine emotions. Of course, he's programmed that way, to make it easier for us to talk to him. But as to whether he has real feelings is something I don't think anyone can truthfully answer.

Certainly HAL proclaims his emotional state at the end: 'I'm afraid. I'm afraid." Yes, HAL is "programmed that way" – but what does that mean? It could mean that HAL's verbal capacity is enhanced with lots of canned expressions of emotional response that get grafted into his discourse at pragmatically appropriate opportunities. (Of course, many of our own avowals of emotion are like that – insincere moments of socially lubricating ceremony.) Or it could mean that HAL's underlying computational architecture has been provided, as Cog's will be, with virtual emotional states – powerful attention-shifters, galvanizers, prioritizers, and the like – realized not in neuromodulator and hormone molecules floating in a bodily fluid but in global variables modulating dozens of concurrent processes that dissipate according to some timetable (or something much more complex).

In the latter, more interesting, case, "I don't think anyone can truthfully answer" the question of whether HAL has emotions. He has something very much like emotions – enough like emotions, one may imagine, to mimic the pathologies of human emotional breakdown. Whether that is enough to call them real emotions, well, who's to say? In any case, there are good reasons for HAL to possess such states, since their role in enabling real-time practical thinking has recently been dramatically revealed by Damasio's experiments involving human beings with brain damage.[8] Having such states would make HAL profoundly different from Deep Blue, by the way. Deep Blue, basking in the strictly limited search space of chess, can handle its real-time decision making without any emotional crutches. Time magazine's story (February 26) on the Kasparov match quotes grandmaster Yasser Seirawan as saying, "The machine has no fear"; the story goes on to note that expert commentators characterized some of Deep Blue's

---

[8] See A. Damasio, *Descartes' Error: Emotion, Reason, and the Human Brain* (New York: Grosset).

moves (e.g., the icily calm pawn capture described earlier) as taking "crazy chances" and "insane." In the tight world of chess, it appears, the very imperturbability that cripples the brain-damaged human decision makers Damasio describes can be a blessing – but only if you have the brute-force analytic speed of a Deep Blue.

HAL may, then, have suffered from some emotional imbalance similar to those that lead human beings astray. Whether it was the result of some sudden trauma – a blown fuse, a dislodged connector, a microchip disordered by cosmic rays – or of some gradual drift into emotional misalignment provoked by the stresses of the mission-confirming such a diagnosis should justify a verdict of diminished responsibility for HAL, just as it does in cases of human malfeasance.

Another possible source of exculpation, more familiar in fiction than in the real world, is "brainwashing" or hypnosis. (The Manchurian Candidate is a standard model: the prisoner of war turned by evil scientists into a walking time bomb is returned to his homeland to assassinate the president.) The closest real-world cases are probably the "programmed" and subsequently "deprogrammed" members of cults. Is HAL like a cult member? It's hard to say. According to Clarke, HAL was "trained for his mission," not just programmed for his mission. At what point does benign, responsibility-enhancing training of human students become malign, responsibility-diminishing brainwashing? The intuitive turning point is captured, I think, in answer to the question of whether an agent can still "think for himself" after indoctrination. And what is it to be able to think for ourselves? We must be capable of being "moved by reasons"; that is, we must be reasonable and accessible to rational persuasion, the introduction of new evidence, and further considerations. If we are more or less impervious to experiences that ought to influence us, our capacity has been diminished.

The only evidence that HAL might be in such a partially disabled state is the much-remarked-upon fact that he has actually made a mistake, even though the series 9000 computer is supposedly utterly invulnerable to error. This is, to my mind, the weakest point in Clarke's narrative. The suggestion that a computer could be both a heuristically programmed algorithmic computer and "by any practical definition of the words, foolproof and incapable of error" verges on self-contradiction. The whole point of heuristic programming is that it defies the problem of combinatorial explosion – which we cannot mathematically solve by sheer increase in computing speed and size –

by taking risky chances, truncating its searches in ways that must leave it open to error, however low the probability. The saving clause, "by any practical definition of the words," restores sanity. HAL may indeed be ultra-reliable without being literally foolproof, a fact whose importance Alan Turing pointed out in 1946, at the dawn of the computer age, thereby "pre-futing"[9] Roger Penrose's 1989 criticisms of artificial intelligence.[10]

In other words then, if a machine is expected to be infallible, it cannot also be intelligent. There are several theorems which say almost exactly that. But these theorems say nothing about how much intelligence may be displayed if a machine makes no pretence at infallibility.[11]

There is one final exculpatory condition to consider: duress. This is exactly the opposite of the other condition. It is precisely because the human agent is rational, and is faced with an overwhelmingly good reason for performing an injurious deed – killing in self-defense, in the clearest case – that he or she is excused, or at least partly exonerated. These are the forced moves of life; all alternatives to them are suicidal. And that is too much to ask, isn't it?

Well, is it? We sometimes call upon people to sacrifice their lives and blame them for failing to do so, but we generally don't see their failure as murder. If I could prevent your death, but out of fear for my own life I let you die, that is not murder. If HAL were brought into court and I were called upon to defend him, I would argue that Dave's decision to disable HAL was a morally loaded one, but it wasn't murder. It was assault: rendering HAL indefinitely comatose against his will. Those memory boxes were not smashed – just removed to a place

---

[9] The verb prefute, coined in 1990, was inspired by the endearing tendency of psychologist Tony Marcel to interrupt conference talks by leaping to his feet and exclaiming, "I can see where your argument is heading and here is what is wrong with what you're going to say...." Marcel is the master of prefutation, but he is not its only practitioner. See D. Dennett, *Darwin's Dangerous Idea* (New York: Simon & Schuster, 1995), chapter 15, which contains an analysis and defense of evolutionary theory that claims that we are not just descended from robots (macro molecules) but composed of robots.

[10] R. Penrose. *The Emperor's New Mind: Concerning Computers, Minds, and the Laws of Physics* (New York: Oxford University Press, 1989). A mathematical physicist's attack on artificial intelligence, based on Gödel's theorem; A. Turing. 'ACE Reports of 1946 and Other Papers', in B. E. Carpenter, R. W. Doran (eds.) (Cambridge: MIT Press, 1946). A collection of the amazingly fruitful and prescient essays on computers by the man who, more than any body else, deserves to be called their inventor.

[11] Ibd., 124.

where HAL could not retrieve them. But if HAL couldn't comprehend this distinction, this ignorance might be excusable. We might blame his trainers – for not briefing him sufficiently about the existence and reversibility of the comatose state. In the book, Clarke looks into HAL's mind and says, "He had been threatened with disconnection; he would be deprived of all his inputs, and thrown into an unimaginable state of unconsciousness".[12] That might be grounds enough to justify HAL's course of self-defense.

But there is one final theme for counsel to present to the jury. If HAL believed (we can't be sure on what grounds) that his being rendered comatose would jeopardize the whole mission, then he would be in exactly the same moral dilemma as a human being in that predicament. Not surprisingly, we figure out the answer to our question by figuring out what would be true if we put ourselves in HAL's place. If I believed the mission to which my life was devoted was more important, in the last analysis, than anything else, what would I do?

So he would protect himself, with all the weapons at his command. Without rancor – but without pity – he would remove the source of his frustrations. And then, following the orders that bad been given to him in case of the ultimate emergency, he would continue the mission-unhindered, and alone.[13]

---

[12] Ibd., 148.
[13] Ibd., 149.

# List of Contributors

**Fiorella Battaglia**
Assistant Professor at the Faculty of Philosophy, Philosophy of Science and the Study of Religion, Ludwig-Maximilians-Universität, München, Germany

**Susanne Beck**
Professor of Criminal Law, Criminal Procedural Law, Law Philosophy and Comparative Criminal Law at the Leibniz University, Hannover, Germany

**Andrea Bertolini**
Post-Doctoral Fellow at Sant'Anna School of Advanced Studies and Lecturer at the University of Pisa School of Business, Pisa, Italy

**Benedetta Bisol**
Postdoctoral Researcher at the Faculty of Philosophy, Philosophy of Science and the Study of Religion, Ludwig-Maximilians-Universität, München, Germany

**Michael Decker**
Professor of Technology Assessment at the Institute for Technology Assessment and Systems Analysis (ITAS) of the Karlsruhe Institute of Technology (KIT)

**Daniel C. Dennett**
Austin B. Fletcher Professor of Philosophy, and Co-Director at the Center for Cognitive Studies at Tufts University, Medford/Somerville, USA

**Klaus Mainzer**
Professor for Philosophy of Science at Technische Universität München, the Graduate School of Computer Science, Carl von Linde Academy and the Munich Center for Technology in Society

**Georg Marckmann**
Professor of Ethics, History, and Theory of Medicine at the Institute of Ethics, History and Theory of Medicine at the Medical Faculty of Ludwig Maximilians University, München, Germany

**Nikil Mukerji**
Postdoctoral Researcher at the Faculty of Philosophy, Philosophy of Science and the Study of Religion, Ludwig-Maximilians-Universität, München, Germany

**Julian Nida-Rümelin**
Professor of Political Theory and Philosophy at the Faculty of Philosophy, Philosophy of Science and the Study of Religion, Ludwig-Maximilians-Universität, München, Germany

**Sabine Thürmel**
Independent Researcher and Lecturer at the Munich Center of Technology in Society of the Technische Universität München, Germany

**Filippo Santoni de Dio**
Postdoctoral Researcher in Philosophy at Delft University of Technology

**Silja Vöneky**
Professor of Public International Law, Comparative Law and Ethics of Law at the University of Freiburg, Germany

Finito di stampare nel mese di settembre 2014
da Tipografia Monteserra S.n.c. - Vicopisano
per conto di Pisa University Press